William Henry Giles Kingston

Adventures among the Indians

William Henry Giles Kingston

Adventures among the Indians

ISBN/EAN: 9783337340803

Printed in Europe, USA, Canada, Australia, Japan

Cover: Foto ©Thomas Meinert / pixelio.de

More available books at **www.hansebooks.com**

ADVENTURES

AMONG THE INDIANS.

BY

W. H. G. KINGSTON,

AUTHOR OF

"PETER THE WHALER," "YOUNG FORRESTERS," ETC.

ILLUSTRATED.

CHICAGO, NEW YORK, SAN FRANCISCO.

BELFORD, CLARKE & CO.

1889.

ROB NIXON,

THE OLD WHITE TRAPPER.

CHAPTER I.

PICTURE a wide, gently undulating expanse of land covered with tall grass, over which, as it bends to the breeze, a gleam of light ever and anon flashes brightly. It is a rolling prairie in North America, midway between the Atlantic and Pacific oceans. On either hand the earth and sky seem to unite, without an object to break the line of the horizon, except in the far distance, where some tall trees, by a river's side, shoot up out of the plain, but appear no higher than a garden hedge-row. It is truly a wilderness, which no wise man would attempt to traverse without a guide.

That man has wandered there, the remnants of mortality which lie scattered about —a skull and the bare ribs seen as the wind blows the grass aside—afford melancholy evidence. A nearer inspection shows a rifle, now covered with rust, a powder-flask, a sheath-knife, a flint and steel, and a few other metal articles of hunters' gear. Those of more destructible materials have disappeared before the ravenous jaws of the hosts of locusts which have swept over the plain. Few portions of the earth's surface give a more complete idea of boundless extent than the American prairie. Not a sound is heard. The silence itself is awe-inspiring. The snows of winter have lain thickly on that plain, storms have swept over it, the rain has fallen, the lightning flashed, the thunder roared, since it has been trodden by the foot of man. Perhaps the last human being who has attempted to cross it was he whose bones lie blanching in the summer sun—that sun which now, having some time passed its meridian height, is sinking towards the west.

Southward appear, coming as it were from below the horizon, some dark specks, scattered widely from east to west, and moving slowly. On they come, each instant increasing in numbers, till they form one dark line. They are animals with huge heads and dark shaggy manes, browsing as they advance, clearing the herbage before them. They are a herd of bison, known by the wild hunters of the west as buffaloes—countless apparently in numbers—powerful and ferocious in appearance, with their short thick horns and long heads. Now they halt, as the richer pasturage entices; now again advance. A large number lie down to rest, while others, moving out of the midst, seem to be acting as scouts to give notice of the

approach of danger. They go on as before,
darkening the whole southern horizon. The
wind is from the west; the scouts lift up
their shaggy heads and sniff the air, but discover no danger. From the east another
dark line rises quickly above the horizon :
the ground shakes with the tramp of horses.
It is a troop of huntsmen—savage warriors
of the desert. What clothing they wear is
of leather gayly adorned. Some have feathers in their heads, and their dark red skins
painted curiously. Some carry bows richly
ornamented: a few only are armed with
rifles. A few, who, by their dress, the
feathers and adornments of the head, appear
to be chiefs, ride ahead and keep the line in
order. Every man holds his weapon ready
for instant use. They advance steadily,
keeping an even line. Their leader waves
his rifle. Instantly the steeds spring forward. Like a whirlwind they dash on : no
want of energy now. The huntsmen are

mong the bewildered herd before their approach has been perceived. Arrows fly in quick succession from every bow—bullets from the rifles. The huntsmen have filled their mouths with the leaden messengers of death, and drop them into their rifles as they gallop on, firing right and left—singling out the fattest beasts at a glance—and never erring in their aim. In a few minutes the plain is thickly strewn with the huge carcasses of the shaggy buffaloes, each huntsman, as he passes on, dropping some article of his property by which he may know the beast he has killed. Now the herd begin to seek for safety in flight, still keeping in the direction they had before been taking, some scattering, however, on each side. The eager hunters pursue till the whole prairie, from right to left, is covered with flying buffaloes and wild horsemen; the crack of the rifles sounding distinctly through the calm, summer air, in which the tiny wreath

A smoke ascends unbroken and marks the hunter's progress.

Among the huntsmen rides one distinguished from the rest by his more complete, yet less ornamented clothing; by a leather cap without feathers, and by the perfect order of his rifle and hunting accoutrements.

On a nearer inspection, his skin—though tanned, and wrinkled, and furrowed, by long exposure to the weather, and by age and toil—might be discovered to have been of a much lighter hue originally than that of his companions. Old as he was, no one was more eager in the chase, and no one's rifle brought down so great a number of buffaloes as did his. To all appearance he was as active and strong as the youngest huntsman of the band. In the course of the hunt he had reached the extreme left of the line. A superb bull appeared before him. "I'll have you for your robe, if not for your meat, old fellow," exclaimed the hunter, galloping on towards the animal's right flank, so as to turn him yet further from the herd, and to obtain a more direct shot at his head or at his shoulders. There are occasions when the most practised of shots will find himself at fault—the firmest nerves will fail. The old hunter had reached a satisfactory position— he raised his rifle, and fired. At that instant, while still at full speed, his horse's front feet sunk into a hole made by a badger, or some other of the smaller creatures inhabiting the prairie ; and the animal, unable to recover itself, threw the hunter violently forward over its head, where he lay without moving, and apparently dead. The horse struggled to free itself; and then, as it fell forward, gave utterance to one of those piercing cries of agony not often heard, and, when heard, not to be forgotten. Both fore-legs were broken. Its fate was certain. It must become the prey of the ravenous wolves, who speedily scent out the spots

where the hunters have overtaken a herd of
buffaloes. Meantime the buffalo, who had
been struck by the hunter's bullet, but not
so wounded as to bring him instantly to the
ground, galloped on for some distance in
the direction he was before going, when,
feeling the pain of his wound, or hearing the
cry of the horse, he turned round to face his
enemies. Seeing both steed and rider prostrate, he tossed his head, and then, lowering
his horns close to the ground, prepared to
charge. The last moments of the old hunter
seemed approaching. The cry of agony
uttered by his favorite steed roused him.
He looked up and saw the buffalo about to
make its charge. His hand had never re-
laxed its grasp of his rifle. To feel for his
powder-flask and to load was the work of an
instant; and, without an attempt to rise, he
brought the muzzle of his piece* to bear on
the furious animal as it was within a few
paces of him. "Rob Nixon never feared

man nor beast, and will not this time, let an old bull bellow as loud as he may," he muttered, as he raised his rifle and fired. The bullet took effect, but did not stop the headlong career of the enraged monster, which came on, ploughing up the ground, towards him. The hunter saw his danger and tried to rise, but in vain. He then made a desperate endeavor to drag himself out of the way of the creature. He but partially succeeded, when the buffalo, sinking down, rolled over and over, crushing, with his huge carcass, the already injured legs and lower extremities of the unfortunate hunter. In spite of the pain he was enduring, the old man, raising himself on his elbow, grimly surveyed his conquered foe: "You've the worst of it, though you nearly did for me, I own," he exclaimed, nodding his head ; " but a miss is as good as a mile, and when I'm free of you, maybe I'll sup off your hump."

To liberate himself from the monster's
carcass was, however, no easy task, injured
as he was already by his fall, and by the
weight of the buffalo pressing on him. He
made several attempts, but the pain was
very great, and he found that his strength
was failing him. While resting, before
making another attempt to move, he perceived his poor horse, whose convulsive
struggles showed how much he had been injured. On looking round, also, he discovered that the accident had taken place in a
slight hollow, which, shallow as it was, shut
him out from the view of his comparions,
who were now pursuing the remainder of
the herd at a considerable distance from
where he lay. Again and again he tried to
drag his injured limbs from beneath the
buffalo. He had never given in while consciousness remained, and many were the ac-
cidents which had happened to him during
his long hunter's life. Would he give in

now? "No, not I," he muttered; "Rob Nixon is not the boy for that." At length, however, his spirit succumbed to bodily suffering, and he sank back exhausted and fainting, scarcely conscious of what had happened, or where he was. Had he retained sufficient strength to fire his rifle he might have done so, and summoned some of the hunters to his assistance; but he was unable even to load it, so it lay useless by his side. Thus he remained; time passed by—no one approached him—the sun sank in the horizon—darkness came on. It appeared too probable that the fate of many a hunter in that vast prairie would be his. How long he had remained in a state of stupor he could not tell; consciousness returned at length, and, revived by the cool air of night, he sat up and gazed about him. The stars had come out and were shining brilliantly overhead, enabling him to see to the extent of his limited horizon. The dead buffalo

still pressed on his legs—a hideous night-
mare; his horse lay near, giving vent to his
agony in piteous groans, and every now and
then making an attempt to rise to his feet.
" My poor mustang, you are in a bad way, I
fear," said the hunter, in a tone of commiser-
ation, forgetting his own sufferings; " I
would put an end to thy misery, and so
render thee the only service in my power,
but that I cannot turn myself to load my
rifle. Alack! alack! we shall both of us
ere long be food for the wolves; but, though
I must meet my fate as becomes a man, I
would save you—poor, dumb brute that you
are—from being torn by their ravenous
fangs while life remains in you." Such
were the thoughts which passed through
the hunter's mind, for it can scarcely be said
he spoke them aloud.

He would probably again have relapsed
into a state of stupor, but that a hideous
howl, borne by the night breeze, reached

his ears. "Wolves!" he exclaimed; "ah! I know you, you brutes." The howl was repeated again and again, its increased loudness, showing that the creatures were approaching. The well-known terrible sounds roused up the old hunter to make renewed exertions to extricate himself. This time, by dint of dragging himself out with his arms, he succeeded in getting his feet from under the buffalo; but he then discovered, to his dismay, that his thigh had either been broken, or so severely sprained by his fall, that to walk would be impossible. He managed, however, to load his rifle. Scarcely had he done so when the struggles of his horse reminded him of the pain the poor animal was suffering. Although he knew that every charge of powder in his flask would be required for his own defence, he did not hesitate in performing the act of mercy which the case required. He uttered no sentimental speech, though a pang of grief passed through his heart as he pointed the weapon at the horse's head. His aim was true, and the noble animal fell dead. " He's gone; not long before me, I guess," he muttered, as he reloaded his piece. " Those brutes will find me out, there is no doubt about that; but I'll have a fight first—Rob Nixon will die game." The old hunter drew a long knife from a sheath at his side, and, deliberately examining its point, placed it on the ground near him while he reloaded his rifle. Thus did the old man prepare for an inevitable and dreadful death, as he believed; yet not a prayer did he offer up, not a thought did he cast at the future. Eternity, heaven, and hell, were matters unknown; or, if once known, long since forgotten. Yet forgetfulness of a fact will not do away with it. They are awful realities, and will assuredly be found such, however much men may strive to banish them from their thoughts.

The young especially are surprised to hear that old men have forgotten what they learned in their youth, that they neglect to pray, to read the Bible, to think about God and their own souls; but let them be assured that if once they give up the habit of praying, of studying God's holy Word, of obeying His commands, there is one ever ready to persuade them that there is no harm in this neglect; that it will save them much trouble; and that it is far more manly to neglect prayers, to be irreligious and profane, than to love, serve, and obey their Maker. A downward course is sadly easy; let them beware of taking the first step. Each step they take in the wrong direction they will find it more and more difficult to recover, till, like the old huntsman, they will cease to care about the matter, and God will no longer be in their thoughts. There lay that old man on the wild prairie, a melancholy spectacle,—not

so much that he was surrounded by dangers
—that he was wounded and crippled—that
wild beasts were near him—that, if he
escaped their fangs, starvation threatened
him,—but that he had no hope for the
future—that he had no trust in God—that
he had not laid hold of the means of
salvation.

As Rob Nixon lay on the ground, supporting his head on his arm, he turned his gaze
round and round, peering into the darkness
to watch for any thing moving near him.
He knew that before the sun set his Indian
comrades would have carried off the flesh
from the buffaloes they had killed, and
that after that they would move their
camp to a distance, no one being likely
to return. He probably would not be
missed for some time, and, when missed,
it would be supposed that he had fallen
into the hands of the Salteux, or Ojibways,
the hereditary enemies of their nation, and

that already his scalp had been carried off
as a trophy by those hated foes. "They'll
revenge me, that's one comfort; and the
Ojibways will get paid for what the wolves
have done." These were nearly the last
thoughts which passed through the brain
of the old hunter, as the howls and yelps
of the wolves, which had formed a dreadful
concert at a distance around him, approached
still nearer. "I guessed the vermin wouldn't
be long in finding me out," he muttered; and,
on looking up, he saw through the darkness,
glaring fiercely down on him from the edge
of the hollow in which he lay, the eyes of a
pack of wolves. "I'll stop the howling of
some of you," he exclaimed, lifting his rifle.
There was no cry; but a gap in the circle of
eyes showed that a wolf had fallen, and instantly afterwards the loud barking and yelp-
ing proved that the savage creatures were
tearing their companion to pieces. This
gave time to the old man to reload and to

pick off another wolf. In this manner he killed several, and, though he did not drive them away, they were prevented from approaching nearer. On finding that such was the case, his hopes of escaping their fangs rose slightly, at the same time that the lightness of his powder-flask and bullet-bag told him that his ammunition would soon fail, and that then he would have his hunting-knife alone on which to depend. He accordingly waited, without again firing, watching his foes, who continued howling and wrangling over the bodies of their fellows. Now and then one would descend a short way into the hollow, attracted by the scent of the dead horse and buffalo, but a sudden shout from the old hunter kept the intruders at a respectful distance. He was well aware, however, that should exhausted nature for one instant compel him to drop asleep, the brutes would be upon him, and tear him limb from limb. Thus the hours

of the night passed slowly along. Many
men would have succumbed; but, hardened
by a long life of danger and activity, Robert
Nixon held out bravely, in spite of the pain,
and thirst, and hunger from which he was
suffering. Never for one moment was his
eye off his enemies, while his fingers were
on the trigger ready to shoot the first which
might venture to approach. More than once
he muttered to himself, "It must be near
morning, and then these vermin will take
themselves off, and let me have some rest.
Ah, rest! that's the very thing I have been
wanting," he continued; "it's little enough
I've ever had of it. I've been working away
all my life, and where's the good I've got
out of it? There's been something wrong,
I suppose, but I can't make it out. Rest!
Yes, that's it. I should just like to find myself sitting in my lodge among a people who
don't care, like these Dakotahs, to be always
fighting or hunting; but they are not a bad

people, and they've been good friends to me,
and I've no fault to find with their ways,
though I'll own they're more suited to young
men than to an old one like me. But there's
little use my thinking this. Maybe, I shall
never see them or any other of my fellow-
creatures again." It was only now and then
that his mind framed any thoughts as co-
herent as these ; generally he remained in a
dreamy condition, only awake to the external objects immediately surrounding him.
Gradually, too, his strength began to fail,
though he was not aware of the fact. The
howls, and barks, and snarling, and other
hideous sounds made by the wolves, increased.   He could see them moving about
in numbers, around the edge of the basin,
their red fiery eyes ever and anon glaring
down on him. At last they seemed to be
holding a consultation, and to have settled
their disputes, probably from not having
longer a bone of contention unpicked

among them. They were evidently, once
more, about to make an attack on him. A
large brute, who had long been prowling
round, first crept on, gnashing his teeth.
The old man lifted his rifle, and the creature, with a loud cry, fell dead. Another
and another came on, and, before he could
load, the foremost had got close up to him.
He fired at the animal's head. It rolled
over, and, the flash of his rifle scaring the
rest, with hideous yelps they took to flight,
the old man firing after them directly he
could reload. He could scarcely believe
that he was to remain unmolested, and,
once more loading his rifle, he rested as
before, on his arm, watching for their re-
appearance. Gradually, however, exhausted
nature gave way, and he sank down uncon
scious on the ground, to sleep, it might be,
the sleep of death.

CHAPTER II.

THE sun rose and shone forth brightly on
the earth. There was the sound of winged
creatures in Robert Nixon's ears as he once
more awoke and gazed languidly around.
His first impulse was to attempt to rise, but
the anguish he suffered the instant he moved
reminded him of the injuries he had received.
Vain were his efforts; to stand up was impossible. Although the wolves for the time
were gone, they, to a certainty, would return
at night, and thus, without ammunition, how
could he defend himself against them? He
might subsist on the meat of the buffalo for
a day or two, but that would soon become
uneatable, and as he could scarcely hope to
recover from his hurt for many days; even if

he escaped the wolves, he must die of starvation. Again he sank into a state of mental stupor, though his eye still remained cognizant of external objects. As the old hunter thus lay on the ground his eye fell on a horseman riding rapidly by. He was a Salteux, or Ojibway Indian, a people having a deadly feud with his friends, the Sioux. The sight roused him. To kill the man and capture his horse was the idea which at once occurred to him. Rousing himself by a violent exertion he levelled his rifle and fired. Not for an instant did he hesitate about taking the life of a fellow-creature. That fellow-creature was a foe of his friends, whose badge he wore, and would, he believed, kill him if he was discovered. He had miscalculated his powers—his eye had grown dim, his arm had lost its nerve; the bullet which once would have proved a sure messenger of death flew wide of its mark, and the Indian sat his horse unharmed. He turned, however, immediately, and galloped towards the spot whence the shot came. The old hunter had expended his last bullet. With grim satisfaction he awaited the Indian's approach, and the expected flourish of the scalping knife, or the kinder blow of the tomahawk, which would deprive him at once of life. "Better so than be torn by the fangs of those vermin the wolves," he muttered, for though he clutched his knife to strike back, he well knew that he was at the mercy of his adversary. The Indian, though a rifle hung at his back, rode steadily up without unslinging it.

" A friend!" he shouted in the Salteux, or Ojibway dialect; "a friend! fire not again."

" A friend! How so?" exclaimed the old hunter. "Your people and mine are mortal foes."

" I would be a friend to all the suffering and distressed," was the unexpected answer. "I see what has happened—you have fought bravely for your life; the remains of the wolves tell me that, but before another sun has risen you would have been torn limb from limb by their fellows. Truly I am thankful that I was sent to save you from death."

"Sent! Who sent you?" cried the old hunter, gazing up at the strange Indian. The other having just dismounted from his horse stood looking compassionately down on him.

"He who watches over the fatherless and widows, and all who are distressed," answered the Indian.

"A generous kind person I doubt not, but I know of none such in this land; He must live far away from here," said the old hunter.

"He lives in heaven, and His eye is everywhere," said the Indian, solemnly. "He loves all mankind; without His will not a sparrow falls to the ground; and I am sure, therefore, that it was His will that I should come to you."

"Truly you speak strange words for a redskin!" exclaimed the hunter. "I have heard long ago white men talk as you, but never an Indian. You are one I see; there is no deceiving me. I cannot understand the matter."

"I will tell you as we go along," said the Indian; "but, we must no longer delay, father; we have many miles to travel before we can reach my people, and I know not how I can restore you to your friends. It would be dangerous for me to approach them, for they could not understand how I can only wish them good."

"I will go with you, friend," said the old man. "I would gladly dwell with your people, and hear more of those strange matters of which you have been speaking."

Without further exchange of words the

Indian, having examined the old man's hurts, gave him some dried meat and a draught from his water-flask, and lifted him with the utmost care on his horse; he then took the hunter's rifle and horse's trappings before moving off. He also secured the tongue and hump, and some slices from the buffalo's back, which he hung to his saddle-bow.

"We may require more provision than our own rifles can supply before we reach our journey's end," he observed; as he did so, pointing to the northeast.

Robert Nixon without hesitation yielded to all his suggestions.

The day was already considerably advanced, and the Indian seemed anxious to push on. Keeping up a rapid pace, he walked by the side of his companion, who, overcome by weakness and want of sleep, would have fallen off, had not his strong arm held him on. Thus they jour-

neyed, hour after hour, across the prairie.
The Indian, from the first, employed various
devices for rendering his trail invisible. On
starting, he moved for some distance westward, till he reached the bed of a small
stream, on which even the sharp eye of a
native could scarcely perceive a trace;
then, circling round, he commenced his
intended course.   Many miles were passed
over, and the bank of a rapid river was
reached, when the setting sun warned him
that it was time to encamp.   Instead, however, of doing so, he at once led his horse
into the stream, and, keeping close to the
shore, waded against the current, often
having the water up to his waist for a considerable distance; then, coming to a ford,
he crossed over and continued along in the
same direction, till he once more returned
to dry ground.   The bank was fringed on
each side by a belt of trees, which in the
warm weather of summer afforded ample

shelter from the dew, and concealment from any passing enemy. The chief trees were poplar, willow, and alder; but there were also spruce and birch. Round the latter lay large sheets of the bark. A quantity of these the Indian at once collected, and with some thin poles, which he cut with his hatchet, he rapidly constructed a small hut or wigwam, strewing the floor with the young shoots of the spruce-fir. On this couch he placed his injured companion, putting his saddle under his head as a pillow. He then brought the old man some food and water, and next proceeded to examine his hurts with more attention than he had before been able to bestow. Bringing water from the river, he fomented his bruises for a long time, and then, searching for some leaves of a plant possessed of healing qualities, he bound them with strips of soft leather round his swollen limbs.

More than once the old hunter expressed his surprise that a stranger should care so much for him, and should actually feed and tend him before he had himself partaken of food and rested.

"I serve a loving Master, and I am but obeying His wishes," was the laconic answer.

"Very strange! very strange!" again and again muttered the old man. "You must tell me something about that Master of yours. I cannot understand who He can be."

"I will not disappoint you, father, for I love to speak of Him," said the Indian; "I will come anon, and sit by your side, and tell you what I know. It will interest you, I doubt not, and maybe you will wish to know more about Him."

Some time passed, however, before the Indian was able to fulfil his promise. He had to tend his horse, and to set some traps to catch any small game which might pass, and to search for certain roots and berries for food. He showed, too, by all his movements, that he considered himself in an enemy's country, or in the neighborhood of an enemy from whom it was necessary to keep concealed. When he came back the old man had fallen asleep.

"Let him sleep on," said the Indian to himself; "our Father in Heaven will watch over and protect us both. I would that I could watch, but my body requires rest."

Having tethered his horse close at hand, strewed the ground with a few spruce fir-tops, and placed his rifle by his side, he knelt down and prayed, not as once to Manitou, to the Great Spirit, the unknown God, but to the true God—a God no longer feared as a worker of evil, but beloved as the source of all good, of all blessings, spiritual and temporal His prayer finished, he stretched himself on his couch, and was in an instant asleep.

The silvery streaks of early dawn were just appearing in the eastern sky, seen amid the foliage of the wood, when the Indian, impulsively grasping his rifle, started to his feet. His quick ear had caught, even in his sleep, the sound of a distant shot. It might be fired by a friend, but very likely by a foe, and it behooved him to be on the alert. The old hunter heard it also, but it did not awake him.

"Ah! they are on us. No matter, we'll fight for our lives," he muttered in his sleep. "Hurrah, lads! Rob Nixon will not yield —never, while he's an arm to strike."

He spoke in English, which the Indian seemed to understand, though the observation he made was in his own language.

"Our own arms will do little for us, father, unless we trust in Him who is all-powerful to save."

His voice awoke the old man, who sat up and looked around from out of his hut. Seeing the Indian in the attitude of listening, he at once comprehended the state of matters.

"Few or many, I'll stand by you, friend Redskin," he exclaimed, apparently forgetting his helpless condition; "load my rifle, and hand it to me. If foes are coming, they shall learn that Rob Nixon has not lost the use of his arms and eyes, whatever he may have of his legs."

"I doubt not your readiness to fight, father," said the Indian, addressing the old man thus, to show his respect for age; "but we may hope to avoid the necessity of having to defend ourselves. Friends, and not foes, may be near us, or we may escape discovery; or, what is better still, we may overcome the enmity of those who approach us with bad intent."

"Your talk is again strange, as it was yesterday," answered the hunter. "I know not what you mean by overcoming enmity. There is only one way that I have ever found answer, both with pale-faces and redskins, and that is by killing your enemy."

"Try what kindness will do, father. Love is the law of the true God," said the Indian; "but we will anon talk of these things. I will go forth and learn what the shot we heard just now means."

"Load my rifle, and give it me first; I pray you," said the white hunter; "I have great faith in my old way of doing things, and am not likely to change."

The Indian loaded the rifle and handed it to him, and, without saying a word more, set off through the wood, and was soon out of sight. Rob Nixon lay still, with his rifle resting across his body, ready to fire should an enemy appear. Over and over again he muttered : "Strange! strange! that a redskin should talk so. I cannot make it out."

Several minutes passed by, and the Indian did not return. The old man grew more anxious than he would have acknowledged to himself. He had some natural feeling on his own account, should his new friend have been cut off, but he was also anxious for that new friend, to whom he could not but be grateful for the service he had rendered him. At length he saw the bushes move, and the Indian appeared, and crept close up to him.

"There are foes, and many of them," he said, in a low voice ; " they are near at hand, but they are not seeking for us; and thus, if they do not cross our trail, we may yet escape discovery."

The Indian had already concealed his horse in a thicket, and by carefully surrounding the spot where they lay with

boughs their little camp was completely
hidden from the sight of any casual passer
by. The boughs he had cut from the interior part of a thicket, for had they been
taken from the outer side the eye of an Indian would at once have observed the white
stumps which were left. Again, by crossing the river in the mode they had done,
there was no trail to lead to their camp.
For these reasons the Indian and the white
hunter had good cause to believe that they
might escape discovery. As their enemies
were as yet at some distance, it was not
deemed necessary to keep altogether silent.
The old hunter was the most loquacious.

" I would, friend Redskin," said he, " that
I had the use of my legs and half a dozen of
my old companions at my back, and I
wouldn't fear as to holding my own against
three-score or more of Crees, or Ojibways ;
no offence to you, friend ; for there are not
many like you, I guess."

"Your people fight bravely but fool-
ishly, according- to Indian notions," answered the Indian; "for, instead of ad-
vancing on their foes under shelter and
trying to take them unawares, they dress
themselves in fine clothes, make a great noise
when going forth to battle, and expose
their bodies to be shot at. I was once
esteemed a mighty warrior, and was a
man of blood; I have engaged in much
fighting, but would now wish to bury the
hatchet of war with all the world. I thank
you for what you say of me; but things of
which I once boasted, I boast of no longer.
I am a chief of many people; but instead,
as at one time, of wishing to lead them to
war, I now desire to lead them to a knowledge of the Lord and Master whom I serve
—the Saviour of the world."

"Every man to his taste, friend Redskin," said the old hunter; "when I was
a young man like you I could not have

fighting or hunting enough. Now, I own, I am growing somewhat weary of the work and if we get to the end of this journey with our scalps on, maybe I'll settle down with your people."

It may seem strange that the old man could not comprehend what was the meaning of the Indian, when he spoke thus. If he had a glimmering of the truth, he turned away from it. Many do the same. Felix has numberless imitators. Both the Indian and Rob Nixon were silent for some minutes, attentively listening for the approach of the strangers. Not a sound, however, being heard, they began to hope that their enemies had gone a different way.

"There'll be no fighting this time, 1 guess, friend Redskin," said the old man. "It's all the better, too, considering that you don't seem much inclined for it; and I'm not in the best trim for work of that sort, or any work, truth to say."

Rob Nixon had remarked that the Indian had winced more than once when addressed as Redskin, which was certainly not a respectful or complimentary mode of addressing him. The reason of this became still more evident when he spoke of himself as a chief. Chiefs in general would not for an instant have suffered such familiarity. Rob Nixon saw that it was time to apologize. He did so in his own way.

"I say, friend, I've just a thing to ask you. You've a name, I doubt not, showing forth some of the brave deeds you have done, the enemies you have slain, the miles you have run, the rivers you have swam across, the bears you have captured, or the beavers you have trapped. Tell me, what is it? for I've a notion the one I've been giving you is not altogether the right or a pleasant one."

The Indian smiled, as he answered quietly,

"The name I bear, and the only one by which I desire to be called, is Peter. It was

given me, not for killing men or slaughtering beasts, but at my baptism, when 1 was
received into the Church of Christ, and undertook to love, honor, serve, and obey Him
in all things as my Lord and Master."

"Peter! Peter! that's a strange name for
an Injun," said the white hunter half to himself. "Why, that's such a name as they
give in the old country to a Christian."

"And I, too, am a Christian, though an
unworthy one, father," answered the Indian,
humbly.

"Never heard before of a Christian Injun!" exclaimed the old man bluntly; "but
strange things happen, I'll allow. I don't
doubt your word; mind that, friend. It
was strange that when you saw I was a
friend of the Dakotahs you didn't scalp me,
without asking questions, and leave me to
be eaten by wolves. That's the true Injun
way. It was strange that you should take
me up, put me on your horse, walk yourself

all these miles, with some hundreds more before you, and risk your own life to save mine. All that is strange, I say; and so, friend, I don't know what other strange things may happen. Well, if so you wish, I'll call you Peter; but I'd rather by far call you by your Injun name. It was a good one, I'll warrant. Come, tell it now. You need not be ashamed of it."

"In the sight of man I am not ashamed of it, for by most of my people I am called by it still; but in the sight of God I am ashamed of it, and still more am I ashamed of the deeds which gained it for me. How, think you, blood-stained and guilty as I was, could I stand in the presence of One pure, holy, loving, and merciful? I tell you, aged friend, neither you nor I, nor any man, could appear before God without fear and trembling, if it were not that He is a God of love, and that through His great love for us, His creatures, whom He has placed on the world, He sent His 'only Son, that all who believe in Him should not perish, but have eternal life."

The young Christian Indian warmed, as he went on in his discourse, which was intermingled with many beautiful illustrations and figures of speech, which it would be vain to attempt to translate. Gradually he thus unfolded the fundamental truths of the Gospel. The old white hunter listened, and even listened attentively; but, far from warming, seemed scarcely to comprehend what was said.

"Strange! very strange!" he muttered frequently; "and that an Injun should talk thus. Forty years I lived among the redskins, and never believed that they knew more than their fathers."

Peter, as he desired to be called,—though his heathen name was Aronhiakeura, or otherwise the Fiery Arrow, from the rapidity of his onslaught and the devastation he caused,—now stated his belief that they might venture to proceed without the like-lihood of being molested. Scarcely, how-ever, had he emerged from their leafy cover when another shot was fired close to them; and, before he could again seek concealment, three fully armed Dakotahs appeared direct-ly in front of him. The Dakotahs instantly rushed behind the trees, to serve as shields should he fire, but he held up his hands to show that he was unarmed, and in a low voice entreated his companion to remain quiet. That resistance would be hopeless was evident by the appearance, directly afterwards, of a dozen or more Indians, who were seen flitting amidst the wood, each man obtaining the best shelter in his power. Peter stood fully exposed to view, without flinching or even contemplating concealing himself. Fearless behavior is sure to obtain the admiration of Indians.

Naturally suspicious, they possibly sup-

posed that he had a strong force concealed
somewhere near at hand, and that they had
themselves fallen into an ambush. Had
they found and followed up his trail, they
would have discovered exactly the state of
the case. That he had a wounded companion would not have escaped their notice, and
that he had but one horse, and travelled
slowly would also have been known to them.
By his having crossed the stream, however,
and come along its bed for some distance,
they were at fault in this respect.

Peter kept his post without flinching; he
well knew that the Dakotahs were watching
him; indeed, here and there he could dis-
tinguish the eye of a red-skinned warrior
glimmering, or the top of a plume waving
among the trunks of the trees or brushwood.

All the time Rob Nixon, on his part, was
watching his preserver with intense anxiety.
He had conceived a warm regard for him,

and, knowing the treachery so often exhibited by the natives, trembled for his safety.

Peter, at length, waved his hand to show that he was about to speak.

"What seek you, friends?" he said in a calm tone ; "I am a man of peace, I desire to be friends with all men, and to injure no one ; moreover, I would that you and all men had the wisdom and enjoyed the happiness which I possess. See, I cannot harm you." As he spoke, he raised up both his hands high in the air.

The Dakotahs, totally unaccustomed to an address of this description, were greatly astonished. Their chief, not to be undone in fearlessness, stepped from behind his covert, completely exposing himself to view.

"Who are you, friend? and whence do you come?" he asked; "you cannot be what you seem?"

"I am a man like yourself, friend, and I

am truly what I seem—a native of this land,
and of a tribe unhappily constantly at enmity with yours," answered Peter firmly;
"but know, O chief, that I differ from many
of my people; that I love you and your
people, and all mankind. Will you listen
to the reason of this? Let your people appear, there is no treachery intended them;
I am in your power—why doubt my word?"

One by one the Dakotahs crept from behind the trees which had concealed them,
and a considerable number assembled in
front of the Indian, who spoke to them of
the Gospel of love, and of the glorious
scheme of redemption.

They listened attentively; most of them
with mute astonishment. Now and then
one of the chief men would give way to his
feelings by a sound signifying either appro-
bation or dissent, but not a remark was
uttered till the speaker ceased.

For a time all were silent, then with

gravity and deliberation one of the chiefs waved his hand and observed—

"These are strange words the man speaks —he must be a great medicine man."

"Truly he has the wisdom of the white faces," said a second; "has he their treachery? Can he be trusted?"

"The things he says may be true, but they concern not us," remarked a third.

"Wisdom is wisdom, whoever speaks it," said a grave old warrior, who had shown himself as active in his movements as the youngest of his companions. "What the stranger tells us of must be as good for one man as for another. Rest is good for the weary; who among my brothers, too, would not rather serve a powerful and kind chief than an inferior and merciless one. He tells us of rest for the weary; of a great and good chief, who can give us all things to make us happy,—I like his discourse, my brothers."

The last speaker seemed to be carrying several with him, when another started up exclaiming —

" What the stranger says comes from the pale-faces—it may be false; there must be some treacherous design in it. Let us rather dance this night the scalp-dance round his scalp than listen to his crafty tales. See, I fear him not."

The savage, as he spoke, lifted his rifle and was about to fire it at Peter, when the rest drew him back, crying out—

" He is a medicine man—a great medicine man, and may work us ill; interfere not with him; though we do not listen to his counsel, let him go free. Even now, while we are speaking, we know not what injury he may be preparing to do us !"

Thus the discussion went on for a considerable time, Peter waiting patiently for its result.

Although the speakers had retired rather

too far off for him to hear all that was said,
he gathered sufficient to know the tenor of
the discussion; still, no fear entered his
bosom, he knew that his life was in the
hand of One mighty to save.

While he stood waiting the result he
prayed for himself certainly, but yet more
earnestly that the truth might be brought
home to the dark hearts of his countrymen.

North American Indians are deliberate in
their councils. Peter knew that his fate would
not be decided quickly; but neither by
word, look, nor action did he show the
slightest impatience. The old white hunter,
meantime, had made up his mind to risk
every thing rather than allow any injury,
which he could avert, to happen to his
new friend. That they would recognize
him, he had no doubt; and the fact that
he was found in company with a member
of a hostile tribe would be considered so
suspicions, that they would possibly put

him to death without stopping to ask
questions. However, should Peter be killed
or made prisoner by the Dakotahs, he
would be left to perish; so that he felt,
indeed, that his fate depended on that
of his friend. · From where he lay he could
see, amid the branches, the Indians holding
their council. His trusty rifle was by his
side, and noiselessly he brought it to cover
their principal chief. His purpose was to
fire at the first hostile movement, hoping
that on the fall of their leader the Indians,
fancying that they had got into a trap,
would take to flight. At length the Dakotahs' leader advanced a few steps. He
little thought that the lifting his hand with
a menacing gesture might cost him his
life.

"Stranger, with you we would gladly
smoke the pipe of peace," he began; "but
your ways are not our ways, or your notions our notions—we have nothing in

common. Go as you came; we wish to
have no communication with you. We
desire not to desert our fathers' ways as
you have done; yet, undoubtedly, the
Spirit you serve will protect you—go—go
—go."

In vain Peter entreated the savages to
hear him once again, assuring them that
he would tell them only what was for
their good. One by one they quitted the
spot where the council had been held;
the first walked off with becoming dignity, but, as more departed, the pace of
each in succession increased, till the last
scampered off almost as fast as his legs
would carry him, fearful lest he should
be overtaken by the strange medicine
man, whose supposed incantations he
dreaded. Peter was less astonished than
a white man would have been at the behavior of his countrymen. Still, he had
gained an unexpected triumph. The Da-

kotahs did not stop, even to look behind
them, but continued their course towards
the west, through the wood and across
the prairie, till they were lost to sight
in the distance. The old hunter, to his
surprise, saw Peter fall on his knees, on
the spot where he had been standing,
to return thanks to Heaven for his deliverance from a danger, far greater than
it might appear to those unacquainted
with Indian customs, for seldom or never
do two parties of the Dakotahs and Ojibways encounter each other, without the
stronger endeavoring to destroy the weaker
with the most remorseless cruelty. Mercy
is never asked for nor expected. The scalping knife is employed on the yet living
victim, should the tomahawk have left
its work unfinished.

CHAPTER III.

"WELL, you are a wonderful man, friend Peter," exclaimed Robert Nixon, when the Indian returned to him and narrated what had occurred; "I never yet have seen the like of it."

"The reason is simply this, father, most men trust to their own strength and wisdom, and fail. I go forth in the strength of One all-powerful, and seek for guidance from One all-wise," answered the Indian, humbly. "It is thus I succeed."

"That's curious, what you say, friend Redskin," answered the old man in a puzzled tone; "it's beyond my understanding, that's a fact."

"The time will come shortly. I hope,

father, when you will see the truth of what I say. But we must no longer delay here, we should be moving on."

The mustang was caught and saddled, the old hunter placed on it, and once more the two travellers were on their way eastward, or rather to the northeast, for that was the general direction of their course. They were compelled, however, to diverge considerably, in order to keep along the course of streams, where many important advantages could be obtained : water, wood for firing, shelter, and a greater supply of game. On the open prairie there was no want of deer of several descriptions, and of small animals, like rabbits or hares ; but, unless by leaving the horse with his burden, the Indian could seldom get near enough to shoot them.

For some distance the open country was of a sterile and arid description ; but as they got farther away from the United

States border it greatly improved, and a well-watered region, with rich grass and vetches, was entered, which extended north, and east, and west, in every direction, capable of supporting hundreds and thousands of flocks and herds, for the use of man, although now roamed over only by a comparatively few wild buffalo, deer, wolves, and bears.

Although they were in British territory, the arm of British law did not extend over this wild region, and Peter, therefore, kept a constant look-out to ascertain that no lurking enemies were near at hand. When he camped at night, also, he selected the most sheltered spot he could find, and concealed his companion and himself amid some thicket or rock, where any casual passerby would not be likely to discover them.

At first, as Peter watched his companion, he thought that he would scarcely reach a place of safety, where he might die in peace

among civilized men; but gradually the old
hunter's strength returned, and each day, as
he travelled on, his health seemed to improve. He also became more inclined to
talk; not only to ask questions, but to speak
of himself. Religious subjects, however, he
avoided as much as possible; indeed, to
human judgment, his mind appeared too
darkened, and his heart too hardened, to
enable him to comprehend even the simplest
truths.

"You'd like to know something about me,
friend Redskin, I've no doubt," said the old
man to Peter, when one day he had got into
a more than usually loquacious mood. "It's
strange, but it's a fact, I've a desire to talk
about my early days, and yet, for forty
years or more, maybe, I've never thought
of them, much less spoken about them. I
was raised in the old country—that's where
most of the pale-faces you see hereabouts
came from. My father employed a great

many men, and so I may say he was a chief; he was a farmer of the old style, and hated any thing new. He didn't hold education in any great esteem, and so he took no pains to give me any, and one thing I may say, I took no pains to obtain it. My mother, of that I am certain, was a kind, good woman, and did her best to instruct me. She taught me to sing little songs, and night and morning made me kneel down, with my hands put together, and say over some words which I then thought very good—and I am sure they were, as she taught me them; but I have long, long ago forgotten what they were. She also used to take me with her to a large, large house, where there were a great number of people singing and often talking together; and then there was one man in a black dress, who got up in a high place in the middle, and had all the talk to himself for a long time, I used to think; but I didn't mind that as I used generally to go to sleep when he began, and only woke up when he had done.

"I was very happy whenever I was with my mother, but I didn't see her for some days, and then they took me into the room where she slept, and there I saw her lying on a bed; but she didn't speak to me, she didn't even look at me, for her eyes were closed, and her cheek was cold—very cold. I didn't know then what had happened, though I cried very much. I never saw her again. From that time I began to be very miserable; I don't know why; I think it was not having my mother to go to and talk to.

"After that I don't know exactly what happened to me; for some time I got scolded, and kicked, and beaten, and then I was sent to a place where there were a good many other boys; and, thinks I to myself, I shall be happier here; but instead of that I was much more beaten and scolded, till I got a feeling that I didn't care what I did.

or what became of me. That feeling never left me. I was always ready to do any thing proposed by other boys, such as rob- bing orchards, or playing all sorts of pranks.

"I now and then went home to see my father; but I remember very little about him, except that he was a stout man, with a ruddy countenance. If he did not scold me and beat me, he certainly did not say much to me; I never felt towards him as I had done towards my mother.

"I must have been a biggish boy, though I was still nearly at the bottom of the school, when another lad and I got into some scrape, and were to be flogged. He pro- posed that we should run away, and I at once agreed, without considering where we should run to, or what we should gain by our run. There is a saying among the pale- faces, 'out of the frying pan into the fire.' We soon found that we had got into a very hot fire.

"After many days' running, sleeping under hedges and in barns, and living on turnips and crusts of bread, which we bought with the few pence we had in our pockets, we reached a seaport town. Seeing a large ship about to sail, we agreed that we would be sailors, if any one would take us. We were very hungry and hadn't a coin left to buy food, so aboard we went. The ship was just sailing,—the cook's boy had run away, and the captain's cabin-boy had just died,—and so we were shipped, without a question being asked, to take their places. They didn't inquire our names, but called us Bill and Tom, which were the names of the other boys. The captain took me into his service, and called me Bill; and my companion, who fell to the cook, was called Tom. I don't know which was the most miserable. Tom had the dirtiest and hardest work, and was not only the cook's but everybody else's servant. I received the most kicks and

thrashings, and had the largest amount of
oaths and curses showered down on my head.
We were both of us very ill, but our masters didn't care for that, and kicked us up to
work whenever they found us lying down.

"Away we sailed; we thought that we
should never come to land again. I didn't
know where we were going, but I found we
were steering towards the south and west.
Week after week I saw a wild, high head-
land on our right hand, and then we had
mist, and snow, and heavy weather, and
were well-nigh driven back; but at last we
were steering north, and the weather became
fire and pleasant. The ship put into many
strange ports; some were in this big country of America, and some were in islands, so
we heard; but neither Tom nor I was ever,
for one moment, allowed to set foot on shore.
Often and often did we bitterly repent our
folly, and wish ourselves back home; but
wishing was of no use. We found that

we were slaves, without the possibility of escape.

"Tom, who had more learning by a great deal than I had, said one day that he would go and appeal to the consul,—I think he was called, a British officer at the port where we lay,—when the mate, who heard him, laughed, and told him, with an oath, that he might go and complain to whomsoever he liked; but that both he and Bill had signed papers, and had no power to get away. By this Tom knew that if we complained the captain would produce the papers signed by the other boys, and that we should be supposed to be them, and have no remedy. Tom then proposed that we should play all sorts of pranks, and behave as badly as we could. We tried the experiment, but we soon found that we had made a mistake; for our masters beat and starved us till we were glad to promise not again do the same.

"Our only hope was that we should some day get a chance of running away; and, if it hadn't been for that, we should, I believe, have jumped overboard and drowned ourselves. Month after month passed by, the ship continued trading from port to port in the Pacific Ocean,—as the big lake you've heard speak of, friend Redskin, is called,— over to the west there; but the chance we looked for never came. We then hoped that the ship would be cast away, and that so we might be free of our tyrants. If all had been drowned but ourselves we shouldn't have cared.

"At last, after we'd been away three years or more, we heard that the ship was going home. We didn't conceal our pleasure. It didn't last long. Another captain came on board one day. I heard our captain observe to him, 'You shall have them both at a bargain. Thrash them well, and I'll warrant you'll get work out of them.'

I didn't know what he meant at the time.

"In the evening, when the strange captain's boat was called away, Tom and I were ordered to get up our bags and jump in. We refused, and said we wanted to go home. We had better have kept silence. Dow: came a shower of blows on our shoulders and amid the jeers and laughter of our ship mates, we were forced into the boat. We found ourselves aboard a whaler just come out, with the prospect of remaining in thos parts three years at least.

"You've heard speak, Peter, of the mighty fish of the big lake. The largest sturgeon you ever set eyes on is nothing to them—just a chipmonk to a buffalo. We had harder and dirtier work now than before— catching, cutting out, and boiling down the huge whales—and our masters were still more cruel and brutal. We were beaten and knocked about worse than ever, and often well-nigh starved by having our rations taken from us. How we managed to live through that time I don't know. I scarcely like to think of it. The ship sailed about in every direction; sometimes where the sun was so hot that we could scarce bear our clothes on our backs, and sometimes amid floating mountains of ice, with snow and sleet beating down on us.

"At last, when we had got our ship nearly full of oil, and it was said that we should soon go home, we put into a port, on the west coast of this continent, to obtain fresh provisions. There were a few white people settled there, but most of the inhabitants were red-skins. The white men had farms, ranchos they were called, and the natives worked for them.

"Tom and I agreed that, as the ship was soon going home, the captain would probably try to play off the same trick on us that our first captain had done, and so

we determined to be beforehand with
him. We were now big, strongish fellows; not as strong as we might have
been if we had been better fed and less
knocked about; but still we thought that
we could take good care of ourselves.
We hadn't much sense though, or knowledge of what people on shore do; for
how should we, when you see that since
the day we left our native country, when
we were little ignorant chaps, we hadn't
once set our feet on dry land. Tom swore,
and so did I, that if we once did reach the
shore, we'd get away as far from the ocean
as we could, and never again smell a breath
of it as long as we lived. How to get there
was the difficulty. We had always before
been watched; and so, to throw our ship-
matos off their guard, we pretended to
think of nothing but about going home;
and our talk was all of what we would
do when we got back to old England.

We said that we were very much afraid
of the savages on shore, and wondered
any one could like to go among them.
After a time, we found that we were no
longer watched as we used to be. This
gave us confidence. The next thing was
to arrange how we were to get on shore.
We neither of us could swim; and, besides, the distance was considerable, and
there were sharks—fish which can bite a
man's leg off as easily as a white-fish
bites a worm in two. We observed that,
in the cool of the evening, some boats
and canoes used to pull round the ship,
and sometimes came alongside to offer
things for sale to the men. Tom and I
agreed that if we could jump into one
of them, while the owner was on board,
we might get off without being discovered.

"Night after night we waited, till our
hearts sunk within us, thinking we should

never succeed; but, the very night before
the ship was to sail, several people came
below, and, while they were chaffering with
the men, Tom and I slipped up on deck.
My heart seemed ready to jump out of
my skin with anxiety as I looked over
the side. There, under the fore-chains,
was a canoe with a few things in her,
but no person. I glanced round. The
second mate was the only man on deck
besides Tom, who had gone over to the
other side. I beckoned to Tom. The
mate had his back to us, being busily
engaged in some work or other, over
which he was bending. Tom sprang over
to me, and together we slid down into
the canoe. The ship swung with her
head towards the shore, or the mate
would have seen us. We pulled as for
our lives; not, however, for the usual
landing-place, but for a little bay on one
side. where it appeared that we could

easily get on shore. Every moment we expected to see a boat put off from the ship to pursue us, or a gun fired; but the sun had set, and it was growing darker and darker, and that gave us some hope. Still we could be seen clearly enough from the ship if anybody was looking for us. The mate had a pair of sharp eyes.

"'He'll flay us alive if he catches us,' said I.

"'Never,' answered Tom, in a low tone; 'I'll jump overboard and be drowned, whenever I see a boat make chase after us.'

"'Don't do that, Tom,' said I; 'hold on to the last. They can but kill us in the end, and we don't know what may happen to give us a chance of escape.'

"You see, friend Peter, that has been my maxim ever since; and I've learned to know for certain that that is the right thing. Well, before long we did see a boat leave the ship. It was too dark to learn who had gone over the side into her. We pulled for dear life for a few seconds, when Tom cried out that he knew we should be taken. I told him to lie down in the bottom of the canoe, and that if the ship's boat came near us I would strip off my shirt and pretend to be an Injun. At first he wouldn't consent; but, as the boat came on, some muskets were fired, and suddenly he said he'd do as I proposed, and he lay down, and I stripped off my shirt, and smoothed down my hair, which was as long as an Injun's. On came the boat. I pulled coolly on, as if in no way concerned. The boat came on—she neared us. Now or never, I thought; so I sang out, in a feigned voice, and pointed with my paddle towards the other side of the harbor.

"I don't think I ever felt as I did at that moment. Did they know me, or should I deceive them? If the mate was there, I knew that we should have no chance. The people in the boat ceased pulling. I didn't move either, though the canoe, with the last stroke I had given, slid on. Again I pointed with my paddle, gave a flourish with it, and away I went as if I had no business with them. I could not understand how I had so easily deceived my shipmates, and every instant I expected them to be after us.

"At last we lost sight of them in the gloom; but Tom, even then, was unwilling to get up and take his paddle. I told him that, if he didn't, we should have a greater chance of being caught. The moment I said that, up he jumped, and paddled away so hard that I could scarcely keep the canoe in the right course for the place where we wanted to land. The stars helped us with their light; and, as we got close in with the shore, we found the mouth of a stream.

"Though we had so longed to get on shore, we felt afraid to land, not knowing what we should do with ourselves. The shore looked so strange, and we expected to see all sorts of wild animals and snakes, which we had heard talk of. Tom was the most timid.

"'It was bad aboard, Bill,' said he, 'but if we was to meet a bear or a buffalo, what should we do?'

"I couldn't just answer him; but, when we found the river, we agreed that we would pull up it as far as we could go, and it would carry us some way into the country, at all events.

"We little knew the size of this mighty land, or of the big, long, long rivers running for hundreds of miles through it. This America of yours is a wonderful country, friend Redskin, if you did but know it.

"Well, up the river we pulled for some miles; it was but a mere brook. you'll understand, but we thought it a great river. It was silent enough, for there were no habitations except a few native wigwams. We had all the night before us; that was one thing in our favor. As on we went, we heard a roaring, splashing noise, which increased.

" 'Hillo! here's a heavy sea got up; I see it right ahead,' cried Tom.

" 'We must go through it, however,' said I; and so I tried to paddle the canoe through it.

" We very nearly got swamped; it was, you see, a waterfall and rapid, and higher up, even, our canoe could not have floated. We now agreed that go on shore we must, like it or not; I stepped out first, and then helped Tom, or in his fright he would have capsized the canoe.

" There we were both of us on firm ground for the first time since, as little boys, we **left** old England. I did fell strange, and when I tried to walk, I could scarcely get along. Tom rolled about as if he was drunk, hardly able to keep his feet. The rough ground hurt us, and we were every instant knocking our toes and shins against stumps and fallen branches. We both of us sat down ready to cry.

"'How shall we ever get along?' asked Tom.

"'We shall get accustomed to it,' I answered; 'but it does make me feel very queer.'

"We found a good supply of provisions in the canoe, and we loaded ourselves with as much as we could carry; and we then had the sense to lift our canoe out of the water, and to carry her some way, till we found a thick bush in which we hid her.

"'If they find out we got away in the canoe, they'll think we are drowned, and not take the trouble to look for us,' observed Tom. as we turned our backs on the spot.

" We were pretty heavily laden, for we didn't know where we might next find any food ; and as we walked on we hurt our feet more and more, till Tom roared out with pain, and declared he would go no further.

" ' Then we shall be caught and flayed alive, that's all, Tom,' said I. ' But let us see if we can't mend matters; here, let us cut off the sleeves of our jackets and bind them round our feet.'

" We did so, and when we again set-off, we found that we could walk much better than before.

" We hadn't been so many years at sea without learning how to steer by the stars. What we wanted was to get to the east; as far from the sea and our hated ship as possible—that one thought urged us on. Through brushwood, which tore our scanty clothes to shreds; and over rough rocks, which wounded our feet; and across marshes and streams, which wetted us well nigh from head to

foot, we pushed our way for some hours—
it seemed to us the whole night—till we got
into an Indian track. 'We didn't know
what it was at the time, but found it was an
easy path; so we followed it up at full speed.
On we ran; we found that it led in the right
direction, and that's all we thought of.

"Unaccustomed to running or walking as
we were, it seems surprising how we should
have held out; but the truth is, it was fear
helped us along, and a burning desire to be
free. Daylight found us struggling up a
high hill or ridge, rather running north and
south; we reached the top just as the sun
rose above a line of lofty and distant mountains. We turned round for a moment to
look on the far-off blue waters which lay
stretched out below us, and on which we had
spent so large a portion of our existence.

"'I've had enough of it,' cried Tom,
fiercely shaking his fist; and then we turned
along again. and rushed down the ridge

towards the east. It was the last glimpse I
ever had of the wide ocean.

"Still we did not consider ourselves safe.
We should have liked to have put a dozen
such ridges between our tyrants and ourselves.

"On we went again till at last our exhausted strength failed, and we stopped to
take some food. Once having sat down, it
was no easy matter to get up again; and before we knew what was happening, we were
both fast asleep. We must have slept a
good many hours, and I dreamed during
that time that the mate, and cook, and a
dozen seamen were following us with flen-
sing-knives, and handspikes, and knotted
ropes, shrieking and shouting at our heels.
We ran, and ran for our lives, just as we
had been running all night, but they were
always close behind us. The mate—oh
how I dreaded him—had his hand on my
shoulder, and was giving a growl of satisfac

tion at having caught me, when I awoke;
and, looking up, saw not the mate, but the
most terrible-looking being I had ever set
eyes on, so I thought.

"I had, to be sure, seen plenty of savages
who came off to the ship from the islands at
which we used to touch, but they were
none of them so fierce as he looked. I
won't describe him, because he was simply
a red-skin warrior in his war paint and
feathers. It was his hand that was on my
shoulder; his grunt of surprise at finding us
awoke me. I cried out, and Tom and I
jumped to our feet and tried to run away;
a dozen Indians, however, surrounded us,
and escape was impossible.

"'Let us put a bold face on the matter,
Tom,' I sang out; 'I don't think they mean
to kill us.'

"Our captors talked a little together, and
they seemed pleased with the way we
looked at them, for they showed us by signs

that they meant us no evil. They were a
portion of a war-party on their way to destroy the pale-face settlement on the coast.
They guessed by our dress and looks, and
from our clothes being torn, that we were
runaway English seamen; and, knowing
that we should not wish to go back to our
ship, considered that we should prove of
more value to them alive, than our scalps
would be if they took them. We understood them to say that they wanted us to go
with them to attack their enemies, but we
showed them by our feet that we could not
walk a step, and as they were not ill-tem-
pered people they did not insist on it.
After a talk they lifted us up—two taking
Tom, and two me between them—and carried us along at a quick rate for some miles
to their camp; there we saw a large number of Indians collected, some armed with
bows, and some few with fire-arms.

"There were a few women, in whose

charge we were placed. We could not make out whether we were considered prisoners or not; at all events, we could not run away. Leaving us, the whole party set forth towards the west on their expedition.

"Two days passed, and then, with loud shoutings, and shriekings, and firing of muskets, the party appeared, with numerous scalps at the end of their spears, and some wretched captives driven before them. I remember, even now, how I felt that night, when the war-dance was danced, and the prisoners tortured; how fearfully the men, and even the women, shrieked, and how the miserable people who had been taken, as they were bound to stakes, writhed under the tortures inflicted on them. While we looked on, Tom and I wished ourselves back again, even on board the ship, thinking that we ourselves might next be treated in the same manner.

"At last the savages brought fire, and then

as the flames blazed up, we saw three people whom we knew well—the captain, and mate, and one of the men, who had been among the worst of our tyrants. Though their faces were distorted with agony and horror, as the light fell on them, there was no doubt about the matter. They might have seen us. If they did, it must have added to their misery. They had come on shore to visit some of the settlers, we concluded, and, at all events, were found fighting with them.

" We got accustomed, after a time, to such scenes, and learned to think little of them, as you doubtless do, friend Peter; but at that time I went off in a sort of swoon, as the shrieks and cries for mercy of the burning wretches reached my ears.

"The Indians had got a great deal of booty, and having taken full revenge for the injury done them, and expecting that they would be hunted out if they remained in the neighborhood, they judged it wise to remove to another part of the country.

"Our feet had sufficiently recovered during the rest of two days to enable us to walk, or I am not certain that we should not have been killed, to save our captors the trouble of carrying us.

"It took us a week to reach the main camp, where most of the women and children were collected. We limped on, with difficulty and pain, thus far concealing our sufferings as much as we could. We could not have gone a mile further, had not the tribe remained here to decide on their future course. The rest, and the care the women took of us, sufficiently restored our strength to enable us to move on with the tribe to the new ground they proposed taking up.

"Your Indian ways, friend Peter, were very strange to us at first, but by degrees we got into them, and showed that we were every bit as good men as the chief braves themselves. Whatever they did, we tried to do, and succeeded as well as they, except in tracking an enemy, and that we never could come up with. They, at first, treated us as slaves, and made us work for then., as they did their women; but when they saw what sort of lads we were, they began to treat us with respect, and soon learned to look upon us as their equals.

"We both of us became very different to what we were at sea, Tom especially. There we were cowed by our task-masters; here we felt ourselves free men; and Tom, who was looked upon as an arrant coward on board ship, was now as brave as the bravest warrior of the tribe. We were braver, indeed; for while they fought Indian fashion, behind trees, we would rush on, and never failed to put our enemies to flight.

"We were of great service to our friends in assisting them to establish themselves in their new territory, and to defend themselves against the numerous foes whom they very soon contrived to make. Still, we held our own, and our friends increased in numbers and power.

"Our chief was ambitious, and used every means to add fresh members to his tribe by inducing those belonging to other tribes to join us. His object, which was very clear, excited the jealousy of a powerful chief especially, of the great Dakotah nation, inhabiting the country northeast of our territory. He, however, disguised his intentions, and talked us into security by pretending the greatest friendship. Through his means, our other enemies ceased to attack us, and we began to think that the hatchet of war was buried for ever.

"Tom and I had been offered wives— daughters of chiefs—and we had agreed to take them to our lodges, when we both of us set out on a hunting expedition to procure game for our marriage feast. and skins

t. pay for the articles we required. We had g eat success, and were returning in high spirits, when night overtook us, within a short distance of the village. We camped where we were, as we would not travel in the dark, hoping to enter it the next morning in triumph.

"About midnight, both Tom and I started from our sleep, we knew not why. Through the night air there came faint sounds of cries, and shrieks, and shouts, and warlike noises. We thought it must be fancy; but presently, as we stood listening, there burst forth a bright light in the direction of the village, which went on increasing, till it seemed that every lodge must be on fire. What could we do? Should we hasten on to help our friends?

"It was too late to render them any assistance. We must wait till daylight to learn what way the foe had gone, and how we could best help our friends: so we stood watching the flames with grief and anger, till they sunk down for want of fuel.

"We had not lived so long with Indians without having learned some of their caution, and, concealing our game and skins, as soon as it was dawn we crept on towards the village.

"As we drew near, not a sound was heard —not even the bark of a dog. We crept amid the bushes on hands and feet, closer and closer, when, from a wooded knoll, we could look down on the lately happy village, or, I should say, on the spot where it lately stood.

"By the gray light of the morning a scene of desolation and bloodshed was revealed to us, which, in all my experience of warfare, I have never seen equalled. Every lodge was burned to the ground; here and there a few blackened posts alone remaining to show where they once stood; but a burnt village I have often seen. It was the sight of the mangled and blackened bodies of our late friends and companions, thickly strewed over the ground, which froze the blood in our reins. For some moments we could scarcely find breath to whisper to each other. When we did, we reckoned up the members of the tribe, men, women, and children, and then counting the bodies on the ground, we found that our foes had killed every one of them, with the exception of perhaps a dozen, who might have been carried off. This told us, too correctly, how the event had occurred.

" In the dead of night the village had been surrounded, torches thrown into it, and, as the people rushed out confused, they were murdered indiscriminately—old and young, women and children. Were our intended wives among them? We almost wished they were; but we dared not descend to as-certain. The place was no longer for us.

" ' I wish that I was back in England, Tom,' said I.

" 'So do I, Bill, right heartily,' said he.

" 'East or west, Tom ?' said I.

" 'Not west!—no, no !' he answered, with a shudder, 'we might be caught by another whaler.'

" 'East, then,' said I, pointing to the rising sun ; 'we may get there some day, but it's a long way, I've a notion.'

" 'If we keep moving on, we shall get there though, long as it may be,' said Tom.

"So we crept back to where we had left our goods, and having taken food for a couple of days, we went and hid ourselves in some thick bushes, where we hoped our enemies would not find us.

" For two days and nights we lay hid, and on the third morning we agreed that we might as well chance it as stay where we were, when the sound of voices, and of people moving through the woods, reached our ears, and, peeping out. we saw several warriors passing along at no great distance. From the way they moved, we knew that they were not looking for any one, nor believing that any enemy was near; but still, should any one of their quick eyes fall on our trail, they would discover us in an instant.

"I never felt my scalp sit more uneasy on my head. Suddenly they stopped and looked about; I thought that it was all over with us; the keen eyes of one of them, especially, seemed to pierce through the very thicket where we lay. We scarcely dared to breathe, lest we should betray ourselves. Had there been only five or six, we might have sprung out and attacked them with some chance of success; but there were a score at least, and more might be following, and so the odds were too great. They were most of them adorned with scalps—those of our slaughtered friends, we did not doubt, and we longed to be avenged on them. On they came; and just as we thought that we had seen the end of them, more appeared, and several of them looked towards us.

"How we escaped discovery, I do not know. Long after the last had passed on into the forest, we came out of our hiding-place, and, gathering up all our property, prepared to commence our journey. We pushed on as fast as our legs would carry us, every moment expecting to come upon some of our enemies, or to have them pouncing out upon us from among the trees or rocks. All day we pushed on, almost without stopping, and for several days resting only during the hours of darkness, till at last we hoped that we had put a sufficient distance between our enemies and ourselves to escape an attack.

"We now camped, to catch more game, and to make arrangements for our course.

"We had got some little learning at school. though most of it was forgotten; but we remembered enough to make us know that England was to the northeast of us, and so we determined to travel on in that direction.

"I won't tell you now all about our journey.

"We had not got far before we found the country so barren, that we were obliged to keep to the north, which brought us into the territory owned by the Dakotah people. We knew nothing of the way then, except from the accounts picked up over the camp-fires of our former friends, and we had managed hitherto to keep out of the way of all strangers. We were ignorant, too, of the great distance we were from England; and of another thing we were not aware, and that was, of the cold of winter.

"We were still travelling on, when the nights became so cold, that we could scarcely keep ourselves from freezing, though sleeping close to our camp-fires. It got colder and colder, and then down came the snow, and we found that winter had really set in. To travel on was impossible; so we built ourselves a lodge, and tried to trap and kill animals enough to last us for food until the snow should disappear. They became, however, scarcer and scarcer, and we began to fear that the supply of food we had collected would not last us out till summer. We had, however, a good number of skins, and, though we had intended to sell them, we made some warm clothing of them instead.

"We had too much to do during the day, in hunting and collecting wood for our fire, to allow of the time hanging very heavy on our hands. At first, we got on very well, but our food decreased faster than we had calculated; and then Tom fell down from a rock, and hurt himself so much, that I could scarcely get him home.

"While he was in this state, I fell sick; and there we two were. in the middle of a desert, without any one to help us. Tom grew worse, and I could just crawl out from our bed of skins and leaves to heap up wood on our fire, and to cook our food. That was growing less and less every day, and starvation stared us in the face. Our wood, too, could not hold out much longer; and though there was plenty at a little distance, I was too weak to go out and fetch it, and cut it up, and poor Tom could not even stand upright.

"Day by day our stock of food decreased. All was gone! There was wood enough to keep our fire alight another day; and then we knew that in one, or, at most, two days more, we must be starved or frozen to death. Tom groaned out that he wished we had but a bottle of rum to keep us warm, and drive away dreadful thoughts. So did I wish we had. That was a hard time, friend Peter."

"Fire-water! Was that all you thought

of? Did you never pray? Did you never ask God to deliver you?". inquired the Indian, in a tone of astonishment.

"No! What had God to do with us poor chaps, in that out-of-the-way place? He wouldn't have heard us if we had prayed; and, besides, we had long ago forgotten to pray," answered the old man, in an unconcerned tone.

"Ah! but He would have heard you; depend on that. The poor and destitute are the very people He delights to help," observed the Indian. "Ah! old friend, you little know what God is, when you fancy that He would not have heard you."

As he spoke, he produced a Testament in the Ojibway tongue, from which he read the words, "God is love;" and added, "This is part of the Bible, which your countrymen, the missionaries, have translated for us into our tongue."

"Ay! maybe." remarked the old man.

after considering a time; "I remember
about the Bible when I was a boy, and it's
all true; but I don't fancy God could have
cared for us."

"Why? is that wisdom you speak, old
friend?" exclaimed Peter. "See God did
care for you, though you did not even ask
Him, or you wouldn't be alive this day.
He has cared for you all your life long.
You have already told me many things
which showed it, and I doubt not if you
were to tell me every thing that has happened to you since you can remember up to
the present day, many, many more would
be found to prove it. Was it God's love
which sent me to you when you were on
the point of death, or was it His hatred?
Was it God's love which softened the hearts
of the Sioux towards us? Come, go on with
your history. I doubt not that the very
next thing that you have to tell me will
prove what I say."

"Well, friend Redskin, what you say may be true, and I don't wish to differ with you," answered the hunter, still apparently unmoved.

"As I was saying, Tom and I expected nothing but starvation. It was coming, too, I have an idea; for my part I had got so bad that I did not know where we were, or what had happened. The hut was dark, for I had closed up the hole we came in and out at with snow and bundles of dry grass, or we should very quickly have been frozen to death.

"The last thing I recollect was feeling cold—very cold. Suddenly a stream of light burst in on my eyes, and, that waking me up, I saw several Indians, in full war-dress, standing looking at Tom and me. I felt as if I did not care whether they scalped me or not: I was pretty well past all feeling. One of them, however, poured something down my throat, and then down,

Tom's throat: it did not seem stronger than water, though it revived me.

"I then saw that their looks were kind, and that they meant us no harm. The truth was that our forlorn condition touched their hearts. It is my opinion, friend Peter, that nearly all men's hearts can be moved, if touched at the right time. These men were Sioux—very savage, I'll allow—but just then they were returning home from a great meeting, where, by means of a white man, certain matters were settled to their satisfaction, and they felt, therefore, well disposed towards us. Who the white man was I don't know, except that he was not a trader, and was a friend of the Indians.

"The Sioux gave us food, and lighted our fire, and camped there for two days, till we were able to move on, and then took us along with them. We lived with them all the winter, and soon got into their ways.

"When we proposed moving on, they

would, on no account, hear of it, telling us that the distance was far greater than we supposed; and that there were cruel, treacherous white men between us and the sea, who were always making war on their people to drive them off their lands, and that they would certainly kill us.

"The long and the short of it is, that Tom and I gave up our intention of proceeding; and, having wives offered to us much to our taste, we concluded to stay where we were. Every day we got more accustomed to the habits of our new friends; and we agreed also, that our friends in England would not know us, or own us, if we went back. We were tolerably happy; our wives bore us children; and, to make a long story short, we have lived on with the same tribe ever since.

"Tom has grown stout and cannot join in the hunt, but his sons do, and supply him with food. If Tom had been with the rest,

he would not have left the neighborhood of
the ground where I fell, without searching
for me. It is through he and I being
together that I can still speak English, and
recollect things about home and our early
days. We have been friends ever since we
were boys, and never have we had a dispute. Four of my children died in infancy,
and I have a son and a daughter. The only
thing that tries me, is leaving Tom and
them, for their mother is dead; and yet I
should like to go and hear more of the
strange things you have told me about, and
see some of my countrymen again before I
die. They won't mourn long for the old
man; it is the lot of many to fall down and
die in the wilds, as I should have died, if you
had not found me. Tom, maybe, will miss
me; but of late years, since he gave up
hunting, we have often been separate, and
he'll only feel as if I had been on a longer
hunt than usual."

"And your children?" said Peter.

"They'll feel much like Tom, I suppose," answered the white hunter. "You know, friend Redskin, that Injun children are not apt to care much for their old parents. Maybe I will send for them, or go for them, if I remain with the pale-faces."

The Indian was silent for some time. He then observed, gravely: "Maybe, old friend, that the merciful God, who has protected you throughout your life, may have ordered this event also for your benefit; yet, why do I say 'maybe?' He orders all things for the best; this much I have learned respecting Him; the wisest man can know no more."

Were not the Indians of North America indued with a large amount of patience, they could not get through the long journeys they often perform, nor live the life of trappers and hunters, nor execute the curious carved work which they produce.

Patience is a virtue they possess in a wonderful degree.

Day after day Peter travelled on, slowly,
yet patiently, with his charge, at length
reaching the banks of the Assiniboine River,
a large and rapid stream, which empties
itself into the Red River, at about the centre of the Selkirk settlement. The banks,
often picturesque, were, in most places, well
clothed with a variety of trees, while the
land on either side, although still in a state
of nature, showed its fertility by the rich
grasses and clover which covered it. The
old hunter gazed with surprise.

"Why, friend Peter, here thousands and
thousands of people might live in plenty,
with countless numbers of cattle and sheep!"
he exclaimed. "I knew not that such a
country existed in any part of this region."

"We are now on the territory of the
English, a people who treat the red man
as they should—as fellow-men, and with

justice," answered the Indian. "It may be God's will that, ere many years are over, all this vast land, east and west, may be peopled by them, still leaving ample room for the red men, who, no longer heathen hunters, may settle down in Christian communities, as cultivators of the soil, or keepers of flocks and herds."

Still more surprised was the old hunter when, a few days after this, they came upon several well-cultivated fields, and saw beyond them a widely scattered village of neat cottages, and the spire of a church rising amid them towards the blue sky.

"What! are those the houses of English settlers?" asked the old man; "it will do my heart good to see some of my own countrymen again."

"You will see few of your countrymen here, father; the inhabitants are settlers, truly, but nearly all my people. There is, however, here a good minister, and a

schoolmaster, white men, who will welcome you gladly. Their hearts are full
of Christian love, or they would not come
to live out here, far removed from relatives and friends, laboring for the souls'
welfare of my poor countrymen."

The old man shook his head.

"No, no; I have no desire to see a parson. I remember well the long sermons—
the last I ever heard was when I was at
school—the parson used to give; and I used
to declare that when I was a man I would
keep clear of them, on this account."

"You would not speak so of our minister
here, were you to hear him," said the Indian. "I will not ask you to do what you
dislike. But here is my house; those within will give you a hearty welcome."

An Indian woman, neatly dressed, with a
bright, intelligent countenance, came forth,
with an infant in her arms, to meet Peter,
several children following her, who clung

around him with affectionate glee. A few
words, which Peter addressed to his wife,
made her come forward, and, with gentle
kindness, assist the old man into the cottage, where the* elder children eagerly
brought a chair, and placed him on it.
One boy ran off with the horse to a stable
close at hand, and another assisted his
mother to prepare some food, and to place
t on a table, before his father and their
guest.

The old man's countenance exhibited
pleased surprise.

" Well! well! I shouldn't have believed
it if I had heard it," he muttered. " I remember many a cottage in the old country
that did not come up to this."

Many and many a cottage very far behind it, the old hunter might have said;
and why? Because, in them the blessed
Gospel was not the rule of life; while in
that of the Indian, God's law of love was

the governing principle of all.   Christ's promised gift, the gift of gifts, rested on that humble abode of His faithful followers.

. Several days passed by, and, to Peter's regret, the old hunter showed no desire to converse with the devoted missionary minister of the settlement.   He came more than once, but the old man, shut up within himself, seemed not to listen to any thing he said.   At length he recovered sufficiently to go out, and one evening, wandering forth through the village, he passed near the church.   The sound of music reached his ears, as he approached the sacred edifice; young voices are raised together in singing praises to God, for His bounteous gifts bestowed on mankind:

> "Glory to Thee, my God, this night,
> For all the blessings of the light;
> Keep me, O keep me, King of kings!
> Beneath Thine own Almighty wings."

The 'old hunter stopped to listen; slowly, and as if in awe, he draws near the open porch. Again he stops, listening still more earnestly.

The young Christians within are singing in the Indian tongue. Closer he draws—his lips open—his voice joins in the melody. Words, long, long forgotten, come unconsciously from his lips. They are the English words of that time-honored hymn, sung by children in the old country. Scarcely does his voice tremble; it sounds not like that of a man, but low and hushed, as it might have been when he first learned, from his long-lost mother, to lisp those words of praise. The music ceases. The old hunter bursts into tears—tears unchecked.

Now he sinks on his knees, with hands uplifted—" Our Father, which art in heaven" —he is following the words of the missionary within. Are a mother's earnest, ceaseless prayers heard—prayers uttered ere she left

this world of trial? Yes; undoubtedly.
But God's ways are not man's ways; though
He tarry long, yet surely He will be found
—ay, "found of them who sought Him
not."

The children's prayer-meeting is over.
The old man remains on his knees, with
head bent down, and hands clasped, till the
shades of evening close over him.

CHAPTER IV.

THAT was the turning-point; from that day Rob Nixon was an altered man. Of course, I do not mean that he at once found all his difficulties gone, his heart full of love, his prayers full of devotion; but from this time he felt, as he had never felt before, that he was " blind, and poor, and naked," and far away from his home. His good and faithful friend, Peter, had given him wise and good advice, and had introduced him to the excellent minister of the settlement, Archdeacon Hunter, who soon became a daily visitor at Peter's cottage.

Skilful in imparting religious knowledge, he was able, by slow degrees, to instruct the old hunter in the leading truths of Christi anity. Once comprehended, the old man grasped them joyfully; and though long unaccustomed to the sight of a book, he set to work again to learn to read, that he might himself peruse the sacred volume. He, of course, learned in English; and it was curious to remark how his countenance beamed with pleasure as he recognized once familiar, but long-forgotten, letters and words, and how rapidly he recovered the knowledge he had possessed as a boy. His great delight was to attend the school-children's service, and to hear them afterwards catechized by the minister; and the gray-headed, gaunt old man, might have been seen constantly sitting among them, truly as a little child, imbibing the truths of the Gospel.

But, after a time, a change came over him. He appeared no longer content to remain, as hitherto, quietly in the cottage of his friend Peter. but spoke of wishing, once more, to be in the saddle, following his calling of a hunter. His rifle and accoutrements had carefully been brought home by Peter, but they would be of no use without a horse, powder and shot, and provisions.

The autumn hunt, in which a large number of the natives of the Red River settlement engage every year, was about to commence, and, to Peter's surprise and regret, Rob Nixon expressed his intention of accompanying them, should he be able to obtain the means of so doing. Peter trembled lest his old friend's conversion should not have been real—lest the seed, which he had hoped would have borne good fruit, had, after all, been sown on stony ground. He delicately expressed his fears, describing the temptations to which a hunter is exposed. A tear appeared in the old man's eye, as he called Peter's eldest boy to him.

"Friend, you love this boy?" he said.

"I do, fondly," was the natural answer.

"And you love his soul?" he asked.

"Far more, surely. It is the most precious part of him," said the Christian father.

"I, too, have a son, and I love him; but I knew that he could take good care of himself, and so I left him with little regret," said the hunter. "But now, friend, I know that he has a so.. which is in danger of perishing, I long to seek him out, to tell him of his danger, to win him back to that Saviour from whom he has strayed so far. I have a daughter and a friend too, and that friend has children. To all I would show how they may be saved. I loved them once, thinking nothing of their souls. How much more do I love their souls, now that I know their value!"

Peter warmly grasped the old hunter's hand, as he exclaimed—

"Pardon me, father, that I had hard thoughts of you. I understand your object, and I doubt not that aid will be afforded you to carry it out, for it is surely one well-pleasing in God's sight. 'He who convert-eth a sinner from the error of his way, shall save a soul from death, and shall hide a multitude of sins.'"

The whole matter being laid before the missionary minister the next day, he highly approved of the old hunter's intention, and promised to aid him as far as he had the power. He was on the point of setting out to visit the settlements, as the Red River colony is called, and he invited Robert Nix-on to accompany him, that he might there obtain the necessary aid for the accomplish-ment of his enterprise.

It was agreed, in the first place, that the old man should not undertake the journey alone. The difficulty was to find a companion for him.

Fortunately, two years before, a young Sioux had been taken prisoner by a party of Crees, a numerous people, who inhabit the country round Lake Winnipeg, their lodges being found far in other directions. They, like the heathen Ojibways, are always at war with the Sioux, and no opportunity is lost of taking each others' scalps.

This young Sioux, to whom the name of Joseph had been given, was anxious to carry the glad tidings of salvation to his countrymen, and hearing of the old hunter's wish, gladly volunteered to accompany him.

Peter would willingly himself have been his companion, but that he had his duties as a teacher to attend to, and his family to care for; besides which, a Sioux would be able to enter the country of his people with less risk of being killed by them, than would one of the Cree, or Ojibway nation. Peter, however, insisted on Nixon taking his horse

" You can repay me for the hire some

day, or your son can repay my children, should you bring him back. If it is not God's will that you should succeed in your mission, yet I fear not that He will repay me, as the loan is for an object well-pleasing in His sight."

A horse for the young Sioux, as well as provisions and articles as gifts to propitiate any chiefs of tribes who might not know him, were still considered necessary, and these could only be procured at the Red River.

The distance between the little colony of Prairie Portage and Red River is about sixty-five miles, but this neither the old hunter nor his companions thought in any way a long journey.

The astonishment of Robert Nixon was very great on finding a well-beaten road the whole distance, over which wheeled carriages could pass with perfect ease; still more when he passed several farms, even to

the west of Lane's Post, which formed the
termination of their first day's journey.

Their course was in the same direction as
that of the Assiniboine, which very winding
river they occasionally sighted. The banks
were generally well clothed with fine wood,
and the soil everywhere appeared to be of
the richest quality.

Considerably greater than before was the
old man's astonishment when, on the second
day about noon, the party arrived at a comfortable farm, where the owner hospitably
invited them to rest, and placed before them
the usual luxuries to be found in a well-
ordered farm-house in the old country, such
as good wheat and maize bread, cheese, butter, bacon, and eggs, with capital beer, and
in addition, preserves and fruit, several
vegetables, and fresh maize boiled, answering the purpose of green peas. A joint of
mutton was roasting at the fire, and pota-
toes were boiling.

After this repast, the farmer brought out a supply of tobacco, which, he told his guests, grew on the farm.

"Indeed, gentlemen, I may say we here live in plenty," he observed; "and all we want are people to settle down about us, and make our lives more sociable than they now are. We have drawbacks, I'll allow; and what farmer, even in the old country, can say that he has not? Ours are, early and late frosts, though chiefly the latter; grasshoppers, which will clear a field of every green thing in a night; and, occasionally, wolves and bears; but those gentry don't like the smell of our gunpowder, and have mostly taken their departure. On the Red River farms, they seldom or never hear of one, and the injury they can do us is but slight."

This was the commencement of a long line of farms, which extends, with few breaks. the whole distance to the Red

River, into which the Assiniboine falls. Often the old hunter was silent, considering the unexpected scenes which met his sight, though he occasionally indulged in quiet remarks on them; but when, at length, the lofty and glittering spire of a large cathedral,* appearing, as the rays of the evening sun shone on it, as if formed of burnished silver; numerous edifices, some of considerable dimensions, scattered about; public buildings and dwelling-houses; other churches in the distance; several windmills, with their white arms moving in the breeze, high above the richly tinted foliage of the trees, which formed an irregular fringe to the banks of the river flowing beneath them; while near at hand, at the point where the Assiniboine flows into the larger

* This cathedral belongs to the Roman Catholics, who have also a large convent near at hand. They maintain a considerable number of missionary sta-tions in different parts of the country.

stream, rose the walls and battlements of a strong fort, whose frowning guns commanded the surrounding plains;—when he saw all this, the scene appeared to his bewildered eyes as if it had sprung up by the touch of the enchanter's wand, in the midst of the desert.

"Well! well!" he exclaimed, "and I have been living all this time but a few weeks' journey from this place, and never should have thought of it."

The sight of the large sails of the freighters' boats made him somewhat uncomfortable, lest he should be carried off to sea; and he could scarcely be persuaded that he was still not far short of two thousand miles from the Atlantic Ocean, and that there was no chance of his being kidnapped. He was even more frightened than his steed, when a steamer came puffing up to a wharf below Fort Garry.

" What creature is that they have aboard

there?" he exclaimed. "Where does the strange craft come from? What is she going to do?" •

He sprang from his horse, and stood looking over the cliff at the steamer. He at once recognized her as a vessel, though of a construction wonderfully strange to his eyes, as no steamers had been built when he left England, and he had never heard of their invention. The stream of steam puffed off, and the loud screams accompanying it, made him somewhat incredulous as to the nature of the vessel. When, however, all was quiet, and he saw a stream of people issuing from her side, he was satisfied that she was of mortal build, and he was at length persuaded to go down and examine her himself. It almost took away his breath, as he said, to find that vessels of far greater size now ploughed the ocean in every direction, and that continents were traversed by long lines of carriages, dragged by single locomotives, at the rate of forty miles an hour.

After hearing of this, he was scarcely surprised at any of the wonders which were told him, and of the numerous discoveries and inventions which have been brought into practical use during half a century.

At the close of the day the travellers reached a well-built rectory, on the banks of the river, where they were hospitably received and entertained. While seated, in the evening, before the fire, with his host, the old man, as he looked round the room, and observed the various comforts which it contained, heaved a deep sigh.

"Ah! I feel now how sadly I have thrown my life away," he exclaimed. "I might, but for my early folly, have enjoyed all the comforts of civilization, and played my part as a civilized man, instead of living the life of a savage among savages."

" Friend," observed the minister, " this is not the only life. There is another and a better—to last forever.

" Then you have no desire to return to your former friends, the Sioux ?" the minister continued, after a pause.

" Ah ! yes ; but not for the pleasure such a life as they lead could give me. There is the friend of my youth, and there are his children, and my children. My great desire is to return to them to tell them that they have souls, and what the Lord, in IIis loving-kindness, has done for their souls."

The object of the old hunter was no sooner known in the settlement than he obtained all the assistance he could re quire. Few persons who had for so long led a savage life could have appreciated, more fully than he now seemed to do, the advantages of civilization, and yet none of them could turn him from his purpose. Within five days he and his young Sioux companion, Joseph, were ready to set out They had a led-horse to carry their provisions and presents, and they had arms, though rather to enable them to kill game for their support than for the purpose of fighting.

"I pray that our hands may be lifted up against no man's life, even though we may be attacked by those who are what we ourselves were but a short time back, and should still be, but for God's grace," said the old man, as he slung his rifle to his saddle-bow.

Once more Robert Nixon turned his back on the abodes of civilized men. Had it not been for the object in view, it would have been with a heavy heart.

"If Tom and I had remained at school, and labored on steadily, we might have been like one of those ministers of the Gospel, or settlers, and our children the same, instead of the young savages they now are, ignorant of God and His holy laws."

Thus he mused as he rode along. He and his young companion did not neglect the usual precautions, when they camped at night, to avoid discovery by any wandering natives who might be disposed to molest them.

The young Indian, though possessing much less religious knowledge than Peter, yet showed a sincere anxiety to fulfil his religious duties, and, without fail, a hymn was sung and prayer was offered up before starting on their day's journey, and when they lay down on their beds of spruce, fir twigs, or leaves, or dry grass, at night.

The travellers rode on day after day without encountering any material impediments to their progress. There were no rugged mountains to ascend, no dense forests to penetrate, or wild defiles amid which they had to find their way. There were rivers and streams; but some were easily forded; across others they swam their horses, and passed their provisions and goods on small rafts, which they towed behind them.

Leaving British territory, and moving west, the country had a barren and arid appearance. In many districts sand predominated, with sand-hills of more or less elevation; in others, grass, growing in tufts out of the parched-up stony ground, was the only herbage. Indeed, from north to south, and east to west, for many hundred miles, there exists an extent of country known as the Dakotah territory, unfitted, from the absence of water, to become the permanent abode of civilized man. Here, however, at certain seasons, herds of buffalo find pasturage on their way to and from the more fertile regions of the north; and thus, with the aid of fish, and other wild animals, and roots and berries, considerable tribes of the Dakotah nation find a precarious existence.

CHAPTER V.

It was in the western portion of the Dakotah territory, described in the last chap-
ter, that a numerous band of the lords of the
soil had pitched their skin tents by the side
of a stream, whose grassy banks, fringed
with trees, contrasted strongly with the dry
and hilly ground before mentioned, which,
as far as the eye could reach, extended on
either side of them Yet the scene was
animated in the extreme. In the centre
of a wide basin, into which a valley opened
from the distant prairie, was erected a high
circular inclosure of stakes, and boughs, and
skins. There was but one entrance towards
the valley, and on either side of this entrance
commenced a row of young trees. or branches

of trees, the distance between each line becoming greater and greater the further off they were from the inclosure. The figure formed by the lines was exactly that of a straight road drawn in perspective on paper, being very wide at one end, and narrowing gradually till it became only the width of the entrance to the inclosure at the other. Between each of the trees or bushes was stationed an Indian, armed with bow or spear, and having a cloak, or a thick mass of branches, in his hand. Outside the inclosure were numerous persons, chiefly women, and old men and boys, the latter armed with bows and arrows, and the former having cloaks or boughs. They were flitting to and fro, apparently waiting some event of interest. As the travellers reached the top of a hill overlooking the inclosure, a cloud of dust was seen approaching the further end.

"There they come, there they come!"

exclaimed the old hunter, with difficulty refraining from dashing down the hill, as, at the instant, a herd of some three or four hundred buffaloes burst, at headlong speed, from out of the dust—tossing their heads and tails, tearing up the earth with their horns, trampling, in their terror, over each other—followed closely by a band of red-skinned huntsmen, with bow or spear in hand, most of them free of clothing, and uttering the wildest cries and shouts, now galloping here, now there, as some fierce bull turned and stood at bay, sending an arrow into the front of one, dashing a spear into the side of another, while they hung on the flanks of the herd, keeping the animals, as nearly as possible, in the centre of the road.

Whenever any of the herd approached the line of bushes on either side, the Indians stationed there shook the cloaks or the boughs they held in their hands, and shout-

ed and shrieked, thus effectually turning the
'bewildered animals into the main stream.

Sometimes the whole herd attempted to
to break through, but were turned with
equal facility. If they attempted to stop,
the hunters behind, closing in on them,
urged them on, until, still more and more
compressed, those in the interior of the herd
being utterly unable to see where they were
going, they were forced, by redoubled
shouts and shrieks in their rear, through
the narrow gateway into the inclosure.
Through it they dashed, a dark stream of
wild fierce heads and manes surging up and
down, till the whole were driven in, and the
hunters themselves, leaping the bar across
the entrance, followed close in their rear.

Now, round and round the confined
pound the affrighted creatures rushed, not
discovering a single opening which might
afford them a chance of escape, bellowing
and roaring, the strong trampling on the

young and weak, the calves soon falling and being crushed to death; showers of arrows from the hunters' bows bringing many low, while others, wounded by the darts and spears of the people outside, or gored by their fellows, sunk down exhausted from loss of blood.

It was truly a spectacle of wanton and barbarous slaughter, which none but those accustomed to it could have watched unmoved. Even Robert Nixon, though he had often joined in similar scenes, regarded it with feelings very different to what he would formerly have done.

"Alas! alas! is it thus God's creatures are destroyed to no purpose, by these poor savages?" he exclaimed to his companion. "Not one-twentieth part of the meat can be consumed by them; and the day will come when they will seek for food, and there will be none for them, and they themselves must vanish away out of the land."

The two travellers had been moving along
the height above the valley, but so entirely
engaged were the Indians in the work of
entrapping the buffalo, that they were observed by no one

They now descended towards the tents.
In front of one of them sat a somewhat
portly man, his countenance, and the hue of
his complexion, rather than his costume,
showing that he was of the white race. The
tents were pitched on a spot sufficiently
elevated above the valley to enable him to
watch all that was taking place within the
pound. His attention, also, was so completely absorbed by the proceedings of his
companions, that he did not perceive, for
some time, the approach of the horsemen.
When he did, starting to his feet, and up-
setting the three-legged stool on which he
was sitting, he exclaimed—

"What, old chum! is it you—you, indeed? I made sure that what they told me

was true, and that you were long, long ago food for the wolves. Let me look at you. I cannot yet believe my senses."

Rob Nixon having dismounted, the two old men stood for some moments grasping each other's hands.

It was some time before old Tom could persuade himself that his friend was really alive; not, indeed, till the latter had given a brief account of the way he had been found and rescued by the Indian, Peter, and the chief events which had occurred to him.

"Well, well! I'm right glad to get you back; and now you must give up your hunting, as I have done, and just take your ease for the rest of your days," said old Tom.

"Hunting I have done with; but I have yet much work to do before I die," answered the old hunter. "You and I are great sinners; we were brought up in a Christian land, and still we have been living the lives of heathens. But, Tom, since I have been away, I have read the Bible; I have there learned about Christ; and I see that we have been living lives as different from His as black is from white, as light is from darkness. Tom, would you like to learn about Him?"

Tom signified his readiness with a nod. It was all Robert Nixon required, and he at once opened on the subject of God's love, and man's sin, and Christ the Saviour from sin. The young Indian stood by holding the horses, and watching the countenances of the speakers. It must have been a great trial for him to remain thus inactive, while his countrymen were engaged in their exciting occupation; but a new rule of life had become his, and duty had taken the place of inclination.

"There, Tom; I've just said a little about the chiefest thing I've got to say to you," were the words with which Rob wound up his address.

Tom looked puzzled, but not displeased, as some men might have been.

His friend was prevented from saying more, by the loud shouts of the Indians, as the last bull of a herd of nearly three hundred animals sank, overcome by loss of blood from numberless arrows and darts, to the saturated ground. There lay the shaggy monsters, in every conceivable attitude into which a violent death could throw them ; some on their backs, as they had rolled over, others with the young calves, which they had run against in their mad career round the pound, impaled on their horns ; many had fallen over each other, and, dying from their wounds, had formed large heaps in every direction. It was truly a sickening spectacle.*

* The chief object of the Indians in thus slaughtering so large a number of buffaloes is to lay in a store of their flesh, which they preserve and call pemmican. It is first cut off, free of fat, and hung up in thin strips to dry in the sun. It is then pounded between stones.

The old hunter, after a pause, pointed towards it:

"There, Tom, that's just a picture of what has been going on in the world, time without mind," he remarked; "the Indians are doing what the spirits of evil do, and the poor buffaloes are like the people in the world, all driven madly together, destroying one another, till none remain alive; but Christ delivers men from the spirits of evil, and leads them into safety and rest."

Hitherto the new-comers had escaped observation, but now numerous Indians

and put into leathern bags, with the boiled fat of the animal poured in and mixed with it. The white fur-traders also purchase this pemmican, as well as the skins known as robes, and also the sinews. Very many more animals are killed than can be used by the thoughtless savages, and thus thousands are left to rot uselessly on the prairie. As the buffaloes decrease in number, so do the red men disappear from the face of the earth. The settlement of civilized men in the territory appears to be the only mode of saving the natives, by affording them the means of subsistence.

crowded round, some to welcome the old white hunter, others to inquire the cause which brought the young man with him.

The first to approach the old man was a young girl; her complexion was fairer than that of several other girls who accompanied her, and her dress was more ornamented with beads and feathers than theirs. She stopped timidly at a short distance—Indian etiquette would not allow her to approach nearer.

She was very beautiful, but her beauty was that of the wild gazelle, it had not yet been destroyed by the hard toil, and often cruel usage, to which the older women of her people were exposed.

"Come, daughter; come!" said the old man in the Dakotah tongue, holding out his arms, "I have good tidings for thee."

The young girl bounded forward, and Rob Nixon, taking her in his arms, imprinted a kiss on her brow.

"Father, father, that you have come back when we thought you lost, is good news enough; you cannot bring me better"— looking up into the old man's face, not without some surprise, however, at the affectionate manner in which she was treated, contrasted with the stern way in which the Indians treat the females of their people.

"I will tell thee of the good news anon. You might not value it as it deserves," said Robert Nixon. "Thy brother, where is he?"

"He left the camp with a score more of our young braves, nearly ten moons ago, to make war on the Crees of the plain, and he has not yet returned. Scouts have been sent out, but no tidings have been received of the party."

The father did not conceal his disap-pointment.

"I have a rich gift to offer him," he

hought; " would that he had been here
to have accepted it. Alas! alas! how
great is my sin, who was born a Christian,
to have allowed my children to grow up
ignorant heathens."

It is sad to think that many white men, in
many parts of the vast territory known as
Rupert's land, may have cause to feel as
did Robert Nixon.

Two of old Tom's sons were also away on
the same hazardous expedition; but, though
anxious about them, for he was a kind-
hearted man, he could not enter into Rob
Nixon's feelings in the matter.

Now, as the evening came on, the people
crowded into the encampment, all eager to
hear how their white friend, and one of their
chief, as well as the oldest, of their leaders,
had escaped death. He used no bitter expressions, but he could not help asking,
ironically, how it was that—among so
many who professed regard for him—no

one had thought of turning back to look for him, when he was missed?

Numerous were the excuses offered, and all were glad when he dropped the subject, and held up a book, out of which he proposed to read to them, in their own language.

Not knowing the nature of a book, they naturally supposed it to be some powerful charm, and declared that he had become a great medicine-man.

"If it is a charm, and I do not say that it is not, it is one that, if you will listen, may do you good, and will make you wiser than you have ever before been," he answered. "Do you, or do you not, wish to hear me?"

There were no dissentient voices, and he then read to them how God, the Great Spirit, so loved the world, that He sent His Son into the world, that all who believe in Him should not perish, but have eternal life, —"men, women, and children, old and young alike," he added. "I will tell you more about the matter by and by, friends. Talk over now what I have said. This book, though small, contains a great deal; many a day must pass before you know its contents. Those who wish to know more may come to my lodge when they will, and I will read to them."

Rob Nixon made a very efficient missionary in his humble, unpretending way. He did not attack Maniton or any of the superstitions, but he placed the better way before them, that they might have the opportunity of comparing it with their own foolish customs and notions.

With his own daughter and his old friend, whom he knew he could trust, he proceeded in a different method; his friend he reminded of what he had been taught in his youth, how he had spent his life, and again and again inquired what hope he had for the future.

To his daughter he pointed out the folly of the religious belief and the customs of red people, and showed her the advantages of those of true Christians. To an artless, unsophisticated mind, where sin has not ruled triumphantly, the Gospel will always prove attractive, if offered—as its divine Originator intended it should be offered—as a blessing—as a charter of freedom, not a code of legal restrictions. The young girl received it joyfully, and day by day increased in knowledge and grace.

He was, however, often in despair with regard to old Tom. His friend listened to what he read and said, but the truth did not appear to find an entrance into his mind; still he listened, and tried to pray, and as he tried, he found praying less difficult; and when he listened, he comprehended better and better what he heard.

Tom's sons and daughters still remaining with him began also to listen, and came oftener and oftener to the old hunter's lodge, as their interest increased, till they declared that they were ready to go wherever they could constantly hear the Word of God, and be more fully instructed in its truths.

A large part of Robert Nixon's object was accomplished, but not the whole. A great grief lay at his heart—the loss, and probable death, of his son.

The winter had now set in, snow covered the whole face of nature in every direction, for many hundreds of miles. Travelling, though not impracticable, had become more difficult and dangerous; it could, however, be accomplished by means of dog-sleighs or carioles, though all the wealth possessed by Nixon and his friend could scarcely furnish dogs sufficient to transport all the party and provisions to the banks of the Assiniboine.

No news had been received of the missing band. Old Tom shared his friend's grief, and now he began to dread their loss for the most important reason.

Nixon's time was also engaged among the tribe generally; even the chief listened to him attentively, and offered no opposition to his proceedings. For himself, he said that he was too old to change, but that his people might follow the new way, if they found it better than the old.

Joseph, the young Sioux, was a great assistance to him. Nixon offered to allow him to go back to his own people, but he declined, saying that he was not strong enough to resist temptations, and might be inclined to go back to their evil ways, if he found himself among them; an example which more civilized youths might wisely follow—not to run into temptation.

CHAPTER VI.

It was during the short spring of the North American continent, which so suddenly breaks into perfect summer, that a camp might have been seen pitched on the side of the bank of a broad and rapid river. The spot selected for the camp formed a bay of the river, or it might be called a nook in the bank. It appeared to have been chosen for the purpose of concealment: for only from one point on the opposite bank could it be seen, while above it was completely sheltered by the thick growth of trees which fringed each side of the river. From the conical shape of the skin-covered tents, the accoutrements of the steeds tethered near, the dog-sleds, for carrying goods and provisions, and the people standing or sitting about, it would have been known at once to be a Sioux encampment.

On a nearer inspection, however, several points of difference would have been discovered. In front of one of the tents sat two old men, whose complexion showed that they were not Indians, while the dress of one of them was that of a civilized man. Several young women and girls were busily preparing the evening meal, some young men were bringing them a supply of firewood and water, while others were engaged in fishing in the river.

Several, both of the young men and girls, had complexions much lighter than those of Indians, though others, from their dark color, were evidently of the native race. They seemed to be fearless of interruption; indeed, they probably relied on due notice of danger being given them by their scouts or sentries. who were watching from some of the more elevated spots in the neighbor-hood.

One of the old men had been reading to the other from the Bible. He closed the sacred volume.

"Let us thank God, old friend, that with-in a week we may hope once more to be among our Christian countrymen, and be able to join with them in His worship and praise, and to thank Him for His loving mercy to us," said Robert Nixon. "For my part, I have only one desire: to recover my boy and yours, and to see them belong-ing to Christ's flock."

"Ah, Bill!"—Tom always called his friend by that name,—"I, too, should like to see the day; but it's far off, I fear. But I hope they'll go to heaven somehow."

This conversation was interrupted by a loud cry of alarm from the young women of the party; and looking up, they saw a dozen red-skin warriors. who had just issued

from among the trees on the summit of the
bank above them.

Several had rifles, others were armed
only with bows. They were in the act of
taking aim with their weapons, when Nixon
saw them.

Forgetting the native language in his agi-
tation, he shouted out to them, in English,
to desist. They hesitated.

Some of the girls took the opportunity of
rushing off to seek for shelter behind the
trees. Tom went into the tent for his gun.

Nixon advanced towards the Indians,
whom he perceived to be Crees, the mortal
enemies of the Dakotahs. His daughter,
believing him to be in danger, instead of
running for shelter, like her companions,
flew after him.

Old Tom reappeared at the moment with
his rifle.

The Crees, believing that resistance was
about to be offered, fired. Their powder or

weapons were bad : some did not go off, the bullets, generally, flew wide, but one, alas! took effect. It was in the bosom of Rob Nixon's daughter. Her cry made him turn round; and, forgetting all else, he caught her in his arms, as she was sinking to the ground.

Before the savages had time to reload, and as they were about to rush down the hill, scalping-knife in hand, to complete their cruel work, they were set upon by an equal number of Sioux, who sprang so suddenly on them from behind, that not one of them had time to use his weapon in self-defence.

A desperate struggle ensued, each man trying to pin his antagonist to the ground. Two Crees, desperately wounded, lay fainting from loss of blood.

Tom, climbing up the hill, still further turned the balance in favor of the Sioux.

The Sioux were, Tom perceived, of his own party. They had been warned by one of their scouts that an enemy was at hand, and without disturbing the rest of the camp had gone out to intercept them. They had, however, missed them, but again discovering their trail, had followed close in their rear, though not fast enough to prevent the unhappy catastrophe which had occurred.

The struggle was fierce and desperate. Neither party expected any mercy from the victors. Three of the Crees were killed, and this releasing three of the Sioux party, aided by old Tom, the latter were able to assist their companions. Their aim was, however, not to kill. The Crees were quickly disarmed, and being bound, stood expecting the usual fate of the vanquished.

At a signal from Nixon, they were led down the bank to where he knelt by the side of his daughter, in vain attempting to stanch the life-blood streaming from her wound.

"Father!" she whispered; "I am leaving you. I feel death coming, but I am happy, for I know One, powerful to save, is ready to receive me. I would have lived to have comforted you, but I believe my prayers are heard, and that my brother will yet be restored to you."

She was silent for some time; then her eyes, opening, fell on the prisoners, as they stood bound on the top of the bank, and she continued:

"I have but one petition to make. It is, that those ignorant men may not be punished. They followed but the ways of their people, and thought not of the wicked act they were doing. I would speak to them."

In a faint voice, the dying girl addressed the prisoners, and urged them to listen to the words her father would speak to them, adding: "Truly do I forgive you, and may you find forgiveness from the Great Good Spirit, whom you know not."

It would be difficult to describe the astonishment of the Crees when they found that not only were they not to undergo torment before being killed, but that they were actually freely pardoned.

After consulting for some time, one of them, who appeared to be the leader, stepped forward and said :

" We have heard that there are praying men among the pale-faces, but that their praying made their people different to us we did not know, for most of the things we do they do; they fight with each other and with us, they drive us from our lands, they cheat us when trading, they shoot us without pity, whenever they catch us, and they bring disease and death among us ; so that, though once we were numerous as the stones which strew the prairie lands of the Dakotahs, now we can count our people while the sun rests at its midday height in the sky. Such was our notion of the pale-faces, but you have given us a different notion. Though we have done you a great injury, though our weapons have cruelly cut down one who is surely the most lovely of the flowers of the prairie, instead of slaying us, you forgive us; she too, even, not only forgives us, but prays to the Great Spirit for us. Our minds are astonished; our hearts are softened, melted within us. We would be your friends, and we wish to prove it. We know the pale-faces who dwell towards the rising of the sun, and we will accompany you on your way to them, and guard you from further attacks. You doubt us. You fear treachery. You are wise. We will prove that we are honest. Some moons past, ere the snows of winter had covered the ground, our tribe was assailed by a party of Dakotah braves. We had notice of their coming, and had an ambush prepared for them. Among them we discerned three whom we knew by their color to be the children of the pale-faces. We judged that they had been carried off when young, and we hoped to obtain a reward by restoring them to their parents or countrymen, our friends. The Dakotahs we slew, but, though they fought desperately and were much wounded, we succeeded in saving the three young men alive. We could not then travel with them, so we kept them in our lodges while the snow remained. We were on our way to the east with them when, in our folly, we resolved to attack your camp. Our prisoners we left with a small number of our band, who are but a short way from this."

"Oh! bring them—haste!—haste!" exclaimed the wounded girl, alone divining who they were of whom the Cree spoke; "I would see my brother ere I die. I have much—much to say to him."

Anxious to gratify his daughter, and satisfied that the Cree chief spoke the truth, and would not prove treacherous, Robert Nixon allowed two of his followers, known as fleet of foot, to hasten to his camp to bring in the young men spoken of, having no doubt that his own son, and his friend's two sons, were the prisoners spoken of.

Meantime, it appeared doubtful whether the dying girl would survive till their arrival. While the rest of the party stood round grieving, she reclined in her father's arms, occasionally whispering a few words of comfort in his ear, and assuring him of her happiness. At length, she lifted up her head in the attitude of listening. Her quick ear had caught the sound of approaching footsteps, even before the rest of the party. It was some time before any one appeared.

" I knew it—I knew it—my brother !" she cried out, as several young men, running at full speed, burst from among the trees at the top of the bank.

One of them, who was leading, taking a

hurried glance around, rushed down, and, with an expression in which surprise and grief were mingled, threw himself by her side.

She took his hand, and strange to his ear were the communications she made.

Another of the youths approached her. She gave him her other hand, and turned her countenance towards him as she did so.

"I was the cause of your going on that expedition. I was ignorant, dark-minded, wicked. I knew well that you loved me. I know it now; but, oh! listen to my father. He will tell you of One who loves you far more than I could do, whose love will make ample amends for the loss of mine; and then we may meet in the realms of happiness, to dwell forever and ever together."

To the young heathen, this language was an enigma. Ere it was solved, the speaker had ceased to breathe.

"The Lord's will be done!" said the old

hunter; and those who knew how he loved his child understood what a mighty change religion had wrought in his heart.

They buried her in that secluded spot, beneath the green turf, on which she had lately trod so full of life and beauty; and those who had loved her, and their late foes, assisted to raise a monument, of materials furnished by the river-bed and the surrounding trees, above her tomb.

Rob Nixon and all the party reached the settlements in safety. He mourned as a father for his daughter, but his mourning was full of hope.

Her dying words were not thrown away on her brother, or on his companions. Before long, they were all baptized, and admitted to the privileges and blessings of Christ's Church. When the father knelt at the Lord's table, for the first time after his daughter's death, and thought of the dead for whom thanks had been given, because they had died in Christ's faith and fear, he felt that his beloved daughter had not died in vain. He declared that he had not been preserved from so many and great dangers of body and spirit, to lead a life of idleness; and while life remained, he never wearied in striving to bring others to a knowledge of Him, whom he had found to be so precious to his own soul ·

THE END.

INDIAN BATTLES

AND

ADVENTURES.

INDIAN HONESTY.

In the character of the Indians of North America there are many traits which their white neighbours would do well to imitate. Among these, strict honesty is one. Mr. Catlin gives the credit of this virtue to all the wild tribes which he visited, not corrupted by intercourse with civilized nations. Bolts and bars, for the protection of property, among them are unknown. He cites many examples to prove this. The following anecdote is from another source.

An Indian being among his white neighbors, asked for a little tobacco to smoke, and one of them, having some loose in his pocket, gave him a handful. The day following, the Indian came back, inquiring for the donor, saying he had found a quarter of a dollar among the tobacco; being told that as it was given him he might as well keep it, he answered, pointing to his breast: 'I got a good man and a bad man here; and the good man say, it is not mine, I must return 't to the owner; the bad man say why he gave it to you, and it is your own now; the good man say, that's not right, the tobacco is yours, not the money ; the bad man say, never mind, you got it, go buy some dram ; the good man say, no, no, you must not do so ; so I don't know what to do, and I think to go to sleep ; but the good man and the bad man keep talking all night, and trouble me ; and now I bring the money back I feel good.'

HONOR AMONG INDIANS.

There is no class of human beings on earth, who hold a pledge more sacred and binding, than do the North American Indians. A sample of this was witnessed during the Winnebago war of 1827, in the person of Dekker-re, a celebrated chief of that nation, who, among four other Indians of his tribe, was taken prisoner at Prairie du Chien. Colonel Snelling, of the 5th regiment of infantry, who then commanded that garrison, despatched a young Indian into the nation, with orders to inform the other chiefs of Dekker-re's band, that unless those Indians who were perpetrators of the horrid murders of some of our citizens, were brought to the fort and given up within ten days, Dekker-re and the other four Indians who were retained as hostages, would be shot at the end of that time. The awful sentence was pronounced in the presence of Dekker-re, who, though proclaiming his own innocence of the

outrages which had been committed by others
of his nation, exclaimed that he feared not
death, though it would be attended with serious consequences, inasmuch as he had two
affectionate wives and a large family of small
children who were entirely dependent on him
for their support: but if necessary, he was willing to die for the honour of his nation. The
young Indian had been gone several days, and
no intelligence was yet received from the murderers. The dreadful day being near at hand,
and Dekker-re being in a bad state of health,
asked permission of the Colonel to go to the
river to indulge in his long accustomed habit of
bathing; in order to improve his health. Upon
which, Col. S. told him that, if he would promise, on the honor of a chief, that he would not
leave the town, he might have his liberty, and
enjoy all his privileges, until the day of the appointed execution. Accordingly he first gave
his hand to the Colonel, thanked him for his
friendly offer, then raised both his hands aloft,
and in the most solemn adjuration, promised
that he would not leave the bounds prescribed,
and said, if he had a hundred lives, he would
sooner lose them all than forfeit his word, or
deduct from his proud nation one particle of its
boasted honor. He was then set at liberty. He
was advised to flee to the wilderness, and make
his escape. "But no," said he, "do you think
I prize life above honor? or that I would betray a confidence reposed in me, for the sake of
saving my life?" He then complacently re

mained until nine days of the ten which he had to live had elapsed, and nothing heard from the nation with regard to the apprehension of the murderers, his immediate death became apparent; but no alteration could be seen in the countenance of the chief. It so happened that on that day, Gen. Atkinson arrived with his troops from Jefferson Barracks, and the order for execution was countermanded, and the Indians permitted to repair to their homes.

INDIAN ELOQUENCE.

The Indian warrior Tecumseh, who fell in the late American war, was not only an accomplished military commander, but also a great natural statesman and orator. Among the many strange, and some strongly characteristic events of his life, the council which the American General Harrison held with the Indians at Vincennes, in 1811, affords an admirable instance of the sublimity which sometimes distinguished his eloquence. The chiefs of some tribes had come to complain of a purchase of lands which had been made from the Kickafoos. The council effected nothing, but broke up in confusion, in consequence of Tecumseh having called General Harrison "a liar." During the long talks which took place in the conference, Tecumseh having finished one of his speeches, looked round, and seeing every one seated, while no seat was prepared for him, a momentary frown passed over his countenance. Instantly General Harrison ordered that a chair should be given him. Some person presented one, and bowing, said to him, "Warrior, your father, General Harrison, offers you a seat." Tecumseh's dark eye flashed. "My father!" he exclaimed .indignantly, extending his arms towards heaven; "the sun is my father, and the earth is my mother; she gives me nourishment, and I repose upon her bosom." As he ended, he suddenly seated himself on the ground.

INDIAN COQUETRY.

The Chawanon Indians, inhabiting the lake of Marcotti, and who are considered the most warlike and civilized of the American Indians, have a manner of courtship which we believe to be peculiar to themselves. When such of their young women as have pretensions to beauty, attain their twelfth year, which is the usual period of their marriage, they either keep themselves quite secluded at home, or when they go out .nuffle themselves up in such a manner, that nothing is seen but their eyes. On these indications of beauty, they are eagerly sought in marriage, and those suitors who have acquired the greatest reputation as warriors or hunters, obtain the consent of the family. After this, the lover repairs to the cabin, where the beauty is lying enveloped on her couch. He gently approaches and uncovers her face, so that his

person may be seen, and if this be to her mind
she invites him to lie down by her side ; if not,
she again conceals her face, and the lover re-
tires.   A husband has the privilege of marry-
ing all his wife's sisters as they arrive at age, so
that after, often before, his first wife is thirty,
he has married and abandoned at least a
dozen.

WEATHERFORD.

"I come, my Wilwullah!
  Guide hither our boy!
I bring from the forest
  Its spirit and joy :
Why lingereth my soft-eyed ?
  And dark grew his brow;
"Thy hunter returneth—
  Where, truant, art thou?"

He enters his wigwam—
  What meaneth that cry ?
His bold form what freezeth?
  What filmeth his eye ?
The work of the white men!
  His mate of the wood,
And their fawns, the light-footed,
  All couched in their blood !

Before a cold foeman
  The Indian is cold ;
But his heart in his wild-wood
  Is like molten gold.
The warrior has clasped them—
  He's red in their gore !
. Has raved and wept o'er them—
  But ne'er will weep more'

" Ye snow-brow destroyers!
    Ye false and ye foul!
For this, by Manito!
    For this shall ye howl!
I swear that pale thousands
    Shall weep for this blow ;
For each drop here wasted,
    Red rivers shall flow !

" When smoke dims the distance,
    And shrieks fill the air,
Then white lips will whisper,
    ' Fly ! Weatherford's there !'
Your warriors shall perish ;
    We'll laugh at their shame,
And the blood of your loved ones
    Shall hiss in the flame !"

How was that vow answered ?
    Ask Mimms : it will tell !
Where the battle was hottest
    There his hatchet fell ;
Where the shriek was the loudest,
    Where freest ran blood,
Be sure, mid his victims,
    There Weatherford stood !

But feeble the red men,
    Though fierce in the fray ;
Like mists in the morning,
    They melted away.
" Give us peace !" prayed the vanquished
    " The white chieftain gives
No peace"—was the answer—
    " While Weatherford lives."

That lion-souled chieftain's*
    Alone in his tent :
'Tis midnight ; still over
    His toil he is bent.

* General Jackson.
2

The drapery is rustled—
   He turns not his ear:
"Ho! Look up, proud warrior,
   Thy foeman is here!"

A dark form stood o'er him,
   His red arm on high;
But quailed not the chieftain
   Beneath his dark eye.
"What art thou, bold savage!
   Sooth, light the foot fell
That stole through the watch
   Of my tried sentinel."

"Where Weatherford willeth,
   Even there will he go;
He heeds not thy sentry
   When seeking his foe."
"I fear thee not, boaster!"
   "Thou needest not fear;
For peace for my people,
   For peace came I here.

"Thou'd'st have me sent to thee,
   And sent to thee bound;
But Weatherford dies not
   The death of a hound:
No recreant, no trembler,
   No captive am I—
I've fetterless lived, and
   Will fetterless die.

"To save my crushed people
   I die, but die free—
A sacrifice worthy
   Of them and of thee!"
"No—back to thy forest—
   Bold warrior go!
I strike not the head
   That is bent to the blow

"Aye, go! but remember
   When meet we again,

Thy lot is the gibbet,
  The cord and the chain.
Be strong for the battle!
  No quarter we yield:
No fear and no mercy!
  Now, back to the field!"

" I long have fought with thee,
  And still would fight on—
But my true Seminoles—
  My warriors are gone!
My brave ones I'd rally,
  And fight at their head;
But where is the warrior
  Can rally the dead!

" At red Talledegha,
  Emuckfaw they stood—
Thou knowest that our valleys
  Are black with their blood.
By the wailing Savannah
  Unburied they lie;
Spare, warrior, the remnant,
  Let Weatherford die!"

No longer the soldier
  The bold plea could hear,
But quick from his bronzed cheek
  He hurried a tear.
" Devoted and brave! As
  Thou will'st shall it be,
Here's peace to thy people,
  And friendship for thee!"

THE FOLLOWING IS THE INCIDENT ON WHICH THE FOREGOING LINES ARE FOUNDED.*

Billy Weatherford, the celebrated savage
warrior, is, at length, vanquished—the desroyer

* Published in the Mobile Com. Register, March, 1824.

is conquered—the hand which so profusely dealt death and desolation among the whites, is now paralyzed—it is motionless. He died at his late residence near Montpelier, in this state, on the 9th inst. His deeds of war are well known to the early settlers in South Alabama, and will be remembered by them while they live : and be talked of, with horror, by generations yet unborn. But his dauntless spirit has taken its flight—" he is gone to the land of his fathers."

Billy Weatherford, denominated 'The Prophet,' was about one-fourth Indian (some say a half breed) his ancestry, on the white side, having been Scottish. It has been said, that he boasted of having no *Yankee* (meaning American) blood in his veins.

This ferocious chief led the hostile Indians to the attack of Fort Mimms, at Tensau, on the 30th of August, 1813; which resulted in the indiscriminate massacre of men, women, and children, to the number of near four hundred. He was also a leader associated with the prophets Francis and Sinquister, at the battle fought on the 23d of December following, at Ekchanachaca, or 'The Holy Ground;' which had been considered by them inaccessible to their enemies, and the 'Grave of White Men.' But it proved a fatal delusion. His party suffered great loss of warriors, and all the provisions, munitions of war, &c., deposited at this place of imaginary security; being, as they supposed, rendered secure by the protecting influence of some supernatural agency ı ıs stated, that—after being sated with the blood of Americans, and witnessing the almost total extinction of his warriors—he voluntarily and dauntlessly flung himself into the hands of General Jackson, and demanded his protection. He is said, on surrendering himself, to have made the following speech to the General—which looks very little like claiming *protection* It displays a spirit, which would have done credit to Napoleon, under similar circumstances, after the battle of Waterloo:

"I am in your power: do with me what you please. I am a soldier. I have done the white people all the harm I could. I have fought them, and fought them bravely. If I had an army, I would yet fight, and contend to the last. But I have done—my people are all gone—I can do no more than weep over the misfortunes of my nation. Once I could animate my warriors to battle: but I cannot animate the dead. My warriors can no longer hear my voice—their bones are at Talladega, Tallaschatchee, Emuckfaw, and Tohopeka. I have not surrendered myself thoughtlessly. Whilst there were chances of success, I never left my post, nor supplicated peace. But my people are gone, and I now ask it for my nation, and for myself.

"On the miseries and misfortunes brought upon my country, I look back with the deepest sorrow, and wish to avert still greater calamities. If I had been left to contend with the Georgian army, I would have raised my corn on one bank of the river, and have fought them on the other. But your people have destroyed my nation. You are a brave man. I rely upon your generosity. You will exact no terms of a conquered people, but such as they should accede to. Whatever they may be, it would now be madness and folly to oppose them. If they, are opposed, you shall find me among the sternest enforcers of obedience. Those who would still hold out, can be influenced only by a mean spirit of revenge; and, to this, they must not, and *shall not*, sacrifice the last remnant of their country. You have told us, where we might go, and be safe. This is a good talk, and my nation ought to listen to it. *They* SHALL *listen to it.*"*

INDIAN CHARACTER.

A striking display of Indian character occurred some years since in a town in Maine. An Indian of the Kennebeck tribe remarkable for his good conduct, received a grant of land from the state, and fixed himself in a new township, where a number of families settled. Though not ill treated, yet the common prejudice against Indians prevented any sympathy

---

* This speech is the most manly and dignified piece of Indian oratory that has ever met our eye. It even surpasses the admired speech of Caractacus, the Briton, when led captive to Rome;—and is, in no wise, inferior to that of Logan.

witn him. This was shown at the death of his only child, when none of the people came near him. Shortly afterwards he went to some of the inhabitants, and said to them. *When white man's child die—Indian man be sorry—he help bury him—when my child die—no one speak to me—I make his grave alone—I cant no live here.*—He gave up his farm, *dug up the body of his child* and carried it with him two hundred miles through the forest, to join the Canada Indians. What energy and depth of feeling does this specimen of Indian character exhibit!

AN INDIAN BEAU.

A young Indian warrior is, notoriously, the most thoroughgoing beau in the world. Bond-street and Broadway furnish no subjects that will undergo as much crimping and confinement, to appear in full dress. We are confident that we have observed such a character constantly occupied with his paints and his pocket-glass, three full hours, laying on his colours, and adjusting his tresses, and contemplating, from time to time, with visible satisfaction, the progress of his growing attractions. When he has finished, the proud triumph of irresistible charms is in his eye. The chiefs and warriors, in full dress, have one, two, or three broad clasps of silver about their arms; generally jewels in their ears, and often in their

noses, and nothing is more common when to
see a thin circular piece of silver, of the size of
a dollar, depending from their nose, a little below the upper lip. Nothing shows more clearly
the influence of fashion. This ornament—so
painfully inconvenient, as it evidently is to
them, and so horribly ugly and disfiguring—
seems to be the utmost finish of Indian taste.
Porcupine quills, stained of different colours,
are twisted in their hair. Tails of animals hang
from their hair behind. A necklace of bears'
or alligators' teeth, or claws of the bald eagle,
hangs loosely down; and an interior and smaller circle of large red beads, or in default of
them, a rosary of red hawthorn berries, sur-
rounds the neck. From the knees to the feet,
the legs are decorated with great numbers of
little perforated cylindrical pieces of silver or
brass, that emit a simultaneous tinkle as the
person walks. If, to all this, he add an American hat, and a soldier's coat, of blue, faced
with red, over the customary calico shirt of the
gaudiest colours that can be found, he lifts his
feet high, and steps firmly on the ground, to
give his tinklers a uniform and full sound; and
apparently considers his person with as much
complacency as the human bosom can be supposed to feel. This is a very curtailed view of
an Indian beau; but every reader, competent
to judge, will admit its fidelity, as far as it goes,
to the description of a young Indian warrior
over the whole Mississippi Valley, when prepared to take part in a public dance.

AN INDIAN TOAST.

When General Wayne was holding his treaty with the Indians at Greenville, a young chief sat down at the dinner table, next to the General. This was not much relished by the *White Chief;* but he did not wish to give open offence to his *Red Brother.* The cloth being removed, the wine began to circulate; when Wayne—thinking to confound and abash the young chief—asked him for a *toast.* This being interpreted and explained to this son of the forest, he filled his tumbler with wine, and gave '*The Great Spirit*'—and after an impressive pause, pressing his hand on his breast—he added, *" Because he put it into the heart of man to make such good liquor !"*

SHREWDNESS.

" He that delivereth it unto thee hath the greater sin."

"I am glad," said the Rev. Dr. Y——s to the chief of the Little Ottowas, "that you do not drink whiskey. But it grieves me to find that your people use so much of it." "Ah, yes," replied the Indian,—and he fixed an arch and impressive eye upon the Doctor, which communicated the reproof before he uttered it—"we Indians *use* a great deal of whiskey, but we do not *make* it."

It is pretty well ascertained that there exists among mankind a universal language of signs, aught by nature herself. Voyagers have always used these signs among savage and previously undiscovered nations. They are always understood, and invariably form the basis of intercourse. The former director of the Hartford Asylum for the Deaf and Dumb, informed the writer, that all the mutes who came to that institution from different parts of the country, brought with them signs and motions which were essentially the same, and which coincided with those used in the institution. This proves that they are *natural*.

Andrew Ellicott, Esq., commissioned by the United States to determine, in conjunction with the Commissioners of Spain, a line of demarcation between the territories of both nations,— related to the writer a curious trait in the savage character.

On his way down the Mississippi, a number of strange Indians came into his camp, from the west side of the river. A Mr. Nolin happened to be there at the time,—well known for his enterprize and skill in catching wild horses in the Internal Provinces of Spanish America. He addressed them in such of the languages as he was acquainted with—but was not understood. He then conversed by certain signs.

hese were understood by the Indians, and were answered in like manner. Thus (if the expression may be allowed) a conversation ensued, in which not a word was spoken:—"and this," said Nolin, "is a sort of universal language common to the Western tribes."—(*See Major Long's Expedition.*)

LOGAN.

This celebrated Indian chief, who had always been a zealous friend of the English, and had often distinguished himself in their service, was taken prisoner, and brought before the General Assembly of Virginia, who hesitated whether he should be tried by court martial as a soldier, or at the criminal bar for high treason. Logan stated that they had no jurisdiction to try him; that he owed no allegiance to the King of England, being an Indian Chief, independent of every nation. In answer to their inquiries as to his motives for taking up arms against the English, he thus addressed the Assembly. "I appeal to any white man, to say if ever he entered Logan's cabin hungry, and I gave him not meat; if ever he came cold or naked, and I gave him not clothing. During the last long and bloody war, Logan remained idle in his tent, an advocate for peace; nay such was my love for the whites, that those of my country pointed at me, as they passed by, and said, 'Logan is the friend o.

white men.' I had ever thought to live with you but for the injuries of one man. Colonel Cressap, the last spring, in cold blood, and un- provoked, cut off all the relations of Logan, not sparing even' my women and children. There runs not a drop of my blood in the veins of any human creature. This called on me for revenge. I have sought it. I have killed many. I have fully glutted my vengeance. For my country, I rejoice at the beams of peace. But do not harbor the thought that mine is the joy of fear. Logan never felt fear. He will not turn his heel to save his life. Who is there to mourn for Logan? Not one !"

This pathetic speech touched the sensibility of all who heard it. The General Assembly applauded his noble sentiments, and immedi- ately set him at liberty. The inhabitants of Virginia vied with each other who should en- tertain him the best, or show him the greatest respect; and he returned to his native country loaded with presents and honors.

THE INDIAN'S VIEWS OF THE TRINITY.

Elliot had been lecturing on the doctrine of the trinity, when one of his auditors, after a long and thoughtful pause, thus addressed him. 'I believe, Mr. Minister, I understand you. The trinity is just like water and ice and snow. The water is one, the ice is another, and the snow is another; and yet they are all one water.'

MORE ROOM.

When General Lincoln went to make peace with the Creek Indians, one of the chiefs asked him to sit down on a log; he was then desired to move, and in a few minutes to move still farther; the request was repeated till the General got to the end of the log. The Indian said, 'Move farther.' To which the General replied, 'I can move no farther.' 'Just so it is with us,' said the chief; 'you have moved us back to the water, and then ask us to move farther.'

INDIAN MENDACITY.

Of all the vices incident to the aborigines of this country, from their intercourse with the whites, that of lying is, probably, not among the least. Some years anterior to the independence of the United States, one Tom Hyde, an Indian famous for his cunning, went into a tavern in Brookfield, Massachusetts, and after a little chat told the landlord he had been hunting, and had killed a fine fat deer, and if he would give him a quart of rum he would tell him where it was. Mine host, unwilling to let slip so good an opportunity of obtaining venison, immediately struck the bargain and measured the Indian his quart of rum, at the same time asking where the deer was to be found. 'Well,' says Tom, 'do you know where the

3

great meadow is ?' ' Yes.' ' Well, do you know the great marked maple tree that stands in it ?' ' Yes.' ' Well, there lies the deer.' Away posted the landlord with his team, in quest of his purchase. He found the meadow and the tree, it is true; but all his searching after the deer was fruitless, and he returned home no heavier than he went, except in mortification and disappointment. Some days after, mine host met the Indian, and feeling indignant at the deception practised on him, accused him in no gentle terms of the trick. Tom heard him out—and, with the coolness of a stoic, replied —' Did you not find the meadow, as I said ?' ' Yes.' ' And the tree ?' ' Yes.' ' And the deer ?' ' No.' ' Very good,' continued he, ' you found *two truths for one lie, which is very well for an Indian.*'

CANONICUS.

Mr. Drake, in his Book of the Indians, thus mentions Canonicus, the sachem of the Narragansets :—

He was contemporary with Miantunnomoh, who was his nephew. We know not the time of his birth, but a son of his was at Boston in 1631, the next year after it was settled. But the time of his death is minutely recorded by Governor Winthrop, in his " Journal," thus. " June 4, 1647, Canonicus, the great sachem of Narraganset, died, a very old man." He is generally supposed to háve been about 85 years of age when he died.

He is mentioned with great respect by Rev. Roger Williams, in the year 1654. After observing that many hundreds of the English were witnesses to the friendly disposition of the Narragansets, he says, "their late famous long-lived Canonicus so lived and died, and in the same most honourable manner and solemnity, (in their way,) as you laid to sleep your prudent peacemaker, Mr. Winthrop, did they honour this their prudent and peaceable prince; yea, through all their towns and countries how frequently do many, and oft times our Englishmen, travel alone with safety and loving kindness?"

ESQUIMAUX INDIANS.

Captain Ross, in the Journal of his Artic Expedition, gives the following account of his first interview with the Esquimaux, in the northern parts of Baffin's Bay:

"These Esquimaux," says he, "conceived he *ships to be living and flying creatures.*" * * * * "I had been employed, with a good telescope, in observing their motions, and beheld the first man approach, with every mark of fear and distrust—looking frequently behind to the other two, and beckoning them to come on, as if for support. They occasionally retreated, then advanced again, with cautious

steps, in the attitude of listening; generally
keeping one hand down by their knees, in
readiness to pull out a knife, which they had in
their boots: in the other hand they held their
whips, with the lash coiled up: their sledges
remained at a little distance—the fourth man
being apparently stationed to keep them in
readiness for escape. Sometimes they drew
back the covering they had on their heads, as
if wishing to catch the most distant sounds.
at which time I could discern their features,
displaying extreme terror and amazement,
while every limb appeared to tremble as they
moved." They were requested to cross a
chasm, which separated them from the interpreter, by a plank; but "appeared still much
alarmed, and requested that Sackhouse (the
interpreter) only should come over. He accordingly passed to the opposite side, on which
they earnestly beseeched him not to touch
them, as, if he did, *they should certainly die.*
After he had used many arguments to persuade them that he was flesh and blood, the
native, who had shown most courage, ventured
to touch his hand; then, pulling himself by the
nose, set up a shout, in which he was joined by
Sackhouse and the other three. The presents
were then distributed, consisting of two or
three articles of clothing, and a few strings of
beads. After which, Sackhouse exchanged his
knife for one of theirs."

Captain Ross and Lieutenant Parry then went
on the ice, and, "by the time they reached it,

the whole were assembled: those who had
originally been left at a distance, with their
sledges, having driven up to join their comrades. The party now, therefore, consisted of
eight natives, with all their sledges, and about
fifty dogs, two sailors, Sackhouse, Lieutenant
Parry, and myself—forming a group of no
small singularity, not a little increased, also, by
the peculiarity of the situation on a field of ice,
far from the land. The noise and clamour may
be easily conceived—the whole talking and
shouting together, and the dogs howling, while
the natives were flogging them with their long
whips, to preserve order." Our arrival produced considerable alarm, causing them to retreat a few steps towards their sledges. On
this, Sackhouse called to us to *pull our noses*,
as he had discovered this to be the mode of
friendly salutation among them. This ceremony was accordingly performed by each of
us, the natives, during their retreat, making use
of the same gesture; the nature of which we
had not before understood." Presents were
then made, and, "on seeing their faces in the
glasses, their astonishment appeared extreme,
and they looked round in silence, for a moment,
at each other, and at us. Immediately afterwards, they set up a general shout, succeeded
by a loud laugh, expressive of extreme delight
as well as surprise—in which we joined, partly
from inability to avoid it, and willing also to
show that we were pleased with our new ac-
quaintances." Confidence shortly after became

3*

established, and uncovering of heads was sub
stituted for pulling of noses—the natives ap
pearing to comprehend the nature of this ceremony more quickly than the seamen did the
other, and probably not considering it a much
more reasonable, although a more inconvenient,
testimony of respect. They were then invited
to the ship, to which one of them thought proper to *address a speech, "pausing between
every question, and pulling his nose with the
utmost solemnity."* All the wonder to be expected was here excited; but the quantity of the
wood and iron appeared to be the chief objects
of surprise.

"Their knowledge of wood seemed to be
limited to some heath of a dwarfish growth,
with stems no thicker than the finger; and,
accordingly, they knew not what to think of
the timber they saw on board. Not being
aware of its weight, two or three of them, successively, seized on the spare topmast, evidently with the view of carrying it off; and, as
soon as they became familiar with the people
around them, they showed that desire of possessing what they admired, which is so universal among savages. The only thing they
looked upon with contempt, was a little terrier
dog;—judging, no doubt, that it was too small
for drawing a sledge. But they shrunk back,
as if in terror, from a pig, whose pricked ears
and ferocious aspect (being of the Shetland
breed) presented a somewhat formidable appearance This animal happening to grunt,

one of them was so terrified, that he became,
from that moment, uneasy, and appeared impa-
tient to get out of the ship. In carrying his
purpose into effect, however, he did not lose
his propensity to thieving, as he seized and
endeavoured to carry off the smith's anvil:
finding that he could not remove it, he laid
hold of the large hammer, threw it on the ice,
and following it himself, deliberately set it on
his sledge, and made off."

A CHOCTAW COUNCIL.

The conduct of the government of the United
States towards the Indian tribes, however politic
it may seem, is certainly not based upon the
Christian precept " to do unto others as we would
that they should do unto us."   All our proceedings towards them have tended to their gradual
extirpation from the land of their birth.   Our
wars, our treaties, our purchases of land, our
system of intercourse with them, have all the
same end.   The following extract will show
how well the Indians understand this.

The reader will recollect, that it has become
the settled policy of the United States to remove
the several tribes of Indians to a country west
of the Mississippi.   In order to discuss and determine on this subject, in 1830 the Choctaw
Indians held a council, in which it was resolved
to sell off their lands to the United States, for
one million of dollars, and to remove without
the States, provided Government would give to
each man a section of land, in fee simple, west
of the Mississippi, and be at the expense of
transporting the tribe to their place of destination, and of supporting them twelve months
after their arrival.   The council sat four days,
and the following is a short sketch of their
proceedings : —

The National Council was organized in the afternoon of the 15th of March. This was a juncture of peculiar interest. To see the rulers of a people, preparing to decide upon a course in which their posterity, to the latest genera- tion, was deeply affected, could not but produce a deep and universal solemnity, and this inte- rest was greatly increased by the bitter tears shed by some of the females present. The voice of sorrow is always eloquent; but, at such a season, never could the female voice speak more forcibly the sympathies of our na- ture. Who could avoid exclaiming, 'O, my native country! Land of my fathers, I must leave thee!'

The Chief presented them with a concise view of the difficulties of their situation, and the alternatives which were before them, and the sad necessity of immediately making their selection. It was at the intimation, that a re- moval was one of the alternatives, that the women wept.

The Chief was followed by an old Captain in the nation, who, in brief simplicity, recounted his sufferings as a warrior and captain, in fight- ing for his White brothers, under General Jack son. He named several places where he had fought, and seen the Choctaws bleed and die At that time, little did he think that his White brothers would ever make it necessary for him, in his old age, to leave his country, and the bones of his father. He would greatly prefer giving up his country, than submit to laws, the nature of which he could not learn, and among a people, the wicked part of whom would harass and ruin them. He expressed a belief that the President would give them a good treaty; and, if he would do so, aged as he was, he would give his voice to go to their lands west of the Mississippi — and, moreover, ex· pressed his belief, that the Great Father above, would go with them. and bless them in their new home.

A Captain of the eastern part of the nation, next came forward. He appeared many years in advance of the first speaker. His white head, palsied limbs, and tremulous voice, made him an object of deepest interest. He was said to have been a warrior under General Wayne. He recounted some of the scenes of his past life, and the hopes which had borne him on-ward in his course; — he touched upon the dis-appointment that had clouded his setting sun; but, awakening, as if by supernatural power, he spoke boldly of his confidence in his GREAT FATHER above, and expressed his full assurance, that HE would accompany his nation, and bless them. The discussion continued until a late hour of the fourth day, when the vote was taken, and found in favour of emigration.

THE YOUNG INDIAN CHIEF.*

This young warrior, of fine size, figure and countenance, is now about 25 years old. At the age of 21 his heroic deeds had acquired for him in his nation the rank of "bravest of the brave." The savage practice of torturing and burning to death their prisoners existed in this nation. An unfortunate female taken in war, of the Paduca nation, was destined to this horrible death. The fatal hour had arrived, the trembling victim, far from her home and her friends, was fastened to the stake; the whole tribe was assembled on the surrounding plain to witness the awful scene. Just when the fire was about to be kindled, and the spectators on the tiptoe of expectation, this young warrior, who sat composedly among the chiefs, having before prepared two fleet horses, with the ne cessary provisions, sprung from his seat, rushed through the crowd, loosed the victim, seized her in his arms, placed her on one of the horses, mounted the other himself, and made the utmost speed towards the nation and friends of the captive. The multitude, dumb and nerveless with amazement at the daring deed, made no effort to rescue their victim from her

* This interesting fact of a young Indian Chief of the Pawnee nation, at the foot of the Rocky Mountains, who was on a visit to Washington in the winter of 1824, is extracted from a letter of the Rev. Richard Reece, to the editor of the London Wesleyan Methodist Magazine.

deliverer. They viewed it as an act of the Great Spirit, submitted to it without a murmur, and quietly returned to their village. The re-leased captive was accompanied through the wilderness towards her home, till she was out of danger. He then gave her the horse on which she rode, with the necessary provisions for the remainder of the journey, and they parted. On his return to the village, such was the respect entertained for him, that no inquiry was made into his conduct; no censure was passed on it, and since the transaction, no human sacrifice has been offered in this or any other of the Pawnee tribes. Of what influence is one bold act in a good cause!

On the publication of this anecdote at Washington, the young ladies of Miss White's Seminary, in that city, presented that brave and humane Indian with a handsome silver medal, on which was engraven an appropriate inscription, accompanied by an address, of which the following is the close:—" Brother, accept this token of our esteem; always wear it for our sake; and when you have again the power to save a poor woman from death and torture, think of this, and of us, and fly to her rescue.''

RED JACKET

It happened during the Revolutionary war, that a treaty was held with the Indians, at which La Fayette was present. The object was to unite the various tribes in amity with

America. The majority of the Chiefs were friendly, but there was much opposition made to it, more especially by a young warrior, who declared that when an alliance was entered into with America, he should consider the sun of his country as set forever. In his travels through the Indian country, when lately in America, it happened at a large assemblage of Chiefs, that La Fayette referred to the treaty in question, and turning to Red Jacket, said, "pray tell me if you can, what has become of that daring youth, who so decidedly opposed all our propositions for peace and amity? Does he still live—and what is his condition?" "I, myself, am the man," replied Red Jacket, "the decided enemy of the Americans, as long as the hope of opposing them with success remained but now their true and faithful ally until death."

INDIAN MODE OF GETTING A WIFE.

An aged Indian, who for many years had spent much of his time among the white people both in Pennsylvania and New Jersey, one day, about the year 1770, observed, that the Indians had not only a much easier way of getting a wife than the whites, but were also more certain of getting a *good* one; 'for (said he in his broken English) 'white man court—court— may be one whole year!—may be two before he marry!—well!—may be then get *very good* wife—but, may be *not*—may be *very cross*!

4

Well now, suppose cross! Scold so soon as get awake in the morning! Scold all day! Scold until sleep!—all one; he must keep *him*. White people have law forbidding throwing away wife, be *he* ever so cross! must keep *him* always! Well? how does Indian do? Indian when he see industrious squaw, which he like, he go to *him*, place his two fore-fingers close aside each other, make two look like one—look squaw in the face—see *him* smile—which is all one *he* say, yes! so he take *him* home—no danger *he* be cross! no! no! Squaw know too well what Indian do if *he* be cross!—throw *him* away and take another! Squaw love to eat meat! no husband! no meat! Squaw do every thing to please husband; he do the same to please squaw! live happy!'

SHENANDOH, THE ONEIDA CHIEF.

Although the dignity of a chief is hereditary in his family, generally, the aristocracy of the Indians is not one of birth merely, nor one of wealth; but it is an aristocracy of merit. A chief is liable to be deposed for misconduct; and a brave warrior takes his place on account of the actions he has performed. Among those who have maintained an ascendancy among their countrymen by the force of individual merit, none is more remarkable than Shenandoh, the Oneida chief.

This celebrated chief, whose life measured a century, died in 1816. He was well known in the wars which occurred while the United States were British colonies; and, also, in the war of the Revolution—as the undeviating friend of the Americans.

In his youth he was very savage, and addicted to drunkenness; but, by the force of reflection, and the benevolent exhortations of a missionary to the tribe, he lived a reformed man for more than sixty years, and died in Christian hope.*

* In 1775 Shenandoh was present at a treaty made in Albany. At night he was excessively drunk; and in the morning, found himself in the street, stripped of all his orna ments, and every article of clothing. His pride revolted at his self-degradation, and he resolved never more to deliver himself over to the power of ' strong water.'

Shenandoh's person was tall and muscular
but well made—his countenance was intelli
gent, and beamed with all the ingenuous dig
nity of an Indian Chief. In youth, he was
brave and intrepid—in his riper years, one of
the ablest counsellors among the North Ameri
can tribes. He possessed a strong and vigor
ous mind; and, though terrible as the tornado.
in war—he was bland and mild as the zephyr,
in peace. With the cunning of the fox, the
hungry perseverance of the wolf, and the
agility of the mountain cat, he watched and
repelled Canadian invasions. His vigilance
once preserved from massacre the inhabitants
of the then infant settlements of the German
Flats. His influence brought his tribe to assist
the Americans, in their war of the Revolution.
His many friendly actions in their behalf,
gained for him, among the Indian tribes, the
appellation of the ' *White Man's Friend.*'

To a friend who called to see him, in his wane
(he was then blind), he thus expressed himself :

"I am an aged hemlock—the winds of a
hundred winters have whistled through my
branches—I am dead at the top. The genera
tion to which I belonged have run away and
left me. Why *I* live, the Great Spirit alone
knows! Pray to my Jesus that I may have
patience to wait for my appointed time to die."

> ' Indulge my native land ; indulge the tear
>   That steals impassioned o'er the nation's doom :
> To me each twig from Adam's stock is near,
>   And sorrows fall upon an Indian's tomb.

INDIAN GRATITUDE AND WIT.

Soon after Litchfield began to be settled by the English, an unknown Indian came into the inn at dusk, and requested the hostess to furnish him with food and drink; stating, that he had had no success in hunting, and could not pay till he had better fortune. The woman refused; calling him a lazy, drunken, good-for-nothing fellow. A man who sat by, noticed the Indian as he turned away from the inhospitable place, and perceiving that he was suffering very severely from want and weariness, he generously ordered the hostess to furnish him with a good supper, and call on him for payment. After the Indian had finished his meal, he thanked his benefactor again and again, and assured him he should never forget his kindness, and would, if it were ever in his power, faithfully recompense it. He observed, that he had one more favor to ask; if the woman was willing, he wished to tell a story. The hostess, whose good nature had been restored by money, readily consented. The Indian, addressing his benefactor, said, "I suppose you read the Bible?" The man assented. "Well, the Bible says, God make the world; and then he took him, and looked on him, and say 'all very good.' Then he made light; and took him, and looked on him, and say, 'all very good.' Then he made land and water, sun and moon,

4*

grass and trees; and he took him, and looked on him, and say, 'all very good.' Then he made beasts, and birds, and fishes; and he took him, and looked on him, and say, 'all very good.' Then he made man; and took him, and looked on him, and say, 'all very good.' Then he made woman; and took him, and looked at him, and —— he no dare say one such word."

Many years after this, the Indian's bene factor was taken prisoner by an Indian scout, and carried into Canada. He was saved from death by one of the tribe, who asked leave to adopt him in the place of a son, who had fallen in battle. Through the winter, he experienced the customary effects of savage hospitality. The following summer as he was at work in the forest alone, an unknown Indian came to him and appointed a meeting at a certain place, on a given day. The prisoner consented; but afterwards, fearing mischief might be intended, he neglected the engagement. The Indian again sought him, reproved him for his want of confidence in him, and assured him the meeting would be for his good. Encouraged by his apparent friendship, the man followed his directions. He found the Indian provided with muskets, ammunition, and knapsacks. The Indian ordered him to arm himself and follow him. Their course was towards the south, and day after day the Englishman followed, without being able to conjecture the motives of his guide. After a

tedious journey, he arrived at the top of an
eminence, commanding a view of a country
somewhat cultivated and populous. "Do you
know that country?" said the Indian, with an
arch smile. "Oh, yes! it is Litchfield," replied
the white man, as he cordially pressed his
hand. "Many years ago, you give weary Indian supper there," said he. "He promise to
pay you, and he pay you now. Go home, and
be happy."

HEAD WORK.

Colonel Dudley, governor of Massachusetts,
in the beginning of the last century, had a
number of workmen employed in building him
a house on his plantation; and one day as he
was looking at them, he observed a stout Indian, who, though the weather was very cold,
was a naked as well as an idle spectator.
· Hark ye, friend,' said the governor, ' why don't
you work like these men, and get clothes to
cover you?' 'And why you no work, governor?' replied the Indian. 'I work,' answered the governor, putting his finger on his
forehead, 'with my head, and therefore need
not work with my hands.' 'Well,' replied the
Indian, 'and if I would work, what have you
for me to do?' 'Go kill me a calf,' said the
governor, 'and I will give you a shilling.' The
Indian did so. The governor asked him why
he did not skin and dress it. 'Calf dead, go

vernor—give me my shilling; give me another
said the Indian, 'and I will skin and dress it.
This was complied with. The Indian then
went to a tavern with his two shillings, and
soon spending one for rum, returned to the
governor, saying, 'Your shilling bad, the man
no take it.' The governor believing him, gave
him another; but soon returning in the same
manner, with the second, the governor dis
cerned his roguery; however, he exchanged
that also, reserving his resentment for a proper
opportunity. To be prepared for it, the go
vernor wrote a letter directed to the keeper of
Bridewell, in Boston, requesting him to take
the bearer and give him a sound whipping
This he kept in his pocket, and in the course of
a few days the Indian came again to stare at
the workmen; the governor took no notice of
him for some time, but at length taking the let
ter out of his pocket, and calling the Indian to
him, said, 'I will give you half a crown if you
will carry this letter to Boston.' The Indian
closed with his proposal, and set out on his
journey. He had not gone far, before he met
with another Indian in the employ of the go
vernor, to whom he gave the letter, and told
him that the governor had sent him to meet
him, and to bid him return with that letter to
Boston, as soon as he possibly could.

The poor fellow carried it with great diligence, and received a severe flogging for his
pains; at the news of which, the governor was
not a little astonished on his return. The other

Indian came no more; but, after the lapse of some months, at a meeting with some of his nation, the governor saw him there among the rest, and asked him how he durst serve him such a trick? The Indian looking him full in the face, and putting his forefinger to his forehead, replied, '*Head work! governor, head work!*'

MAGNANIMITY AND DISINTERESTED GENEROSITY:

WITH STRIKING TRAITS IN THE SAVAGE CHARACTER.

The Pawnee Loups (Wolf Pawnees) a tribe of Missouri savages, lately exhibited the anomaly among the American aborigines of a people addicted to the superstitious rite of offering human victims, in propitiation of '*Venus, the Great Star.*' The inhuman ceremony was annually performed at the period immediately preceding their horticultural operations, in order to insure a bountiful return from the earth:—the neglect of which duty, it was believed, would occasion a total failure of crops. To obviate, therefore, a national calamity so formidable, any person was at liberty to offer up a prisoner, of either sex, whom the fortune of war had placed in his power.

The devoted individual was clad in the gayest attire, pampered with a profusion of the choicest food, and constantly attended by the conjurers, alias priests, who anticipated all his

wants—cautiously concealed from him the rea.
object of their sedulous attentions—and endeavoured to preserve his mind in a state of cheer-
ful composure:—with the view of promoting
obesity, and thus rendering the sacrifice more
acceptable to their Ceres.

When the victim was sufficiently fattened, a
day was appointed for the sacrifice, that all
might attend the celebration. In the presence
of the assembled multitude, he was bound to a
cross; a solemn dance was performed; and,
after certain ceremonies, the warrior who had
captured him, cleft his head with a tomahawk;
and, at the same moment, numerous arrows
were discharged at the body.

It appears, this barbarous rite has lately been
abolished. *Latelesha*. or Knife Chief, principal
of the nation, having long regarded this sacrifice as cruel and unnecessary, had vainly endeavoured to wean his countrymen from the
observance of it. At length an Iotan woman,
brought captive into the village, was doomed to
the Great Star. Having undergone the necessary treatment. she was bound to the cross. At
this critical juncture, *Petalesharoo*, son of *Latelesha*, stepped forward, and declared, that it
was his father's wish to abolish a custom so inhuman; that, for his part, he was determined
to release the victim, at the risk of his life. He
now cut the cords that bound her, carried her
swiftly through the crowd, and placed her on a
horse; mounted another himself, and conveyed
her beyond the reach of pursuit

Notwithstanding the success of this enterprise, it was reserved for another display of the firmness of this young warrior, to abolish the sanguinary sacrifice — we hope for ever. The succeeding spring, a Spanish boy was captured, and confided, by the warrior who took him, to the priests, to undergo the usual preparation for sacrifice. The Knife Chief consulted with his son how to avoid the repetition of the horrible rite. "*I* will rescue the boy," said *Petalesharoo*, "as a warrior ought—by force." But the father, unwilling that his son should again expose himself to imminent danger, devised other means for rescuing the devoted victim: — that is, by ransom. For this purpose he repaired to a Mr. Pappon, then trading in the village, who generously contributed a quantity of merchandize. Other contributions were added by the Knife Chief himself, and by Petalesharoo, and other Indians. The whole was laid up in a heap, in the Chieftain's lodge, and the warrior was summoned to attend.

Latelesha, armed with his war-club, commanded the warrior to accept of the merchandize, as a ransom for the boy, or prepare for instant death. The warrior refused to comply: the chief flourished his club in the air. "Strike!" said Petalesharoo, "I will meet the vengeance of his friends." But the more politic Chief preferred adding to the mass of merchandize a few more articles, in order to give the warrior another opportunity of complying, without breaking his word The expedient

succeeded. The goods were reluctantly ac
cepted; the boy was liberated, and afterwards
conducted to St. Louis by the traders. The
merchandize was sacrificed in his place: the
cloth was cut in shreds, and suspended on poles,
and many of the valuables were consumed by
fire, to appease and propitiate the Indian Ceres

TECUMSEH, WHEN A YOUTH.

Tecumseh was one of the most remarkable men that has ever figured in our aboriginal history. He gained an ascendancy over the minds of his countrymen entirely by the commanding force of his character, and the persuasive power of his eloquence. These instruments enabled him to produce a degree of union and combination among the North-western tribes, by no means less remarkable than the confederacies which signalized the times of king Philip and of Pontiac. His brother, the prophet, was a pusillanimous driveller, compared with Tecumseh; and exerted all his influence by addressing the superstitious fears of his countrymen; whereas the great warrior addressed himself to the higher principles of their nature, and made successful appeals to their reason, and even to their humanity. Of the last we have a signal example in his arresting the massacre of the American prisoners at Fort Meigs.

It has somewhere been observed, that "every circumstance relating to this extraordinary man will be read with interest." We believe it, and therefore proceed with the following account, which appeared in a western periodical of 1826.

"About thirty years ago (as the writer received the narrative from Captain Thomas Bryan, of Kentucky) the said Bryan was employed as a surveyor of the Virginia Military Lands, northwest of the Ohio river. While engaged in completing a chain of surveys, ex-

tending from the head waters of Brush Creek
to those of Paint Creek (now the central part
of the State of Ohio), his provisions became
scant, and at length entirely exhausted. He
directed his hunter—who had been unsuccessful on a recent excursion—to make another
attempt to procure subsistence, and to meet
him at a particular point then designated;
where, after closing the labour of the day, he
should encamp with his chain-men and marker.

"Towards evening, the men became exhausted with hunger. They were in the heart
of a solitary wilderness, and every circumstance was calculated to produce the greatest
dejection of spirit. After making great exertions to reach the point designated, where they
were to encamp upon their arrival, they met
their hunter, who had been again unsuccessful.
Feeling for himself and his comrades every
emotion of a noble heart, he was alarmed for
their situation. The hunter declared he had
used every exertion in pursuit of game, but all
his attempts were of no avail; that the whole
forest appeared to him to be entirely destitute
both of birds and beasts! Under these awful
apprehensions of starvation, he knew that it
would be a vain attempt to reach the settlement;—he trembled, and shed tears. Captain
Bryan, at this critical juncture, felt his spirits
roused at the reflection of their desperate situation; he thrust his jacob-staff in the earth, and
ordered his men to prepare a camp, and make
a good fire; he seizes the gun and ammunition

of the unsuccessful, hunter, and darted forth in pursuit of game. The weather had become exceedingly cold, for it was in the depth of winter—every rivulet was bound in ice. He had not proceeded far before he was gratified with the cheering sight of three elks, making towards him. He succeeded in killing two, and, shortly after, a bear. He now called for his men, and ordered his game to be carried to the camp. No one, but those similarly situated, can conceive the feelings excited on such an occasion.

But, perilous as the situation of the surveyor and his party might appear, there were others who were threatened with the like appalling distress. Three or four Indians, who had been out on a hunting excursion, hearing the report of Captain Bryan's gun, made immediately in that direction, and had arrived at the camp before Bryan returned. On his appearance there, they informed him, as well as they could (some of them speaking a little English), of their wretched situation. They told him that, for three days, their whole party had subsisted on one skunk, and that was exhausted. They described the absence of the game, in the language of the hunter, as if "the whole forest was entirely destitute both of *birds* and *beasts.*" They were informed by Captain Bryan, that he had plenty for himself, his men, and themselves; desired them to fix their camp, make a good fire, and assist his men in flaying the bear and elks, which were now brought into camp—

and then to cut, carve, and cook for themselves
Their very looks were expressive of the joy
they now felt for a deliverance so unexpected—
nor did they spare the provisions.   Their hunger was such, that, as soon as one round was
served, another—another—and another, in succession—was greedily devoured.

A fine-looking, tall, dignified savage, then
approached the surveyor's camp—rather young
in appearance than otherwise.   He very gracefully stepped up to Captain Bryan (who was
now reposing in his camp, on account of rheu-
matism, occasioned by his recent exposure),
and informed him, that the old man in his
camp was a Chief; that he felt under great
obligations to the Great and Good Spirit for so
signal an interposition in their favour; that he
was about to make a prayer, and address the
Good Spirit, and thank him : that it was the
custom, on such occasions, for the Indians to
stand up in their camp; and that his Chief requested the captain and his men, to conform,
in like manner, by standing up in *their* camp.
The captain replied, that his men would all
conform, and order should be preserved; but,
as for himself, his affliction would compel him
to keep his seat—but this must not be con-
strued into disrespect.   The captain remarked
to me, that he was not himself a religious cha
racter, though a man of feeling.

" The old Chief raised himself upon his feet,
as did those around him; and, lifting up his
hands commenced his prayer and thanksgiving

with an audible voice.   And such an address to Diety, on such an occasion—as far as I could understand him—I never before heard flow from mortal lips!   The tone—the modulation of his voice—the gestures—all corresponded to make a very deep impression upon us.   In the course of his thanksgiving—as I gathered from the Indians—he recapitulated the doleful situation in which they were so recently placed— the awful horrors of starvation, with which they were threatened—the vain attempts they had made to procure food, until He, the Great and Good Spirit, had sent that good White man, and had crowned his exertions with success; and so directed him and them to meet, and to find plenty."   Who can fully describe the abundant overflowings of a grateful heart? He continued in this vehement strain for about half an hour, "when," remarked Captain B., "my own men reflecting on their own recent situation, retrospecting what had taken place, and beholding the pious gratitude of a 'Child of the Forest,' feeling the same sensations, they were melted into tenderness—if not into tears."

The person who so gracefully addressed Captain Bryan, in behalf of his Chief, was TECUMSEH.

INDIAN LOGIC.[*]

A few years since, whilst the mistaken zea. of many good men, led them to think that their red brethren of the forest might be Christianized before they were civilized,—a missionary was sent out among them to convert them to the Christian faith. The missionary was unfortunately one of those preachers who delight in speculative and abstruse doctrines, and who teach the inefficacy of all human exertions in obtaining salvation. He called the Indians together to hear what he called the Gospel. The Sachem or Chief of the tribe to which he was sent, came with the rest. The missionary in the course of his sermon, (which was upon the very simple and intelligible doctrine of *election*) undertook to prove, that some were made to be saved, and some to be damned, without any regard to their good or bad conduct. As an illustration of his doctrine, he cited the case of Jacob and Esau, and attempted to show that God loved the one and hated the other before either of them was born. The Sachem heard him attentively, and after meeting invited him to his wigwam. After some conversation, the

[*] The Editor of the Indian Anecdotes, is not responsible for the sentiments, which any of the Anecdotes of this collection may seem to illustrate. And although he has carefully omitted such as would tend to corrupt, or exert an immoral influence on the character; he disclaims every political or religious partiality. The above has been introduced as an interesting specimen of Indian logic.

Sachem thus addressed the Missionary. "Sir, me tell you a story: My wife have two boys, twins; both of them as pretty as the two you tell me about to-day. One of them she love and feed him; the other she let lie on the ground crying. I tell her take him up, or he die. She no mind me. Pretty soon he die. Now what shall I do to her?"—Why, said the Missionary, she ought to be hung!—"Well," said the Sachem, "then you go home and hang your God, for you say he do just so. You no preach any more here, unless you preach more good than this." The Missionary finding himself amongst a people too enlightened to give credence to his narrow and heart-revolting principles, thought it expedient to seek a new field of labor.

THE INDIAN AND THE DUTCH CLERGYMAN.

A Dutch clergyman in the then province of New York, 1745, asked an Indian, whom he had baptized, whether he had been in Shekomeko, and had heard the Moravian missionary preach, and how he liked him? The Indian answered, 'That he had been there, and had attended to the missionary's words, and liked to hear them; that he would rather hear the missionary than him, for when the former spoke, it was as though his words laid hold of his heart, and a voice within said, 'that is truth;' but that *he* was always playing about

the truth, and never came to the point.   Tha
he had no love for their souls, for when he nad
once baptized them, he let them run wild, never
troubling himself any further about them.   That
he acted much worse than one who planted
Indian corn; for, added he, 'the planter sometimes goes to see whether his corn grows or not.'

"INDIAN, WHO IS YOUR CAPTAIN?"

An English captain, in the year 1759, who
was beating up for recruits in the neighbour-
hood of Bethlehem, met one day a Moravian
Indian, and asked him whether 'he had a mind
to be a soldier.'   'No,' answered he, 'I am
already engaged.'   'Who is your captain?'
asked the officer.   'I have a very brave and
excellent captain,' replied the Indian, 'his name
is Jesus Christ; Him will I serve as long as I
live: my life is at his disposal;' upon which
the British officer suffered him to pass unmolested.

INDIAN BON MOT.

One of the Moravian Indians who had been
baptized by the name of Jonathan, meeting
some white people, who had entered into so
violent a dispute about baptism and the holy
communion, that they at last proceeded to
blows—'These people,' said he, 'know nothing
of our Saviour; for they speak of Him as we
do of a strange country.'

INDIAN FIDELITY.

Some time after the commencement of the Revolutionary war, when the northern Indians were beginning to make inroads on the people living on the east side of the Ohio river, General O'Hara having come out to the upper Moravian town, on the Muskingum, on business and there taken lodging with a respectable and decent family of Indians in the village — I had one evening scarcely laid down to sleep when I was suddenly roused from my bed by an Indian runner, (or messenger) who in the night had been sent to me, 9 miles, with the following verbal message: "My friend, see that our friend O'Hara, now at your town, be immediately taken off to the settlement of white people, avoiding all paths leading to that river. Fail not in taking my advice, for there is no time to lose—and hear my son further on the subject."

The fact was, that eleven warriors from Sandusky, were far advanced on their way to take or murder O'Hara; who at break of day would be at this place for the purpose. I immediately sent for this gentleman, and told him that I would furnish him with a conductor, on whom he might depend, and having sent for Anthony, (otherwise called Luke Holland) informed him of the circumstance and requested his services; he (the Indian) wished first to know, whether my friend placed *confidence* in him, and trusted to his fidelity; which question being answered by O'Hara himself, and to his full satisfaction, he replied, ' well, our lives cannot be separated ' we must stand or fall together ! but take cou rage, for no enemy shall discover us !'

The Indian then took Mr. O'Hara through the woods, and arriving within a short distance of the Ohio river, pointed out to him a hiding place, until he, by strolling up and down the river, should discover white people on the opposite shore ; when finally observing a house where two white men were cleaning out a canoe for use, he hurried back to bring on his friend, who, when near the spot, advised his Indian conductor to hide himself, knowing those people to be bad men, he feared they might kill him, for his services. The Indian finally seeing his friend safe across the river, returned and made report thereof.

The young Indian, who had been the bearer of the message from his father to me, had im mediately returned on seeing O'Hara off, in order to play a further deception on the war party, for the purpose of preventing them even from going to our town, fearing, that if there, and not finding their object, they might pro bably hunt for his track, and finding this, pursue him. He indeed effected his purpose so completely, that while they were looking for him in one direction, his conductor was taking him off in another.

The father of the young lad, who was the principal cause that O'Hara's life had been saved. had long been admired by all who knew nim for his *philanthropy ;* on account of which the traders had given him the name of "*the gentleman.*" Otherwise this Indian was not in connection with the Christian Indian Society, though a friend to them. He lived with his family retired and in a decent manner.

While I feel a delight in offering to the relatives and friends of the deceased, as also to the public, this *true* and *faithful* picture of Indian *fidelity*—I regret that, on necessarily having had to recur to the names 'Anthony' and 'Luke Holland,' I am drawn from scenes of pleasure, to crimes of the *blackest hue.* The very Indian just named, who at that time joyfully reported to me his having conducted his friend out of danger, to a place of safety, some years after approached me with the doleful news that every one of his children, (all minors) together with his hoary headed parents, *had been murdered by the white people*, at Gradenhutten, on the Muskingum.   JOHN HECKELWELDER.

INDIAN HOSPITALITY.

I can give, says Colden, in his history of the five Indian Nations, two strong instances of the hospitality of the Mohawks, which fell under my own observation; and which will show, that they have the very same notion of hospitality which we find in the ancient poets. When I was last in the Mohawk's country, the sachems told me that they had an Englishman among their people, a servant who had run away from his master in New York. I immediately told them they must deliver him up. 'No,' they answered, 'we never serve any man so, who puts himself under our protection.' On this I insisted on the injury they did thereby to his master: they allowed it might be an injury, and replied, 'Though we will never deliver him up, we are willing to pay the value of the servant to the master.' Another man made his escape from the jail in Albany, where he was in prison on an execution of debt: the Mohawks received him, and, as they protected him against the sheriff and officers they not only paid the debt for him, but gave him land over and above, sufficient for a good farm, whereon he lived when I was last there.

KINDNESS OF AN INDIAN HUSBAND.

There was a famine in the land, and a sick Indian woman expressed a great desire for a mess of Indian corn. Her husband having heard that a trader at Lower Sandusky had a little, set off on horseback for that place, one hundred miles distant, and returned with as much corn as filled the crown of his hat, for which he gave his horse in exchange, and came home on foot, bringing his saddle back with him.

INDIAN RECORDS.

At certain seasons the Indians meet to study the meaning, and renew their ideas of their strings and belts of wampum. On such occasions, they sit down around the place in which they are deposited, and taking out a string or belt, one after another, hand them to every person present; and in order that they may all comprehend its meaning, repeat the words pronounced on the delivery, in their whole connexion. By these means they are enabled to remember the promises reciprocally made; and, as they admit young boys who are related to the chiefs, they become early acquainted with all their national concerns; and thus the contents of their wampum documents are transmitted to their posterity. The following instance may serve to show how well this mode of communication answers the purpose of refreshing the memory:—A gentleman in Philadelphia, once gave an Indian a string of wampum, saying, 'I am your friend, and will serve you to the utmost of my power.' Forty years after, the Indian returned the string, adding. 'Brother, you gave me this string of wampum, saying, I am your friend, and will serve you to the utmost of my power.' 'I am now aged, infirm, and poor; do now as you promised.' The gentleman honourably redeemed his promise, and generously assisted the old Indian.

BURNING OF BROOKFIELD.

It has been remarked, that the history of every ncursion of the Indians into the territory of the whites may be written in the words *surprise massacre, plunder* and *retreat.* They fall upon the defenceless village in the dead of night, " as falls the plague on men," or as the lightning falls on the forest. No vigilance seems to have been sufficient effectually to guard against these attacks, and no prudence or foresight could avert them. The Indians made their approaches to the isolated villages by creeping cautiously through the surrounding woods in the dead of night. The outposts were seized, and the sentinels silently tomahawked, ere the warwhoop roused the sleeping families from their beds.

During the early settlements of New England, the inhabitants suffered much from the incursions of the Indians. The most celebrated war, perhaps, which ever took place with the natives, however, was King Philip's war. During its continuance, the town of Brookfield, Massachusetts, was attacked. The inhabitants collected in one house which was immediately besieged by the savages, who set fire instantly to every other building in the town. For two days and nights the Indians shot upon the people in the house incessantly, but were met with a most determined defence on the part of the besieged They then attempted to fire the house by flaming torches at the ends of long poles; but the garrison continued to defend themselves by firing from the windows, and throwing water upon the flames, as they fortunately had a pump within the house. These attempts failing, the Indians then prepared a cart loaded with flax, hemp, and other combustible matters, and under cover of a barricade of boards, thrust the burning mass, by means of long timbers, against the house. In this movement one of the wheels came off, which turned the machine aside, and exposed the Indians to the fire of the garrison; a shower of rain coming on at the same time extinguished the flames. Shortly afterwards a reinforcement of forty men arrived from Boston, forced their way through the enemy, and joined the garrison. The Indians then abandoned the siege and retired, having suffered a heavy loss.

THE HEROIC COLLAPISSA.

In the heart of the savage, there are some noble and redeeming qualities; he can be faithful, even unto death, to the friend or the stranger who has dwelt beneath his roof, or sat under the shadow of the same tree. He can be generous also; can endure all tortures, rather than show weakness or fear.

"An instance of this occurred," says Bossu, " when the French were in possession of New Orleans: a Chactaw, speaking very ill of them,

said the Collapissas were their slaves; one of
the latter, vexed at such words, killed him with
his gun. The nation of Chactaws, the greatest
and most numerous on the continent, armed
immediately, and sent deputies to New Orleans
to ask for the head of the murderer, who had
put himself under the protection of the French.
They offered presents to make up the quarrel,
but the cruel people would not accept any!
they even threatened to destroy the village of
the Collapissas. To prevent the effusion of
blood, the unhappy Indian was delivered up to
them: the Sieur Ferrand was charged with the
commission. The Indian was called Tichou;
he stood upright in the midst of his own people
and of his enemies, and said, "I am a true man,
that is, I do not fear death; but I pity the fate
of a wife and four children, whom I leave behind me very young; and of my father and
mother, who are old, and for whom I got subsistence by hunting." (He was the best hunter
in the nation.)

He had hardly spoken the last word of this
short speech, when his father, penetrated with
his son's love, rose amidst the people, and
spoke as follows:—

"It is through courage that my son dies;
but, being young and full of vigour, he is more
fit than myself to provide for his mother, wife,
and four little children: it is therefore necessary
he should stay on earth to take care of them.
As to myself, I am near the end of my career;
I am no longer fit for anything: I·cannot go

like the roebuck, whose course is like the winds, unseen; I cannot sleep like the hare, with my ears never shut; but I have lived as a man, and will die as such, therefore I go to take his place."

At these words, his wife, his son, his daughter-in-law, and their little children, shed tears round the brave old man: he embraced them for the last time. The relations of the dead Chactaw accepted the offer; after that, he laid himself on the trunk of a tree, and his head was cut off with one stroke of a hatchet. Every thing was made up by this death; but the young man was obliged to give them his father's head: in taking it up, he said to it, "Pardon me thy death, and remember me in the country of spirits."

All the French who assisted at this event were moved even to tears, and admired this noble old man. A people among whom such things could be done, hardly deserved the sweeping censures of Mather and other good men, who painted them rather as fiends in human shape. Courage is, of course, the virtue held in most honour: those who run away or desert in an action are not punished, they are considered as the disgrace of human nature: the ugliest girls will not accept of them for husbands: they are obliged to let their hair grow, and to wear an alcoman, or apron, like the women. "I saw one of them," says Bossu, who dwelt a long time among the Indians "who, being ashamed of his figure, went by

6*

himself to fight the Chicachas, for his misery was more than he could bear: for three or four days he went on creeping like a snake, and hiding himself in the great grass, without eating or drinking; so he came to their country, and watched a long time to do some exploit; often lying down in the rushes, when his enemies came near, and putting out his head above the water from time to time, to take breath. At last he drew near a village in the night, cried the cry of death, killed one of the people, and then fled with the speed of an arrow. He was out three months upon this expedition: when he drew nigh to his own village, weary, and bearing the head of his enemy, they came down the hill to meet him. The women were loud in his praises—the warriors gathered round him; and then they gave him a wife."

JOHN ELIOT'S FIRST MISSION TO THE INDIANS.

On the 28th of October, 1646, Eliot set out from his home, in Roxbury, Massachusetts, in company with three friends, to the nearest Indian settlement: he had previously sent to give this tribe notice of his coming, and a very large number was collected from all quarters. If the savages expected the coming of their guest, of whose name they had often heard, to be like that of a warrior or sachem, they were greatly deceived. They saw Eliot on foot, drawing near, with his companions; his translation of the scriptures, like a calumet of peace and love, in his hand. He was met by their chief, Waubon, who conducted him to a large wigwam After a short rest, Eliot went into the open air and standing on a grassy mound, while the people formed around him in all the stillness of strong surprise and curiosity, he prayed in the English tongue, as if he could not address heaven in a language both strange and new. And then he preached for an hour in their own tongue, and gave a clear and simple account of the religion of Christ, of his character and life, of the blessed state of those who believed in him.

Of what avail would it have been to set before this listening people the terrors of the Almighty, and the doom of the guilty? This wise man knew, by long experience as a minister, that the heart loves better to be persuaded than terrified—to be melted than alarmed. The whole career of the Indian's life tended to freeze up the finer and softer feelings, and make the more dark and painful passions familiar to him. He resolved to strike a new chord, and when he saw the tear stream down their stern faces, and the haughty head sink low on the breast, as he painted the ineffable love of Christ, he said it was "a glorious and affecting spectacle to see a company of perishing forlorn outcasts, so drinking in the word of salvation." The impressions this discourse produced, were of a very favourable nature : as far as the chief,

Waubon, was concerned, they were never effaced. Afterwards the guest passed several hours conversing with the Indians, and answering their questions. When night came, he returned to the tent with the chief, and the people entered their wigwams, or lay down around, and slept on the grass. What were Eliot's feelings on this night? At last, the longing of years was accomplished; the fruit of his prayers was given to him.

"Could the walls of his loved study speak," says his friend, "they would tell of the entreaties poured forth before the Lord, of the days and nights set apart with fasting — that thus, thus it might be." A few of the chiefs' friends alone remained, after the people were retired. One of the Christians perceived an Indian, who was hanging down his head, weeping; the former went to him, and spoke encouraging words, after which he turned his face to the wall, and wept yet more abundantly: soon after, he rose and went out. "When they told me of his tears," said Eliot, "we resolved to go forth, and follow him into the wood, and speak to him. The proud Indian's spirit was quite broken: at last we parted, greatly rejoicing for such sorrowing."

He now resolved to continue his labours · but, on the 26th of November, when he met the assembly of the Indians for the third time, he found that, though many of them had con structed wigwams at the place of meeting, for the more readily attending his ministry, h audience was not so numerous as on the former occasions. The Powahs (or soothsayers) had strictly charged the people not to listen to the instructions of the English, and threatened them with death in case of disobedience. Having warned his auditors against the impositions of these men, he proceeded to discourse as formerly, and was heard with the greatest attention. "It is wonderful," observed one of his friends, "to see what a little light will effect, even upon hearts and spirits most incapable."

On the night after this third meeting, many were gathered in the tent, looking earnestly at Eliot, with the solemn gravity and stillness which these savages affected; when the chief, Waubon, suddenly rose, and began to instruct all the company out of the things he had heard that day from Eliot, with the wild and impressive eloquence of the desert. And waking often that night, he many times was heard speaking to some or other of his people, of the words of truth and mercy that he had heard.

Two or three days after these impressions had been made, Eliot saw that they were likely to be attended with permanent consequences. Wampas, an intelligent Indian, came with two of his companions to the English, and desired to be admitted into their families. He brought his son, and several other children with him, and begged that they might be educated in the Christian faith: the example quickly spread and all the Indians who were present at the fourth meeting, on the 9th of December, offered their children to be instructed.

The missionary was himself surprised at the success of his first efforts, as well as at his facility of preaching and conversing in the Indian tongue; it was the reward of his long and patient application. "To think of raising," says Mather, "these hideous creatures unto the elevations of our holy religion, must argue a more than common or little soul in the undertaker: could he see any thing angelical to encourage his labours?—all was diabolical among them."

Eliot saw that they must be civilized ere they could be christianized; that he must make men of them, ere he could hope to see them saints. It is, no doubt, far easier and more flattering to the soul of the agent, to see men weep and tremble beneath his word, than to teach them to build, to plant, to rear the walls and the roof-tree, and sit at their own hearth-side: this is slow and painful work for a man of lofty mind and glowing enthusiasm. But in his own words, "he abhorred that he should sit still, and let that work alone;" and lost no time in addressing himself to the General Court of the colony, in behalf of those who showed a willingness to be placed under his care. His appli cation was successful; and the Indians, having received a grant of land on which they migh build a town, and enjoy the Christian instruc uon which they desired, met together, and gave their assent to several laws which he had framed, to enforce industry and decency — to secure personal and domestic comfort.

The ground of the town having been marked out, Eliot advised the Indians to surround it with ditches and a stone wall; gave them instruments to aid these objects, and such rewards, in money, as induced them to work hard. It was a strange and novel thing to see these men of the wilderness, to whom a few months previous all restraint was slavery, and their lakes and forests dearer than the palaces of kings, submit cheerfully to this drudgery of bricks and mortar — chief as well as serf; the very hands that were lately red with slaughter, scooping the earth at the bidding of Eliot, from morn to night. He soon had the pleasure of seeing Nonanetum completed.

The progress of civilization which followed, was remarkable for its extent and rapidity : the women were taught to spin, and they soon found something to send to the nearest markets all the year round : in winter they sold staves, baskets, and poultry ; in spring and summer fish, grapes, strawberries, &c.

In the mean while, he instructed the men in husbandry, and the more simple mechanical arts : in hay-time and harvest, he went forth into the fields with them. All this was not done in a day, for they were neither so industrious nor so capable of hard labour as those who had been accustomed to it from early life.

At a funeral, on the 7th of October, 1647, a change in the usages and prejudices of the Indians was evinced in a striking manner. The deceased was a man of some consequence. Their custom had been to mourn much for the dead, and to appear overcome with grief, especially when the earth shrouded them from their sight. The departed was borne to the grave on a light bier, and interred in a sitting posture: in his hand was placed a calumet and some tobacco, that he might present the ensigns of peace to the people of another world. If the corpse was that of a warrior, his quiver full of arrows, a bow, and a hatchet, were placed by his side, and also a little mirror, that he might see how his face looked after passing through the region of death; and a little vermilion to take away its extreme paleness. His was a bold hand that could at once tear aside these loved usages, and make the dust of the warrior of no more consequence than that of the meanest of his followers. The cemetery of the new town was in the woods, and the procession of all the inhabitants moved slowly beneath their shadow, in deep and solemn silence; with the missionary at their head: no wail was heard—no wild gush of sorrow. To estimate this sacrifice, it is necessary to recur to the Indian oelief, "that after death they should go to a very fertile country, where they were to have

many wives, and, above all, lovely places for
hunting:" often, no doubt, the shadowy chase
of the bear and the stag came on the dreams
of the dying man; and afterwards, beautiful
women would welcome him, weary to his
home. When the dead was laid in the grave,
Eliot read the funeral service over him, and
then told the many people, that in heaven they
neither married nor were given in marriage;
that the passions of this world, the wild chase
or the warrior's joy, could never come there;
there was neither chieftain nor slave; that in
the love of Christ, who was the resurrection
and the life, all these things would be lost.
And they believed him—those fierce and brutal
men—and wept, not for the dead, but for themselves; "so that the woods," says a gentleman
who was present, "rang with their sighs and
prayers;" he also adds these words,—" God
was with Eliot, and the sword of his word will
pierce deep, in the hand of the mighty." His
opinion of the mental powers of this people
was not a very low one:—"There is need,"
he says, in one of his letters, " of learning, in
ministers who preach to Indians, much more
than to Englishmen and gracious Christians;
for these had sundry philosophical questions,
which some knowledge of the arts must help
to give answer to, and without which they
would not have been satisfied. Worse than
Indian ignorance hath blinded their eyes, that
renounce learning as an enemy to gospel ministers" So acute were many of the question

7

proposed by the Indians, and so deeply expressive of a gentler and better nature, that more than one educated stranger was induced to attend regularly the assemblies of the missionary.

LOVEWELL'S FIGHT.

Captain John Lovewell, of Dunstable, raised a volunteer company and met with great success. At one time he fell in with an Indian trail and pursued it till he discovered them asleep on the bank of a pond. They were all killed, and their scalps, stretched upon hoops, served to decorate their triumphal return. They, of course, received the bounty, which amounted to ten pounds.

(1725.) Lovewell, having augmented his company to 46 men, again set out with the intention of attacking an Indian town on the Saco. They built a fort on the Great Ossapy pond, and then proceeded, leaving one of their number sick, and eight men to guard the fort.

When about 22 miles from the fort they rested on the banks of a pond, where they discovered a single Indian at a distance, on a point of land, and rightly judging that he was attached to a large party of Indians, Lovewell determined to advance and attack them. Accordingly the whole company threw off their packs in one place among the brakes; and, to gain the advantage, the men were spread so as partially to surround the water. Lovewell had, however, mistaken the position of the Indians, who were already on his track, and coming to the place where the packs were deposited, by counting them discovered the number of English to be less than their own. They, therefore marched to assault the English in the rear, and actually hemmed them in between the mouth of a brook, a rocky point, a deep bog, and the pond. The company, completely surrounded, fought desperately till nightfall, when the Indians, tired of the conflict, moved off. The number of killed and wounded amounted to 23, Lovewell being among the former. The remainder of the party returned to the fort which had been deserted, in consequence of the arrival of one of Lovewell's men who fled at the beginning of the fight, and reported all the rest killed. After resting, they started for home, where they arrived, to the great joy of their friends, after enduring the severest hardships. The survivors were liberally compensated, and the widows and families of the slain were provided for by the government of the province.

COTTON MATHER'S ACCOUNT OF THE INDIANS OF HIS TIME.

"These shiftless Indians," says Mather, "their housing is nothing but a few mats tied about poles fastened into the earth, where a good fire is their bed-clothes in the coldest season: their diet has not a greater dainty; a handful of meal and a spoonful of water being their food for many days; for they depend on the produce of their hunting and fishing, and badly cultivated grounds: thus they are subject to long fastings. They have a cure for some diseases, even a little cave: after they have terribly heated it, a crew of them go and sit there with the priest, looking in the heat and smoke like so many fiends, and then they rush forth on a sudden, and plunge into the water: how they escape death, instead of getting cured, is marvellous; they are so slothful, that their poor wives must plant, and build, and beat their corn. All the religion they have is a belief in many gods, who made the different nations of the world, but chiefly in one great one of the name of Kicktan, who dwelt in the south-west regions of the heavens, who created the original parents of mankind, who, though never seen by the eye of man, was entitled to their gratitude, that we have in us immortal souls, which, if good, should go to a splendid entertainment with Kicktan; but, otherwise, must wander about in a restless horror for ever."

THE VALIANT OLD MOHAWK.

(1696.) On one occasion, when Count Frontignac succeeded in capturing a Mohawk fort, it was found deserted of all its inhabitants except a sachem in extreme old age, who sat with

the composure of an ancient Roman in his ca-
pitol, and saluted his civilized compeer in age
and infirmity, with dignified courtesy and venerable address. Every hand was instantly raised
to wound and deface his time-stricken frame
and while French and Indian knives wer
plunged into his body, he recommended to his
Indian enemies rather to burn him with fire,
that he might teach their French allies how
to suffer like men. "Never, perhaps," says
Charlevoix, "was a man treated with more cruelty; nor ever did any endure it with superior
magnanimity and resolution."

OPECHANCANOUGH'S LAST WAR.

Opechancanough was by no means backward
in taking advantage of the repose afforded by
the treaty of 1632. For the long period which
elapsed between its conclusion and his final
effort, in 1644, he was industriously occupied in
making preparations for a renewal of hostilities. An opportunity at length presented itself
for executing his long-cherished purpose. The
colony was involved in intestine dissensions.
An insurrection had taken place in consequence
of the unpopularity of the governor, and at a
moment when the people were occupied with
internal disorders and heedless of danger from
without, their great enemy struck a powerful
and almost fatal blow.

He was now advanced to extreme old age,

7*

being supposed to have numbered nearly a
hundred years, but the powers of his mind
were still so vigorous, that he was the leading
spirit of a confederacy embracing all the Indian
tribes distributed over a space of country six
hundred miles in extent. Unable to walk, he
was borne in a litter to the scene of action
(April 18th, 1644,) and thus led his warriors to
the attack. Such was the skill with which his
measures had been concerted that the whole
force of the Indians commenced their operations upon the entire line of the frontier at the
same instant of time, with the intention of car-
ying a war of extermination down to the sea,
and thus annihilating the colony at a single
blow. In two days, five hundred persons had
fallen in the massacre. Of course, every ope-
ration of industry was instantly abandoned, and
all who were able to bear arms were embodied
to oppose so terrible an invasion. Governor
Berkeley, at the head of a chosen force, consisting of every twentieth man in the colony,
marched into the enemy's country, and thus
gave him the first check. Of the details of the
campaign, in consequence of the confusion and
distress prevailing at the time, no details are
furnished by the contemporary historians. Be-
verly's account, the only one which survived
the ravages of the time, is meagre and unsatis-
factory. One result of the war, however, is
sufficiently well attested, since it terminated the
horrors of the season. This was the capture of
the aged Onechancanough, who was surprised

and taken prisoner by a squadron of horse under the command of Governor Berkeley, who forthwith conducted him in triumph to James-Town.

It was the governor's intention to have sent this remarkable person to England; but he was shot after being taken prisoner, by a soldier, in resentment of the calamities he had inflicted on the province. He lingered under the wound for several days, and died with the pride and firmness of an old Roman. Indignant at the crowds who came to gaze at him on his death-bed, he exclaimed; "If I had taken Sir William Berkeley prisoner, I would not have exposed him as a show to the people." Perhaps he remembered that he had saved the life of Captain Smith, and forgot the numberless instances in which he had exposed other prisoners to public derision and lingering torture.

After the decease of their great enemy, the colonists had no difficulty in concluding a treaty with the Indians, which gave tranquillity to the province for a long term of years.

THE BURNING OF SCHENECTADY.

The incursions of the Indians on our frontiers in early times were usually the result of Spanish influence in the South, or French influence in the North. The French reduced the incitement of Indian hostilities to a complete system, and their officers and soldiers were not ashamed to accompany the savages in their murdering and marauding expeditions into New England and New York. Among all the recorded instances of this kind, none appears to have been attended with more atrocious circumstances of cruelty and rapine, than the burning of Schenectady. This affair is marked by many traits of the very worst description. The inhumanity of murdering in their beds the very people who had formerly relieved their wants, is, perhaps, without a parallel.

In 1690, Count de Frontignac, governor general of Canada, sent out three expeditions against the American colonies. The first of these proceeded against Schenectady, then a small village, situated on the Mohawk river. This party, after wandering for twenty-two days through deserts rendered trackless by snow, approached the village of Schenectady in so exhausted a condition, that they had determined to surrender themselves to the inhabitants as prisoners of war. But, arriving at a late hour on an inclement night, and hearing from the messengers they had sent forward that the inhabitants were all in bed, without even

the precaution of a public watch, they exchanged their intention of imploring mercy to
themselves, for a plan of nocturnal attack and
massacre of the defenceless people, to whose
charity their own countrymen had once been so
highly indebted. This detestable requital of
good with evil was executed with a barbarity
which, of itself, must be acknowledged to form
one of the most revolting and terrific pictures
that has ever been exhibited of human cruelty
and ferocity. Dividing themselves into a number of parties, they set fire to the village in various places, and attacked the inhabitants with
fatal advantage when, alarmed by the confla-
gration, they endeavoured to escape from their
burning houses. The exhausted strength of
the Frenchmen appeared to revive with the
work of destruction, and to gather energy from
the animated horror of the scene. Not only
were all the male inhabitants they could reach
put to death, but women were murdered, and
their infants dashed on the walls of the houses.
But either the delay caused by this elaborate
cruelty, or the more merciful haste of the
flames to announce the calamity to those who
might still fly from the assassins, enabled many
of the inhabitants to escape. The efforts of
the assailants were also somewhat impeded by
a sagacious discrimination which they thought
it expedient to exercise. Though unmindful
of benefits, they were not regardless of policy ;
and of a number of Mohawk Indians who
were in the village, not one sustained an injury

Sixty persons perished in the massacre, and twenty-seven were taken prisoners. Of the fugitives who escaped half naked, and made their way through a storm of snow to Albany, twenty-five lost their limbs from the intensity of the frost. The French, having totally de-stroyed Schenectady, retired loaded with plunder from a place where, we think, it must be acknowledged that even the accustomed atro-cities of Indian warfare had been outdone.

REMARKABLE CUSTOM OF THE NATCHES.

The Natches were a very considerable nation; they formed several villages, that were under some peculiar chief, and these obeyed one superior of the whole nation. All these chiefs bore the name of suns; they adored that luminary, and carried his image on their breasts, rudely carved. The manner in which the Natches rendered divine service to the sun has something solemn in it. The high-priest got up at break of day, and marched at the head of the people with a grave pace, the calumet of peace in his hand. He smoked in honour of the sun, and blew the first mouthful of smoke towards him; when he rose above the horizon, they howled by turns after the high-priests, and contemplated it with their arms extended to heaven. They had a temple in which they kept up an eternal fire.

So proud were these chiefs, who pretended to trace their origin to the sun, that they had a law, by which every Natchez, who had married a girl of the blood of the suns, must follow her in death, as soon as she had breathed her last. There was an Indian, whose name was Etteacteal; he dearly loved a daughter of one of these suns, and married her; but the consequence of this honour had nearly proved very fatal to him. His wife fell sick: he watched over her day and night, and with many tears he besought her not to die, and they prayed together to Wachil, or the sun, that he would spare her life; at last he saw her at the point of death, and then he fled: for the moment she ceased to breathe, he was to be slain. He embarked in a piragua on the Mississippi, and came to New Orleans. He put himself under the protection of M. de Bienville, the then governor, who interested himself for him with the Natches; they declared that he had nothing more to fear.

Etteacteal, being thus assured, resolved to return to his nation; and without settling among them, made several voyages thither; he happened to be there, when the chief called the **Stung Serpent**, brother to the head of the nation, died; he was a relation of the late wife of Etteacteal, and the people resolved to make the latter pay his debt, and arrested him. When he found himself in the hut of the grand chief of war, he gave vent to the excess of his grief.

The favourite wife of the deceased Stung Serpent, who was likewise to be sacrificed, and who saw the preparations for her death with firmness, hearing the complaints and groans of Etteacteal, said to him, " Art thou no warrior?" he said, " Yes, I am one." " However," said she, " thou criest, life is dear to thee; and as that is the case, it is not good that thou shouldst go along with me—go with the women." Etteacteal replied, " True, life is dear to me: it would be well if I walked yet on earth; wa t, O wait till the death of the great sun, and I will die with him." "Go thy way," she said, "it is not fit that thou die with me, and thy heart remain behind on earth; the warriors will obey my word, for now, so near to the Spirit of life, I am full of power: go away, and let me see thee no more." He did not stay to have this order repeated; he disappeared like lightning. Three old women, two of whom were his relations, offered to pay his debt; their age and their infirmities had disgusted them with life, none of them had been able to walk for a great while; but the hair of the two that were willing to kitearnes, was no more grey than that of young women: the third was a hundred and twenty years old; they were sacrificed in the evening, at the going down of the sun.

The generosity of these women gave the Indian life again, acquired him the degree of *Considered*, and cleared his honour, that had been sullied by his fearing death. The hour being come for the sacrifice of the favourite wife of the deceased chief, she came forth, and called her children round her, while the people stood a little way off: "Children," she said, "this is the day on which I am to tear myself from your arms, and to follow your father's steps, who waits for me in the country of the spirits; if I were to yield to your tears, I should injure my love, and fail in my duty. I have done enough for you by bearing you next to my heart, and by suckling you with my breasts. You that are descended of his blood, a'id fed by my milk, ought you to shed tears? rejoice, rather, that you are suns and warriors: go, my children, I have provided for all your wants, by procuring you friends; my friends, and those of your father, are yours too. And you, Frenchmen," she added, turning herself towards our officers, "I recommend my or phan children to you;—you ought to protect them; we shall be longer friends in the coun try of the spirits than here, because we do not die there again. And now the day is sinking behind the hills; yet a few moments, my husband, and I come!"

Moved by these words, a noble woman came to join herself to the favourite wife, of her own accord, being engaged, she said, by the friendship she bore the Stung Serpent, to follow him into the other world. The Europeans called her the Haughty Lady, on account of her majestic deportment, and proud and beautiful features: on this account the French officers regretted very much her resolve, and strove to dissuade her from it, but in vain: the moving sight filled them all with grief and horror.

PONTIAC.

Great as were many of the western Indian warriors, none was greater than Pontiac, a chief whose fame was not only spread throughout America, but widely diffused in Europe. He was the chief of all the Indians on the chain of lakes: the Ottawas, to which he belonged, the Miamis, Chippewas, Wyandots, Pottawatomies, Winnebagoes, Shawanese, Ottagamies, and Mississagas, all of which tribes afterwards were led by Tecumseh. Pontiac is said to have possessed a majestic and princely appearance, so pleasing to the Indians, and this in part accounts for his popularity among them.

In 1760, after the capture of Quebec, Major Rogers was sent into the country of Pontiac to drive the French from it. Being informed of his approach, Pontiac sent word to him to wait until he came to him. The major waited, and when Pontiac came, that chief asked him why he entered his dominions without permission. The major answered that he came not against the natives but the French; and at the same time gave the chief several belts of wampum; whereupon Pontiac replied, "I stand in the path you travel until to-morrow morning." By this was meant that he must not proceed until the next morning. Upon an offer of the Indian, Major Rogers bought a large quantity of parched corn, and other provisions. The next day Pontiac offered him every facility for the undertaking. Messengers were sent to the different tribes to assure them that the English had his permission to pass through the country, and he even accompanied the major and troops as far as Detroit. He was noted for the desire of knowledge, and while the English were in his country, he was very curious in examining their arms, clothes, &c., and expressed a wish to go to England. He said that he would allow white settlements within his domains; and was willing to call the king of England *uncle* but not master. He further told the soldiers that they must behave themselves peaceably while in his country, or he would stop the way.

Pontiac had distinguished himself at Detroit and Michillimackinac. When the French gave up Canada (1760), their Indian allies still preserved their hatred towards the English, and as Pontiac was the most considerable enemy of that nation, the adjacent tribes *all came* to him as a support against them. Pontiac had advanced farther in civilization than any of the neighbouring chiefs: he appointed a commissary during the war of 1763, called Pontiac's war, and issued bills of credit, on each of which was pictured the thing desired, and the figure of an otter, the symbol of his tribe. In 1763 Major Rogers sent a bottle of brandy to him, which Pontiac was counselled not to drink, as it probably contained poison. But with the greatest magnanimity he exclaimed, " It is not in his power to *kill him* who has so lately saved his life."

THE IDOL OF THE PEORIAS.

(FROM AN OLD TRAVELLER.)

"We arrived at the village of the Peorias, allies of the Illinois, through a fine large meadow, which is many leagues long. This village is situated on the banks of a little river, and surrounded with great pales and posts: there are many trees on the banks, and the huts are built beneath them. When we arrived there, I inquired for the hut of the grand chief: I was well received by him and his first warriors. They had just been beaten by the Foxes, their mortal enemies, and were now holding a consultation about it. A young Indian lighted the calumet of peace; then they brought me a dish of maize flour, called sagamité, sweetened with the syrup of the maple-tree; and afterwards a dessert of dry fruits, as good as Corinth raisins. The next day I saw a great crowd in the plain: they were for making a dance in favour of their new Manitou; the high priest had a bonnet of feathers, like a crown, on his head. I was at the door of the temple of their false deity; he begged me to go in. Judge of my astonishment, for this is the picture of their Manitou: his head hung upon his breast, and looked like a goat's; his ears and his cruel eye were like those of a lynx, with the same kind of hair; his feet, hands, and thighs were in form something like those of a man.

"The Indians found him in the woods, at the

8 *

foot of a ridge of mountains, and the priests
had persuaded them to adopt him for a divinity.
This general assembly was called, to invoke his
protection against their enemies.   I let the Indians know that their Manitou was an evil
genius; as a proof of it, I said that he had just
permitted the nation of Foxes, their most cruel
enemies, to gain a victory over them, and they
ought to get rid of him as soon as possible, and
be revenged on him.   After a short time, they
answered, 'Houé nigeié, tinai labé,' — 'we believe thee, thou art in the right.'   They then
voted that he should be burnt; and the great
priest, after some opposition, pronounced his
sentence, which, according to the interpreter's
explanation, was in these terms : 'O thou, fatal
to our nation, who has wrongfully taken thee
for her Manitou! thou hast paid no regard to
the offerings which we have made thee, and
hast allowed our enemies, whom thou dost
plainly protect, to overcome us; therefore our
old men, assembled in council, have decreed,
with the advice of the chief of the white warriors, that to expiate thy ingratitude towards
us, thou shalt be burnt alive.'   At the end of
this sentence, all the assembly said, 'Hau, hau,
which signified 'yes.'

   "As I wished to get this monster, I went to
the priest, made him a small present, and bid
my interpreter tell him that he should persuade
his countrymen, that if they burnt this evil genius, there might arise one from his ashes that
could be fatal to them; that I would go on pur-

pose across the great lake, to deliver them from it. He found my reasons good, and got the sentence changed, so that it was strangled. I got it instantly dissected, in order to bring it to France, where its skeleton is now in the cabinet of natural history of M. de Fayolles. The assembly dispersed, and returned to their village by the river side. In the evening you might see them sitting in groups at their doors, and on the shore, with many fires made of the branches of the trees, whose light was on the water and the grove; while some of them danced the dance of war, with loud shrieks, that were enough to strike an awe into the heart."

DEATH OF A MOHAWK CHIEF.

Count Frontignac, whose sprightly manners and energetic character supported the spirits of his countrymen amidst every reverse, was so provoked with what he deemed the ingratitude of the Five Nations for his kindness to them at Schenectady, that, besides encouraging his own Indian allies to burn their prisoners alive, he at .ength condemned to a death still more dreadful, two Mohawk warriors who had fallen into his hands.   In vain the French priests remonstrated against this sentence, and urged him not to bring so foul a stain on the Christian name : the count declared that every consideration must yield to the safety and defence of his people, and that the Indians must not be encouraged to believe that they might practise the extreme of cruelty on the French without the hazard of having it retorted on themselves.   If he had been merely actuated by politic considerations, without being stimulated by revenge, he might have plainly perceived, from the conduct of all the Indian tribes in their wars with each other, that the fear of retort had no efficacy whatever to restrain them from their barbarous practices, which he now undertook to sanction as far as his example was capable of doing.   The priests, finding that their humane intercession was ineffectual, repaired to the prisoners, and laboured to persuade them to embrace the Christian name, as a preparation for the dreadful fate which they were about to receive from Christian hands; but their instructions were rejected with scorn and derision, and they found the prisoners determined to dignify, by Indian sentiments and demeanour, the Indian death which they had been condemned to undergo. Shortly before the execution, some Frenchman, less inhuman than his governor, threw a knife into the prison, and one of the Mohawks immediately dispatched himself with it: the other, expressing contempt at his companion's mean evasion from glory, walked to the stake, singing in his death-chant, that he was a Mohawk warrior, that all the power of man could not extort the least expression of suffering from his lips, and that it was ample consolation to him to reflect that he had made many Frenchmen suffer the same pangs that he must now himself undergo. When attached to the stake, he looked round on his executioners, their instruments of torture, and the assembled multitude of spectators, with all the complacency of heroic fortitude; and, after enduring for some hours, with composed mien and triumphant language, a series of bar barities too atrocious and disgusting to be re-cited, his sufferings were terminated by the interposition of a French lady, who prevailed with the governor to order that mortal blow, to which human cruelty has given the name *of* *coup de grace* or stroke of *favour.*

MURDER OF MISS MACREA.

Mr. Jones, an officer of the British army, had gained the affections of Miss Macrea, a lovely young lady of amiable character and spotless reputation, daughter of a gentleman attached to the royal cause, residing near Fort Edward; and they had agreed to be married. In the course of service, the officer was removed to some distance from his bride, and became anxious for her safety and desirous of her company. He engaged some Indians, of two different tribes, to bring her to camp, and promised a keg of rum to the person who should deliver her safe to him. She dressed to meet her bridegroom, and accompanied her Indian conductors; but by the way, the two chiefs, each being desirous of receiving the promised reward, disputed which of them should deliver her to her lover. The dispute rose to a quarrel; and, according to their usual method of disposing of a disputed prisoner, one of them instantly cleft the head of the lady with his tomahawk. This simple story, sufficiently tragical and affecting in itself, was blazoned in the American newspapers with every amplification that could excite the imagination or touch the heart; and contributed in no slight degree to embitter the minds of the people against those who could degrade themselves by the aid of such allies. The impulse given to the public mind by such atrocities more than counterbalanced any advantages which the British derived from the assistance of the Indians.

AN INDIAN IN COLLEGE.

The first serious disappointment whic 1 John Eliot, the Indian Apostle, experienced, was in his efforts for the instruction of the Indian youth in the classic languages; many of the ablest and most promising among them were set apart for this purpose; his ambition was to bring them up "with our English youth in university learning." Where was the use of this? Eliot's best purposes were prone to be carried to excess. He gave away a whole year's salary, at a wretched cottage, while his wife was probably expecting it at home for household demands. He had learned his Indians to read and write; many could read English well; and now he wished to give them a polite education, that must have sat as gracefully on them as the full-sleeved gown and bands of the divine. Considerable sums were expended in their board and education: a substantial building of brick, which cost between three and four hundred pounds, was erected; it was large enough to accommodate twenty scholars. It must have been Spartan discipline to the heads as well as hearts of the poor Indians, to labour morn and night through the Greek and Roman authors, to try to discover and relish the beauties of style and the splendour of imagery. No doubt, their thoughts sometimes fled away to their deserts, where their fathers roved in dignity and freedom, and

books never came. The design might be praise-
worthy, but Providence did not smile upon it,
most of these young men died when they had
made great proficiency in their studies, as if the
languages wore out their hearts; others abandoned their books, even when they were pre
pared to enter Harvard College, in the town of
Cambridge; their patience was probably exhausted, and the boon of literary dignity could
lure them no further. A few of these, passing
from one extreme to the other, burst their bonds
at once; and as if mind and body panted together to be free, hastened back to the wilderness again, into its wigwams and swamps;
where neither Homer nor Ovid was like to
follow them.

"These circumstances proved very discou-
raging to the godly in New England," says a
contemporary. "Some were so far affected by
them, as to conceive that they were manifest
tokens of the Divine disapprobation. Mr. Eliot,
however, whose faith was more vigorous, considered them merely as trials, to which they
ought to submit without reluctance." In consequence of the death and failure of those who
entered the aforesaid building, it was soon after
chiefly occupied by the English. Only one of
these Indian students appears to have obtained
his degree at Harvard College; and at the conclusion of two Latin and Greek elegies, which
he composed on the death of an eminent minister, subscribed himself " Cheesecaumuk, Se

nior Sophista." What an incongruous blend-
ing of sounds!

Eliot at last saw his error, and, instead of
the classics, applied with fresh ardour to his
more useful translations, of which the circula-
tion was so rapid, that he printed a fresh edi-
tion of the "Practice of Piety." He also soon
after established a lecture at Naticke, in which
he explained the leading doctrines of theology
and logic: here he was on safe ground, and his
labours were eminently useful. During the
summer months they assembled eagerly once
a fortnight, and many of them gained much
knowledge; yet he was far from being satisfied
with his oral instructions, and he printed a
thousand copies of a logic primer, and made
little systems of all the liberal arts, for the use
of the Indians. The same minds that had pined
and sunk beneath the study of the classic
tongues, embraced these things with ardour.

9

AN INDIAN WARRANT.

Judge Davis, in his Appendix to the Memo
rial, observes, that the employment of the more
intelligent and energetic Indians as rulers, was
particularly grateful to them.   He had often
heard of amusing anecdotes of the Indian
rulers.   The following warrant is recollected,
which was issued by one of these magistrates,
directed to an Indian constable, and will not
suffer in comparison with our more verbose
forms.

'I, Hihoudi, you Peter Waterman, Jeremy
Wicket, quick you take him, fast you hold him
straight you bring him before me, Hihoudi.'

CAPTAIN JOHN SMITH.

This gentleman figures, in the early history of our country, as the most strenuous promoter of colonization, the most wise founder, and the most active governor, of colonies. In New England he acted as discoverer and settler; in Virginia he sustained both these characters, as well as that of the most efficient and able governor of the first permanent colony. When he landed upon the soil, he was a private citizen; but the misgovernment of others soon made it necessary to call him to the office of governor.

Under his directions James-Town was fortified by such defences as were sufficient to repel the attacks of the savages; and, by dint of great labour, which he was always the foremost to share, the colonists were provided with dwellings that afforded shelter from the weather, and contributed to restore and preserve their health. Finding the supplies of the savages discontinued, he put himself at the head of a detachment of his people, and penetrated into the country; and by courtesy and liberality to the tribes whom he found well disposed, and vigorously repelling the hostilities of such as were otherwise minded, he obtained for the colony the most abundant supplies

In the m.dst of his successes he was surprised on an expedition, by a hostile body of savages, who, having succeeded in making him prisoner, after a gallant and nearly successful defence, prepared to inflict on him the usual fate of their captives. His eminent faculties did not desert him on this trying occasion. He desired to speak with the sachem or chief, and, presenting him with a mariner's compass, expatiated on the wonderful discoveries to which it had led, described the shape of the earth, the vastness of its lands and oceans, the course of the sun, the varieties of nations, and the singularity of their relative positions, which made some of them antipodes to the others.

With equal prudence and magnanimity he refrained from all solicitations for his life, which would only have weakened the impressions which he hoped to produce. The savages listened with amazement and admiration. They had handled the compass, and viewing with surprise the play of the needle, which they plainly saw, but found it impossible to touch, from the intervention of the glass, this marvellous object prepared their minds for the reception of those vast impressions by which their captive endeavoured to gain ascendency over them.

For an hour after he had finished his harangue, they seem to have remained undecided; till their habitual sentiments reviving, they resumed their suspended purpose, and, having bound him to a tree, prepared to dispatch him with their arrows. But a stronger impression had been made on their chief; and his soul, enlarged for a season by the admission of knowledge, or subdued by the influence of wonder, revolted from the dominion of habitual ferocity. This chief was named Opechancanough, and destined at a future period to invest his barbarous name with terror and celebrity. Holding up the compass in his hand, he gave the signal of reprieve, and Smith, though still guarded as a prisoner, was conducted to a dwelling where he was kindly treated, and plentifully entertained. But the strongest impressions pass away, while the influence of habit remains.

After vainly endeavouring to prevail on their captive to betray the English colony into their hands, they referred his fate to Powhatan, the king or principal sachem of the country, to whose presence they conducted him in triumphal procession. The king received him with much ceremony, ordered a plentiful repast to be set before him, and then adjudged him to suffer death by having his head laid on a stone and beat to pieces with clubs. At the place appointed for this barbarous execution, he was again rescued from impending fate by the interposition of Pocahontas, the favourite daughter of the king, who, finding her first entreaties disregarded, threw her arms around the prisoner, and declared her determination to save him or die with him. Her generous affection prevailed over the cruelty of her tribe, and the king not only gave Smith his life, but soon after went

9*

him back to James-Town, where the beneficence of Pocahontas continued to follow him
with supplies of provisions that delivered the
colony from famine.

ANECDOTES OF KING PHILIP'S WAR.

COMMENCEMENT OF THE WAR.

In the year 1674, the number of Eliot's towns
and settlements, in which industry, comfort,
good order, and the best instruction, were established, amounted to more than twelve, when
an unforeseen event happened, that threw a
cloud over all his prospects. This was the war
in which the colonists of New England were
involved with Philip, son of Massasoit, the celebrated chief, and, for the last years of his life,
the firm friend of the English. " O, thou sword
of the wilderness, when wilt thou be quiet?"
says Mather, forgetful that it was bared by the
aggressions of the settlers, as well as by the
fierce and restless spirit of the Indian prince.
Ever since the foundation of the colonies, the
former had conducted themselves, says more
than one divine of the period, with great kindness to their heathen brethren. The truth of
this assertion is very doubtful. The missionary
took no part in the disputes, save to urge his
countrymen to forbearance and peace. " We,
the poor church of Naticke," he writes to them,
" hearing that the honoured rulers of Plymouth

are pressing and arming of soldiers to go to
war with the Indians, do mourn greatly on account of it, and desire that they may not be
destroyed, because we have not heard that they
have done any thing worthy of death. It is
your duty to offer, accept, and desire peace, and
we pray you, for God's sake, and for your
souls' sake, obey this word; we long to hear
of a happy peace, that may open a clear passage for the gospel among that people." Simple as these words are, they unfold an affection
on the part of the missionary and his converts,
for those who had few claims on their regard;
for Philip, and most of his chiefs, had sternly
rejected all persuasions to Christianity. But
Eliot was not of the sentiment of another divine, who rejoiced in the rejection of the proposals by the Indians, that "this thing was of
the Lord." He saw only on one side an ex-
quisite jealousy, roused by many wrongs, a
heart burning with vindictive feelings; on the
other, a sordid ambition, an unhallowed love
of glory. It was a source of sorrow, that the
torch of discord was first kindled by one of his
own people. In the end of the year 1674, John
Seusoman, a converted Indian, after having
apostatized from the faith, devoted himself to
the service of Philip, as secretary. He informed
the English that his countrymen had resolved
to adopt measures for their destruction. "He
could write," says the historian, "though the
king, his master, could not read."

This renegade, fearing the consequences of
what he had done, returned to the protection
of the settlers, and was soon after slain by two
of the·Indian captains.   The English arrested
the perpetrators of the deed, and, on a trial by
jury, finding them guilty, they were executed.
Philip was alarmed at the condemnation of his
counsellors, and, conscious that he had given
cause for suspicion, resolved to be the first in
the field.   He had probably long waited for an
opportunity.   Rash, headstrong, and vindictive,
with the courage but not the talents of his
father, Massasoit, the slow and artful aggressions of the settlers stung him to the quick.
He began to gather his warriors around his
dwelling-place, at the strong forts near the Naraganset river; he received the accession of
several other tribes.   In the mean time, it was
said, strange sights and sounds foreboded, in
many parts of the colonies, the woes that were
near; the singing of bullets, and the awful
passing away of drums in the air; invisible
troops of horses were heard riding to and fro;
and in a clear, still, sunshiny morning, the phan-
toms of men, fearfully flitting by! Philip, heedless of omens and dreams, sent away the women and children, and took his stand on Mount
Hope, a low and beautiful eminence, on which
was his strongest fort.   Ere matters came to a
fatal extremity, and all the evils of war were
let loose on his settlements, Eliot did his utmost
to turn them aside; he saw that many of his

people would inevitably be involved with one party or the other. His town of Pakeunit was very near Mount Hope; he had visited the latter during the life of Massasoit, and though he felt not the same regard or esteem for his son, a friendly intercourse had subsisted between them. His applications to the colonists for peace being fruitless, he resolved to try them also on the former.

INTERVIEW BETWEEN ELIOT AND PHILIP

A few miles only distant, the encampmen
of the Indians around their Mount was distinctly visible from Pakeunit; and Eliot, with
two or three of his people, went to have an interview with the chieftain. Philip respected
his character, though he disliked his proceedings, for he had always treated his mission with
contempt and slight; among the warriors, however, both of his own and other tribes, were
many who had heard Eliot preach, and had received him beneath their roof. The interview
was without any success; the spirit of the In
dian was made up to the desperate struggle,
and all that could be done was to beseech him
to spare the settlements of the converts.

The contrast between the two men must
have been sufficiently striking. Philip was in
the prime of life, with a frame nerved by early
hardship, and the usages of savage warfare, in
which he was very expert; he was dressed like
his chiefs, save that he wore a silver-laced tu-
nic, or coat, and that his arms were more rich
his chief ensign of dignity was his princely, yet
cruel and gloomy features, where the thirst of
revenge was stamped. The frame of the missionary was not bowed even by seventy years,
though they had turned his hair white; the
leathern girdle was about his loins, that he
always wore, and the simple apparel that he

.oved; he stood among these fierce and exasperated men as calm and fearless as in his own assembly at Naticke : he could not but foresee the devastation about to be let loose on the land ; that the fire and the sword would waste all his pleasant places, and scatter his converts ; and he returned with a heavy heart to his home. Several of the latter afterwards sided with the forces of Philip : whether from this circumstance, or from the nearness of the settlement of Pakeunit to the camp of the prince, the colonists contracted the strongest dislike and mistrust of the Christian Indians. Eliot, when he saw there was no longer a chance of peace, exhorted his people in the above town, and at Naticke, as well as the other congregations, not to be moved by the example or seductions of either party.

CHRISTIAN INDIANS ENGAGE IN THE WAR.

The contagion was, however, too strong; and Eliot at last saw many of them also take up arms against their infidel countrymen. The order and harmony of their dwelling-places were for a time utterly blasted; on the hills around Na-ticke and Pakeunit the watch-fires were blaz-ing; the war-whoops were often heard in the night; at intervals, a solitary musket, and then a signal cry, came from the neighbouring woods; and yet nearer, the poor Indians at last saw their plantations without the town, burning; for Philip began hostilities by a sud-den attack on them, so that their taking up arms was partly in self-defence. After several actions, he retired from Mount Hope to the woods, swamps, and fastnesses of the interior, in the dominion of the great tribe of the Nara-ganset Indians, who, for his sake, had now broken treaty with the English. It was the depth of winter, yet the latter resolved to fol-low him to his retreats, and an army of fifteen hundred men, under the command of the Hon. J. Winslow, marched to the abode of the In-dians. This was on an island of about five or six acres, the only entrance to which was upon a long tree over the water, so that but one man could pass at a time: but the water was frozen; the trees and thickets were white with their burden of snow, as was the surface of the earth, so that the smallest movement of the Indians could be seen.

Within the isle were gathered the powers of the Pequot and Naraganset tribes, with their wives, families, and valuable things; the want of leaves and thick foliage allowed no ambush, and the savage must fight openly beside his own hearth and store.   It was the close of day when the colonists came up to the place; a fort, a blockhouse, and a wall that passed round the isle, proved the skill, as well as resolution, of the assailed; the frozen shores and water were quickly covered with the slain, and then the Indians fought at their doors and around their children, till all was lost, and a thousand of them fell.   Philip fled with his surviving forces to a distant position, where it was impossible to follow him.   Concord, one of the first settlements of Eliot, and one or two other towns, were this winter destroyed, and its poor people turned from their dwellings into all the rigours of the winter; many perished in the woods or amidst the snows, or by the secret and sudden ambushes of the enemy.

10

MISFORTUNES OF PHILIP.

The last defeat, in which his best fighting men were slain, had broken the power, but not the spirit, of Philip. Unable to meet the colonists in the open field, he harassed them in a thousand ways, so that, as the spring advanced, the more industrious and timid were thrown into the extremity of despair, and said, " How shall we wade through another summer like the last ?" But the chief was now a wandering exile ; his paternal dominion was taken ; the singular friendship of Quanonchet, " the mighty sachem of the Naragansets," was his last support. The fidelity of this man was tried to the uttermost : he had received the fugitive with open arms ; rallied all his forces around him ; they fought, side by side, with the heroism of men on the last strand of their country ; were defeated, and fled together, without a reproach or complaint on either side ; they retreated yet farther into the interior, and, by their persuasions, engaged other tribes in the cause ; but, at this moment, the Maquas, a powerful nation in the west, made a descent on them, and wasted their band. In spite of these disasters, they again advanced.

CLOSE OF THE WAR.

Eliot, during these troubles, was subjected to much contempt and reproach. His efforts to protect his people, and watch over their interests, were incessant; but so strong was the suspicion against them, that the colonists, not content with confining a great number of them in Long Island, inflicted on them many sufferings, and a few of the more cruel said that they were worthy of death.

But the war began to draw to a close: Quanonchet, venturing out with a few followers near the enemy, was pursued and taken. His behaviour under his misfortunes was very noble and affecting; for when repeated offers were made him of life, if he would deliver up Philip, and submit his own people to the English, he proudly rejected them. They condemned him to die, and, by a refinement of cruelty, by the hands of three young Indian chiefs. The heroic man said, "that he liked it well, for he should die before his heart was soft, or he had spoken any thing unworthy of himself."

Philip was deeply moved by the death of the chieftain, for their friendship was like that of David and Jonathan, strongest in misery and exile. He was not yet left desolate: his beloved wife and only child were with him. They had shared all his sufferings; in his flights, his inroads, his dwellings in the swamps, they seem never to have left his side. The un-

fortunate prince now returned to Mount Hope,
the scene of his former power and happiness,
it was for no purpose of defence that he came,
for it was too near the English settlements, but
merely to visit it once more. "He finds it,"
says Mather, "to be Mount Misery, Mount
Confusion!"

No doubt it was so to his bleeding spirit;
for, with all his savage propensities, this prince
was susceptible of some of the finest feelings
of our nature. He sat down mournfully on the
beautiful Mount, on which were now the ruins
of his fortress and camp; but he could not remain long here, for the feet of his pursuers
were nigh, and he was compelled to seek his
distant retreats again:—there was a greater
agony in store for him than the sight of his
ruined home.

Early one morning, his quarters were surprised by the English, most of his followers
slain, and his wife and son made captive. The
chief fled, broken-hearted, but unsubdued, leaving all he loved on earth in the hands of those
who had no mercy. "This was no small torment to him," quaintly says the historian. "Wo
to him that spoileth! His peag, or silver belt,
the ensign of his princedom, also remained in
our hands, so hardly did he escape." The measure of his woes was not yet full. The Indian
princess of Pocasset was warmly attached to
his cause, and had more than once aided him
in his extremity; she had received him beneath
her roof, soothed his sorrows, and, what was

more, summoned her people to fight for him, and saved him and his people in her canoes the year before. Now, she followed him in his flight, and, as the more devout said, as if by a judgment, could not find a canoe to transport her, and, venturing over the river upon a raft, it broke under her, and she was drowned. Her body was soon after washed on shore, and the English, forgetful of all decency and delicacy to a woman of her rank, though a savage, cut off her head, and placed it on high, which, when the Indians who were her people saw, they gathered round, and gave way to the most sad and touching lamentations.

Philip now began, like Saul of old, when earth was leaving him, to look to the powers beyond it, and to apply to his magicians and sorcerers, who, on consulting their oracles, assured him that no Englishman should ever kill him. This was a vague consolation, yet it seems to have given him, for a while, a confidence in his destiny, and he took his last stand in the middle of a distant and almost inaccessible swamp. It was a fit retreat for a despairing man, being one of those waste and dismal places to which few ever wandered, covered with rank and dense vegetation. The moist soil was almost hidden by the cypress and other trees, that spread their gloomy shades over the treacherous shallows and pools beneath.

In the few drier parts, oaks and pines grew, and, between them, a brushwood so thick, that the savage could hardly penetrate : on the long

10 *

rich grass of these parts, wild cattle fed, un-
assailed by the hand of man, save when they
ventured beyond the confines of the swamp.
There were wolves, deer, and other animals·
and wilder men, it was said, were seen here; it
was supposed that the children of some of the
Indians had either been lost or left here, and
had thus grown up like denizens of this wild.
Here the baffled chieftain gathered his little
band around him, like a lion baited by the
hunters, sullenly seeking his gloomy thickets,
only to spring forth more fatally; despair was
his only friend; for what other was now left:
his love was turned to agony; his wife was in
the hand of his enemies; and would they spare
her beauty? His only son, the heir of his long
line, must bow his head to their yoke; his chief
warriors had all fallen, and he could not trust
the few who were still with him.

Quanonchet, whose fidelity and attachment
were stronger than death, was in the land of
spirits, chasing the shadowy deer, and solaced
with many wives; for Philip, to the last, believed in the religion of his country. In this
extremity, an Indian proposed to seek peace
with the English;—the prince instantly laid him
dead at his feet. This man had a friend, who,
disgusted with the deed, soon after fled from the
place to Rhode Island, where the English were
recruiting their weary forces, and betrayed the
place of his retreat. On this intelligence, a
body of forces instantly set out.

DEATH OF PHILIP.

The night befoie his death, Philip, "like him in the army of Midian," says the historian, "had been dreaming that he was fallen into the hands of the English; he awoke in great alarm, and told it to his friends, and advised them to fly for their lives, for that he believed it would come to pass." The place was well suited to awake all the terrors of the imagination; to any eye but that of the savage, it was like the "valley of the shadow of death;" the cypress and oak trees hung heavy and still, over the accursed soil; the faint gleam of the pools and sluggish lakes on every side, in the starlight, and the howl of the wolf, fitfully, as if it warned that the hour was nigh. "Now, just as he was telling his dream, Captain Church, with his company, fell in upon them." They had been guided by the deserter to the swamp, and, with great difficulty, across some felled trees, into its labyrinths. The battle was fierce and short: Philip fought till he saw almost every follower fall in his defence, then turned, and fled; he was pursued by an Englishman and an Indian; and, as if the oracle was doomed to be fulfilled, the musket of the former would not go off; and the latter fired, and shot him through the heart.

With his death, all resistance ceased; his dominions fell into the hands of the colonists, and peace was restored to the settlements, but prosperity came not with it. It was a cruel blow to Eliot, nearly all whose life had been given to his beloved cause, to look around on the plantations ravaged, the dwellings empty, the defences broken, and, more than all, the spirit of his people in despair. Of twelve towns, at the beginning of the war, four only were now undestroyed.

CANONICUS.

The *Narragansets*, possessed the country about Narraganset Bay, including Rhode Island, and other Islands in that vicinity, and a part of Connecticut. *Canonicus* was their great warrior Sachem. This tribe is described by our early historians 'as a great people,' capable of raising 4000 warriors. Canonicus lived to an advanced age, and died according to Gov. Winthrop, June 4th, 1647. He discovered a generous mind in receiving Rev. Roger Williams when in great distress, and affording him a friendly protection. Mr. Williams mentioned his name with respect and acknowledged his obligation to him thus in a manuscript letter to the Governor of Massachusetts. After observing that many hundreds of the English were witnesses to the friendly disposition of the Narragansets, he says: 'Their late long lived Canonicus so lived and died, in the same most honorable manner and solemnity (in their way) as you laid to sleep your prudent peace-maker

Mr. Winthrop, did they honor this their prudent and peaceable prince; yea, through all their towns and countries how frequently do many and oft times of Englishmen travel alone with safety and loving kindness?' On one occasion Canonicus thus addressed Roger Williams: 'I have never suffered any wrong to be done to the English since they landed, nor never will. If the English speak true, if he mean truly, then shall I go to my grave in peace, and I hope that the English and my posterity shall live in love and peace together.' 'His heart,' says Mr. Williams, 'was stirred up to love me as his son to the last gasp.' However partial Canonicus may have been to Rev. Mr. Williams, he was not uniformly friendly to the settlers in general. It appears in Gov. Winslow's Good News from New England, that in February, 1622, this chief sent into Plymouth, a bundle of arrows bound together with a rattle-snake's skin. This was received as it was intended, a challenge for war. Gov. Bradford filled the rattle-snake skin with powder and shot and returned it to *Canonicus*, with a message of defiance which produced the desired effect. Canonicus was so frightened that he dared not touch the article and soon returned it to Plymouth and became silent and peaceable.

CHICKATAUBUT.

Chickataubut, was a sachem of considerable note among the *Massachusetts* tribe, and one of those who, in 1621, acknowledged themselves the subjects of King James. He was Sachem of Passonagesit (Weymouth,) where his mother was buried. In Drake's Indian Biography the following is related from Thomas Morton's New Canaan. In the first settling of Plymouth, some of the company in wandering about upon discovery, came upon an Indian grave, which was of the mother of Chickataubut. Over the body a stake was set in the ground, and two huge bear skins sewed together spread over it; these the English took away. When this came to the knowledge of Chickataubut, he complained to his people and demanded immediate vengeance. When they were assembled, he thus harangued them: ' When last the glorious light of all the sky was underneath the globe and birds grew silent, I began to settle as my custom is to take repose ; before mine eyes were fast closed, me thought I saw a vision, at which my spirit was much troubled, and trembling at that doleful sight cried aloud ; Behold ! my son, whom I have cherished, see the paps that gave thee suck, the hands that clasped thee warm, and led thee oft, canst thou forget to take revenge on those wild people that hath my monument defaced in a despiteful manner; disdaining our ancient antiquities, and honorable customs. See now the Sachem's grave lies, like unto the common people of ignoble race, defaced. Thy mother doth complain, implores thy aid against this thievish people newly come hither; if this be suffered I shall not rest in quiet within my everlasting habitation.' Battle was the unanimous resolve, and the English were watched and followed from place to place, until at length as some were going ashore in a boat, they fell upon them, but gained little advantage. After maintaining the fight for some time, and being driven from tree to tree, the chief captain was wounded in the arm and the whole took to flight. This action caused the natives about Plymouth to look upon the English as invincible, and was the reason that peace was maintained so long after."

When Boston was settled *Chickatabut* visited Governor *Winthrop*, and presented him with a hogshead of corn. Many of his ' sanops and squaws' came with him, but were most of them sent away after they had all dined, Chickatabut probably fearing they would be burdensome, although it thundered and rained and the Governor urged their stay. At this time he wore English clothes, and sat at the Governor's table, where he behaved himself soberly, &c. as an Englishman. "Not long after he called on Governor Winthrop and desired to buy of him a suit of clothes for himself, the governor informed him that 'English Sagamores did not use to truck;' but he called his tailor and gave him orders to make him a suit of clothes, whereupon he gave the governor two large skins of coat beaver. The clothes being ready, the governor put him into a very good new suit from head to foot, and after, he set meat before them; but he would not eat till the governor had given thanks, and after meat he desired him to do the like, and so departed."

CONDITION OF THE INDIAN WOMEN.

Polygamy is not uncommon among them and the husband occasionally finds it necessary to administer a little wholesome castigation to his more quarrelsome or refractory squaws. But many are satisfied with one wife. The care of the tent and the whole drudgery of the family devolve on the women. They gather fuel, cook the provisions, and repair every article of dress; cultivate the ground, where any is cultivated; carry the baggage on a journey; and pitch the tent when they halt. In these and similar employments, their lordly fathers, husbands, and brothers, think it degrading to assist them, and unworthy of warriors to engage in such employments.

Mr. Catlin whose long residence among the Indians, and careful observation of their habits, entitle his opinion to great respect, regards the assignment of drudgery to the women as no more than an equitable distribution of the labour necessary to the support of the household He considers the toils of war and the chase, which are almost incessant, and are solely performed by the men, as a complete offset to the domestic and agricultural cares of the women. On the whole he thinks that the condition of the Indian women is as comfortable as it is possible to render it by any arrangement which would not completely change their mode of life. To withdraw the men from the chase and confine them to the culture of the ground, would render the Indians an agricultural and not a hunting people. Still the condition of the Indian woman is a miserable and degraded one,—a condition of incessant labour and care.

In none of the tribes do the women experience much tenderness; but among the Sioux they are so harshly treated, that they occasionally destroy their female infants, alleging that it is better for them to be put to death than to live as miserably as they themselves have done. Even suicide is not uncommon among them, although they believe it offensive to the Father of Life.

INDIAN EDUCATION.

The Indians never chastise their children, especially the boys; thinking that it would damp their spirits, check their love of independence. and cool their martial ardour, which they wish above all things to encourage. " Reason," say they, " will guide our children, when they come to the use of it; and before that, their faults cannot be very great." They avoid compulsory measures, and allow the boys to act with uncontrolled freedom; but endeavour, by example. instruction, and advice, to train them to diligence and skill in hunting; to animate them with patience, courage, and fortitude in war; and to inspire them with contempt of danger, pain, and death,—qualities of the highest order in the estimation of an Indian.

By gentleness and persuasion they endeavour to imbue the minds of their children with virtuous sentiments, according to their notions of virtue. The aged chiefs are zealous in this patriotic labour, and the squaws give their cordial co-operation.

Ishuchenau, an old Kanza warrior, often admonished the group of young auditors who gathered around him, of their faults, and exhorted them never to tell a lie, and never to steal, except from an enemy, whom it is just to injure in every possible way. "When you become men," said he, "be brave and cunning in war, and defend your hunting grounds against all encroachments: never suffer your squaws and little ones to want; protect them and strangers from insult. On no occasion betray a friend; be revenged on your enemies; drink not the poisonous strong water of the white people, for it is sent by the bad spirit to destroy the Indians. Fear not death; none but cowards fear to die. Obey and venerate old people, particularly your parents. Fear and propitiate the bad spirit, that he may do you no harm: love and adore the Good Spirit, who made us all, who supplies our hunting grounds, and keeps all alive." After recounting his achievements, he was wont to add, "Like a decayed prairie tree, I stand alone :—the friends of my youth, the companions of my sports, my toils, and my dangers, rest their heads on the bosom of our mother. My sun is fast descending behind the western hills, and I feel it will soon be night with me." Then with hands and eyes lifted towards heaven, he thanked the Great Spirit for having spared him so long, to show the young men the true path to glory and fame.

Their opinions, in many instances, are false, and lead to corresponding errors in conduct. In some tribes, the young person is taught to pray, with various superstitious observances, that he may be a great hunter, horse-stealer, and warrior; so that thus the fountain of virtue is polluted.

The Indians are entirely unacquainted with letters; but they have a kind of picture writing, which they practise on the inside of the bark of trees, or on skins prepared for the purpose, and by which they can communicate the knowledge of many facts to each other.

The Indian names are descriptive of the real or supposed qualities of the person to whom they belong: they often change them in the course of their lives. The young warrior is ambitious of acquiring a new name; and stealing a horse, scalping an enemy, or killing a bear, is an achievement which entitles him to choose one for himself, and the nation confirms it.

SPEECH OF AN INDIAN TO JOHN ELIOT

The following instance is very expressive of the fine use the Indians make of simple and natural images:—the speaker was dressed in a robe of several marten-skins sewed together; it was fastened to his right shoulder, and passed under his left arm : he wrapped himself up in this robe, and said—

"My heart laughs for joy on seeing myself before thee : we have all of us heard the word which thou hast sent us. How beautiful is the sun to-day ! but lately it was red and angry, for our hands were stained with blood ; our tomahawks thirsted for it; our women howled for the loss of their relations; at the least shriek of the birds of night, all our warriors were on foot; the serpents angrily hissed at us, as we passed. Those we left behind sang the songs of death.

"But now our whole nation laughs for joy to see us walk on the same road with thyself, to join the Father of spirits : our hearts shall make but one : come with us to the forests; come to our homes by the great river; we shall plant the tree of life, of which thou speakest, there, and our warriors shall rest beneath its leaves; and thou shalt tell us more of that land where there is no storm or death, and the sun is always

oright. Will not that be good? What dost
thou say to it, my father?"

RELIGION OF THE INDIANS.

Of the religion of the Indians we have no
full and clear account. Indeed, of the opinions
of a people who have nothing more than a
few vague and indefinite notions, no distinct
explanation can be given. On this subject the
Indians are not communicative; and to obtain
a thorough knowledge of it would require
familiar, attentive, unsuspected, and unpreju-
diced observation. But such observation is not
easily made; and a few general, and on some
points uncertain, notices only can be given.

On looking at the most renowned nations of
the ancient heathen world, we see the people
prostrating themselves before innumerable di-
vinities; and we are ready to conclude that
polytheism is the natural belief of man, unen-
lightened by revelation. But a survey of the
vast wilds of America will correct this opinion.
For there we find a multitude of nations, widely
separated from each other, all believing in One
Supreme God, a great and good spirit, the father
and master of life, the maker of heaven and
earth, and of all other creatures. They believe
themselves entirely dependent on him, thank
him for present enjoyments, and pray to him for
the good things they desire to obtain. They
consider him the author of all good; and believe

11*

he will reward or punish them according to their deeds.

They believe in inferior spirits also, both good and bad; to whom, particularly to the good, they give the name of *Manitou*, and consider them tutelary spirits. The Indians are careful observers of dreams. and think them selves deserted by the Master of life, till they receive a manitou in a dream; that is, till they dream of some object, as a buffalo or beaver, or something else, which they think is an intima tion that the Great Spirit had given them that object as a manitou, or medicine. Then they are full of courage, and proud of their powerful ally. To propitiate the manitou, or medicine every exertion is made, and every personal consideration sacrificed. "I was lately the proprietor of seventeen horses," said a Mandan, "but I have offered them all to my medicine, and am now poor." He had turned all these horses, which constituted the whole of his wealth, loose into the plain, committed them to nis medicine, and abandoned them for ever But, although they offer oblations to the man-itous, they positively deny that they pay them any adoration, and affirm that they only worship the Great Spirit through them.

They have no regular periodical time eithe. of private or public religious worship. They have neither temples, altars, stated ministers of religion, nor regular sacrifices; for the jugglers are connected rather with the medical art than with religious services. The Indians in general, like other ignorant people, are believers in witchcraft, and think many of their diseases proceed from the arts of sorcerers. These arts the jugglers pretend to counteract, as well as to cure natural diseases. They also pretend to predict the weather and to make rain; and much confidence is placed in their prognostications and their power.

The devotional exercises of the Indians consist in singing, dancing, and performing various mystical ceremonies, which they believe efficacious in healing the sick, frustrating the designs of their enemies, and securing their own success. They often offer up to the Great Spirit a part of the game first taken in a hunting expedition, a part of the first produce of their fields, and a part of their food. At a feast, they first throw some of the broth, and then of the meat, into the fire. In smoking, they generally testify their reverence for the Master of life, by directing the first puff upwards, and the second downwards, or the first to the rising, and the second to the setting sun: at other times they turn the pipe to every point of the compass.

They firmly believe in the immortality of the soul, and in a state of future retribution: but their conceptions on these subjects are modified and tinged by their occupations in life, and by their notions of good and evil. They suppose the spirit retains the same inclinations as when in the body, and rejoices in its old pursuits. At times, an Irdian warrior, when about to kill and scalp a prostrate enemy, addresses him in such terms as the following:—

"My name is Cashegra: I am a famous warrior, and am going to kill you. When you reach the land of spirits, you will see the ghost of my father: tell him it was Cashegra sent you there." The uplifted tomahawk then descends upon his victim.

The Mandans* expected, when they died, to return to the original subterraneous abode of their fathers: the good reaching the ancient village by means of the lake, which the weight of the sins of the bad will render them unable to pass. They who have behaved themselves well in this life, and been brave warriors and good hunters, will be received into the town of brave and generous spirits; but the useless and selfish will be doomed to reside in the town of poor and useless spirits.

The belief of those untutored children of nature has an influence on their conduct. Among them the grand defect is, an erroneous estimate of good and evil, right and wrong.

* The Mandan tribe is now entirely extinct.—Catlin.

DESTRUCTION OF THE PEQUOTS IN 637.

"An army of a hundred and sixty men, under the command of Captain Underhill, were despatched, and with them was Uncas, an Indian chief: when they landed from the river, they were joined by five hundred Narraganset Indians. We were now informed that the Indians had retired into two impregnable forts, one of which was the hold of Sassacus, the chief tyrant; that fierce tiger, at the very mention of whose name the Narragansets trembled, saying, "He was all one a God, nobody could kill him." The council of war determined to fall first upon the fort which they could first find; and on their silent march in the moon-shiny night, an Indian spy brought them word that the Pequots were in a profound sleep. Our guide was one Wequash, an Indian revolted from them; and now the Narragansets retired into the wood, and behind the trees—they were overcome with fear. The English advanced against the nearest fort, when a dog, that stood sentinel like another Cerberus, barking, awoke them all; their cry, when they sprung from their sleep, was dreadful to hear in the silent night; and thereupon followed a bloody en counter; many were killed; but we set fire to their huts, and a high wind caused them to be quickly consumed; many of the Indians climbed to the tops of the palisadoes, and were a mark for the bullets; some of the trees also turning threw such a fiery light, that with the howlings, and cries also, the place was like the pit of torment. Samson was not in greater distress by thirst after his exploit upon the Philistines, than was the mighty Sassacus when his strong holds were thus burned, and his barbarians dismissed from a world that was burdened with them. The next day, as we were returning, three hundred of the enemy again came up, like bears bereaved of their young; they fought, and made a fort of every swamp in the way, covering their bodies with the green boughs and the long grass, so that we were sometimes in the very midst of them, and knew it not, save by the sudden yell and the volley."

INDIAN COOLNESS.

Sam Barrow was a famous warrior in Philip's war, and for a long time dreaded as a ferocious enemy by the inhabitants. He was at length captured by Captain Church at Cape Cod. Church, in his history, says, that 'he was as noted a rogue as any among the enemy.' Church told him that the government would not permit him to grant him quarter, because of his inhuman murders and barbarities, and therefore ordered him to prepare for execution. Barrow replied, that the sentence of death against him was just, and that indeed he was ashamed to live any longer, and desired no more favor than to smoke a whiff of tobacco before his execution. When he had taken a few whiffs, he said, 'I am ready,' when one of Church's Indians, being prepared, sunk his hatchet into his brains.

THE GREAT MASSACRE OF VIRGINIA.

The peace which had subsisted since the marriage of Pocahontas had lulled the English into security, and disposed them to extend their plantations along the banks of the rivers, as far as the Potomac, in situations too remote from each other.   Their houses were open and free to the natives, who became acquainted with their manner of living, their hours of eating, of labor and repose, the use of their arms and tools, and frequently borrowed their boats, for the convenience of fishing and fowling, and to pass the rivers.   This familiarity was pleasing to the English, as it indicated a spirit of moderation, which had been always recommended, by the Company in England, to the planters ; and, as it afforded a favourable symptom of the civilization and conversion of the natives; but by them, or their leaders, it was designed to conceal the most sanguinary intentions.

In the spring of the next year, (1622) an opportunity offered, to throw off the mask of friendship, and kindle their secret enmity into a blaze.   Among the natives who frequently visited the English, was a tall, handsome, young chief, renowned for courage and success in war, and excessively fond of finery in dress.   His Indian name was Nematanow ; but by the English he was called Jack of the Feather. Coming to the store of one Morgan, he there viewed several toys and ornaments, which were

very agreeable to the Indian taste; and per
suaded Morgan to carry them to Pamunky,
where he assured him of an advantageous
traffic. Morgan consented to go with him; but
was murdered by the way.

In a few days, Nematanow came again to the
store, with Morgan's cap on his head; and
being interrogated by two stout lads, who
attended there, what was become of their
master, he answered that he was dead. The
boys seized him, and endeavoured to carry him
before a magistrate; but his violent resistance,
and the insolence of his language, so provoked
them, that they shot him. The wound proved
mortal; and when dying, he earnestly requested
of the boys, that the manner of his death might
be concealed from his countrymen, and that he
might be privately buried among the English.

As soon as this transaction was known, Opechancanough demanded satisfaction; but being
answered that the retaliation was just, he formed
a plan for a general massacre of the English,
and appointed Friday, the twenty-second day
of March, for its execution; but he dissembled
his resentment to the last moment. Parties of
Indians were distributed through the Colony, to
attack every plantation, at the same hour of the
day, when the men should be abroad and at
work. On the evening before, and on the
morning of that fatal day, the Indians came as
usual to the houses of the English, bringing
game and fish to sell, and sat down with them
to breakfast. So general was the combination,

and so deep the plot, that about one hour before noon, they fell on the people in the fields and houses; and, with their own tools and weapons, killed, indiscriminately, persons of all ages, sexes and characters; inhumanly mangling their dead bodies, and triumphing over them, with all the expressions of frantic joy.

Where any resistance was made, it was generally successful. Several houses were defended, and some few of the assailants slain. One of Captain Smith's old soldiers, Nathaniel Causie, though wounded, split the skull of an Indian, and put his whole party to flight. Several other parties were dispersed by the firing of a single gun, or by the presenting of a gun, even in the hands of a woman.

James-Town was preserved by the fidelity of Chanco, a young Indian convert, who lived with Richard Pace, and was treated by him as a son. The brother of this Indian came to lie with him, the night before the massacre, and revealed to him the plot, urging him to kill his master, as he intended to do by his own. As soon as he was gone in the morning, Chanco gave notice of what was intended, to his master; who, having secured his own house, gave the alarm to his neighbours, and sent an express to James-Town. Three hundred and forty-nine people fell in this general massacre; of which number, six were members of the Council.

EXPLOIT OF CAPTAIN STANDISH.

"The 23d of March (1623) being a yearly court day, we came to this conclusion; that Captain Standish should take as many men as he thought sufficient to make his party good, against all the Indians in the Massachusetts Bay; and because it is impossible to deal with them upon open defiance, but to take them in such traps as they lay for others; therefore that he should pretend trade, as at other times; but first go to the English, and acquaint them with the plot and the end of his own coming, that by comparing it with their carriage toward them, he might better judge of the certainty of it, and more fitly take opportunity to revenge the same; but should forbear, if it were possible, till such time as he could make sure of Wittuwamat, a bloody and bold villain, whose head he had orders to bring with him. Upon this, Captain Standish made choice of eight men, and would not take more, because he would prevent jealousy. On the next day, before he could go, came one of Weston's company to us with a pack on his back, who made a pitiful narration of their lamentable and weak estate, and of the Indians' carriage; whose boldness increased abundantly, insomuch as they would take the victuals out of their pots, and eat before their faces; yea, if in any thing they gainsayed them, they were ready to hold a knife at their breasts. He said that, to give them content, they had

hanged one of the company, who had stolen
their corn, and yet they regarded it not; that
another of them had turned savage; that their
people had mostly forsaken the town, and made
their rendezvous where they got their victuals,
because they would not take pains to bring it
home; that they had sold their clothes for corn,
and were ready to perish with hunger and cold,
and that they were dispersed into three companies, having scarcely any powder and shot.
As this relation was grievous to us, so it gave
us good encouragement to proceed; and the
wind coming fair the next day, March 25th,
Captain Standish being now fitted, set forth for
Massachusetts.

"The Captain being come to Massachusetts,
went first to the ship, but found neither man nor
dog therein.   On the discharge of a musket, the
Master and some others shewed themselves,
who were on shore gathering ground-nuts and
other food.   After salutation, Captain Standish
asked them how they durst so leave the ship,
and live in such security? they answered, like
men senseless of their own misery, that they
feared not the Indians, but lived and suffered
them to lodge with them, not having sword nor
gun, nor needing the same.   To which the
Captain replied, that if there were no cause, he
was glad.   But upon further inquiry, understanding that those in whom John Sanders had
reposed most confidence were at the plantation,
thither he went, and made known the Indians'
purpose, and the end of his own coming; and

INDIAN ANECDOTES. 137

told them that if they durst not stay there, it was the intention of the Governor and people of Plymouth, to receive them, till they could be better provided for. These men answered that they could expect no better, and it was of God mercy that they were not killed before his coming, desiring that he would neglect no opportunity to proceed; hereupon he advised them to secrecy and to order one third of their company that were farthest off to come home, and on pain of death to keep there, himself allowing them a pint of Indian corn, to a man, for a day, though that was spared out of our feed. The weather proving very wet and stormy, it was the longer before he could do any thing.

"In the mean time an Indian came to him and brought some furs, but rather to get what he could from the Captain than to trade; and though the Captain carried things as smoothly as he could, yet, at his return, the Indian reported that he saw by his eyes that he was angry in his heart, and therefore began to suspect themselves discovered. This caused one Pecksuot, who was a Pinese (chief) being a man of a notable spirit to come to Hobamock (Standish's Indian guide and interpreter) and tell him that he understood the Captain was come to kill himself and the rest of the savages there: 'Tell him, said he, we know it, but fear him not, neither will we shun him; but let him begin when he dare, he shall not take us at unawares.' Many times after, divers of them,

12*

severally or a few together, came to the planta
tion, where they would whet and sharpen the
point of their knives before his face, and use
many other insulting gestures and speeches.
Among the rest, Wittuwamat bragged of the
excellency of h.s knife, on the handle of which
was pictured a woman's face. 'But, said he,
I have another at home, wherewith I have
killed both French and English, and that hath a
man's face on it, and by and by, these two mus.
be married.' Further he said of that knife
which he there had, *Hinnaim namen, binnaim
michen, matta cuts*, that is to say, *by and by
it should see, by and by it should eat, but not
speak*. Also Pecksuot being a man of greater
stature than the Captain, told him 'though you
are a great Captain, yet you are but a little
man ; though I be no Sachem, yet I am a man
of great strength and courage.' These things
the Captain observed, but, for the present, bore
them with patience.

"On the next day, seeing he could not get
many of them together at once, but Pecksuot
and Wittuwamat being together, with another
man and the brother of Wittuwamat a youth
of eighteen, putting many tricks on the weaker
sort of men, and having about as many of his
own men in the same room, the Captain gave
the word to his men ; and the door being fast
shut, be begun himself with Pecksuot and
snatching the knife from his neck, after much
struggling killed him therewith ; the rest killed
Wittuwamat and the other man ; the youth

ney took and hanged. It is incredible, how
many wounds these men received, before they
died, not making any fearful noise, but catching
at their weapons, and striving to the last. Hobamock stood by as a spectator, observing how
our men demeaned themselves in the action;
which being ended, he, smiling, brake forth and
said, 'Yesterday Pecksuot bragged of his own
strength and stature, and told you that though
you were a great Captain, yet you were but a
little man; but, to-day, I see you are big enough
to lay him on the ground.'

"There being some women, at the same time
there, Captain Standish left them, in the custody
of Weston's people, at the town; and sent word
to another company, to kill those Indian men
that were among them. These killed two more;
himself with some of his own men, went to
another place and killed another; but through
the negligence of one man, an Indian escaped,
who discovered and crossed their proceedings.

"Captain Standish took one half of his men
with one or two of Weston's and Hobamock,
still seeking them. At length they espied a file
of Indians, making toward them; and, there
being a small advantage in the ground, by
reason of a hill, both companies strove for it.
Captain Standish got it; whereupon the Indians
retreated, and took each man his tree, letting
fly their arrows amain, especially at himself and
Hobamock. Whereupon Hobamock cast off
his coat, and chased them so fast, that our
people were not able to hold way with him

They could have but one certain mark, the arm
and half the face of a notable villian, as he
drew his bow at Captain Standish, who with
another, both discharged at him, and brake his
arm.   Whereupon, they fled into a swamp;
when they were in the thicket, they parlied but
got nothing but foul language.   So our Captain
dared the Sachem to come out and fight like a
man, showing how base and woman-like he
was, in tonguing it as he did; but he refused
and fled.   So the Captain returned to the plantation; where he released the women and took
not their beaver coats from them, nor suffered
the least discourtesy to be offered them.

"Now were Weston's people resolved to
leave the plantation, and go to Monhegan,
hoping to get passage and return to England
with the fishing ships.   The Captain told them,
that for his own part, he durst live there with
fewer men than they were; yet since they were
otherwise minded, according to his orders from
the Governor and people of Plymouth, he would
help them with corn, which he did, scarce
leaving himself more than brought them home.
Some of them disliked to go to Monhegan;
and desiring to go with him to Plymouth, he
took them into the shallop; and seeing the
others set sail, and clear of Massachusetts Bay,
he took leave and returned to Plymouth, bringing the head of Wittuwamat, which was set
up on the fort.

"This sudden and unexpected execution,
hath so terrified and amazed the other people

who intended to join with the Massachusencks against us, that they forsook their houses, running to and fro like men distracted; living in swamps, and other desert places, and so brought diseases upon themselves, whereof many are dead; as Canacum, Sachem of Manomet; Aspinet, of Nauset; and Ianough, of Matachiest. This Sachem, (Ianough) in the midst of these distractions, said, 'the God of the English was offended with them, and would destroy them in his anger.' From one of these places, a boat was sent with presents to the Governor, hoping thereby to work their peace; but the boat was lost, and three of the people drowned; only one escaped, who returned; so that none of them durst come among us."

In one of his later voyages at sea he met with tempestuous weather of long continuance, in which his ships were so shattered, that with the utmost difficulty he kept them above water, till he ran them ashore on the island of Jamaica. By his extraordinary address, he procured from the natives two of their largest canoes; in which two of his most faithful friends, Mendez and Fiesco, accompanied by some of his sailors and a few Indians, embarked for Hispaniola. After encountering the greatest difficulties in their passage, they carried tidings of his misfortune to Ovando, and solicited his aid. The merciless wretch detained them eight months, without an answer; during which time, Columbus suffered the severest hardships, from the discontent of his company, and the want of provisions. By the hospitality of the natives, he at first received such supplies, as they were able to spare; but the long continuance of these guests had diminished their store, and the insolence of the mutineers gave a check to their friendship. In this extremity, the fertile invention of Columbus suggested an expedient which proved successful. He knew that a total eclipse of the moon was at hand, which would be visible in the evening. On the preceding day, he sent for the principal Indians, to speak with them, on a matter of the utmost importance. Being assembled, he directed his interpreter to tell them, that the GOD of heaven, whom he worshipped, was angry with them, for withholding provision from him, and would punish them with famine and pestilence; as a token of which, the moon would, in the evening, appear of an angry and bloody colour. Some of them received his speech with terror, and others with indifference; but when the moon rose, and the eclipse increased as she advanced from the horizon, they came in crowds, loaded with provision, and begged the Admiral to intercede with his GOD, for the removal of his anger. Columbus retired to his cabin; and when the eclipse began to go off, he came out and told them, that he had prayed to his GOD, and had received this answer; that if they would be good for the future, and bring him provision as he should want, GOD would forgive them; and as a token of it, the moon would put on her usual brightness. They gave him thanks, and promised compliance; and whilst he remained on the island there was no more want of provision.

ADVENTURES OF JAMES CARTIER IN CANADA.

After spending some time in exploring the northern coast, to find an opening to the northward; in the beginning of September, 1535, he sailed up the river St. Lawrence and discovered several islands; one of which, from the multitude of filberts, he called Coudres; and another, from the vast quantity of grapes, he named Bacchus, (now Orleans.) This island was full of inhabitants who subsisted by fishing.

When the ships had come to anchor between the N. W. side of the island and the main, Cartier went on shore with his two young Savages. The people of the country were at first afraid of them; but hearing the youths speak to them in their own language, they became sociable, and brought eels and other fish, with a quantity of Indian corn in ears, for the refreshment of their new guests; in return for which, they were presented with such European baubles as were pleasing to them.

The next day, Donacona, the prince of the place, came to visit them, attended by twelve boats; but keeping ten of them at a distance, he approached with two only, containing sixteen men. In the true spirit of hospitality, he made a speech, accompanied with significant gestures, welcoming the French to his country and offering his service to them. The young savages, Taignoagni and Domagaia answered him, reporting all which they had seen in

France, at which he appeared to be pleased. Then approaching the Captain, who held out his hand, he kissed it, and laid it round his own neck, in token of friendship. Cartier, on his part, entertained Donacona with bread and wine, and they parted mutually pleased.

The next day Cartier went up in his boat to find a harbour for his ships; the season being so far advanced that it became necessary to secure them. At the west end of the isle of Bacchus, he found "a goodly and pleasant sound, where is a little river and haven; about three fathom deep at high water." To this he gave the name of St. Croix, and determined there to lay up his ships.

Near this place was a village called Stadacona, of which Donacona was the Lord. It was environed with forest trees, some of which bore fruit; and under the trees, was a growth of wild hemp. As Cartier was returning to his ships, he had another specimen of the hospitable manners of the natives. A company of people, of both sexes, met him on the shore of the little river, singing and dancing up to their knees in water. In return for their courtesy, he gave them knives and beads; and they continued their music till he was beyond hearing it.

When Cartier had brought his ships to the harbour and secured them, he intimated his intention to pass in his boats up the river to Hocheloga. Donacona was loath to part with him; and invented several artifices to prevent his going thither. Among others, he contrived

13

to dress three of his men in black and white skins, with horns on their heads, and their faces besmeared with coal, to make them resemble infernal spirits. They were put into a canoe and passed by the ships; brandishing their horns and making an unintelligible harangue. Donacona, with his people, pursued and took them, on which they fell down as if dead. They were carried ashore into the woods, and all the savages followed them. A long discourse ensued, and the conclusion of the farce was, that these demons had brought news from the God of Hochelaga, that his country was so full of snow and ice, that whoever should adventure thither would perish with the cold. The artifice afforded diversion to the French, but was too thin to deceive them. Cartier determined to proceed; and on the 19th of September, with his pinnace and two boats, began his voyage up the river to Hochelaga.

Among the woods on the margin of the river were many vines loaded with ripe grapes, than which nothing could be a more welcome sight to Frenchmen, though the fruit was not so delicious as they had been used to taste in their own country. Along the banks were many huts of the natives; who made signs of joy as they passed; presented them with fish; piloted them through narrow channels; carried them ashore on their backs, and helped them to get off their boats when aground. Some presented their children to them, and such **as were of proper age were accepted.**

The water at that time of the year being
low, their passage was rendered difficult; but
by the friendly assistance of the natives they
surmounted the obstructions. On the 28th of
September they passed the rapids between the
islands in the upper part of the lake Ango-
leme, (now called St. Peter's) and on the second
of October they arrived at the island of Hochelaga; where they had been expected, and
preparations were made to give them a welcome reception. About a thousand persons
came to meet them, singing and dancing, the
men on one side, the women on the other, and
the children in a distinct body. Presents of
fish and other victuals were brought, and in return were given knives, beads and other trin-
kets. The Frenchmen lodged the first night in
their boats, and the natives watched on the
shore, dancing round their fires during the
whole night.

The next morning Cartier, with twenty-five
of his company, went to visit the town, and
were met on the way by a person of distinction,
who bade them welcome. To him they gave
two hatchets and two knives, and hung over
his neck a cross which they taught him to kiss.
As they proceeded, they passed through groves
of oak, from which the acorns were fallen and
lay thick on the ground. After this they came
to fields of ripe corn, some of which was gathered. In the midst of these fields was situate
the town of Hochelaga.

It was of a round form, encompassed with

three lines of palisades, through which was
one entrance, well secured with stakes and bars.
On the inside was a rampart of timber, to
which were ascents by ladders, and heaps of
stones were laid in proper places for defence.
In the town were about fifty long huts built
with stakes and covered with bark. In the
middle of each hut was a fire, round which
were lodging places, floored with bark and
covered with skins. In the upper part was a
scaffold, on which they dried and preserved
their corn. To prepare it for eating, they
pounded it in wooden mortars, and having
mixed it with water, baked it on hot stones.
Besides corn they had beans, squashes and
pumpkins. They dried their fish and preserved
them in troughs. These people lived chiefly
by tillage and fishing, and seldom went far
from home. Those on the lower parts of the
river were more given to hunting, and considered the Lord of Hochelaga as their sovereign,
to whom they paid tribute.

When the new guests were conducted to an
open square in the centre of the town, the females came to them, rubbing their hands and
faces, weeping with joy at their arrival, and
bringing their children to be touched by the
strangers. They spread mats for them on the
ground, whilst the men seated themselves in a
large circle on the outside. The King was then
brought in a litter, on the shoulders of ten men,
and placed on a mat next to the French Captain. He was about fifty years old, and had no

n .rk of distinction but a coronet made of porcupine's quills dyed red; which he took off and gave to the Captain, requesting him to rub his arms and legs which were trembling with a palsy. Several persons, blind, lame, and withered with age, were also brought to be touched; as if they supposed that their new guests were messengers from heaven invested with a power of healing diseases. Cartier gratified them as well as he could, by laying his hands on them and repeating some devotional passages from a service book, which he had in his pocket; accompanying his ejaculations with significant gestures, and lifting up his eyes to heaven. The natives attentively observed and imitated all his motions.

Having performed this ceremony, he desired men, women and children to arrange themselves in separate bodies. To the men he gave hatchets, to the women beads, and to the children rings. He then ordered his drums and trumpets to sound, which highly pleased the company and set them to dancing.

Being desirous of ascending the hill, under which the town was built, the natives conducted them to the summit; where they were entertained with a most extensive and beautiful prospect of mountains, woods, islands and waters. They observed the course of the river above, and some falls of water in it; and the natives informed them that they might sail on it for three months; that it ran through two or three great lakes, beyond which was a sea of

13*

fresh water, to which they knew of no bounds; and that on the other side of the mountains there was another river which ran in a contrary direction to the southwest, through a country full of delicious fruits and free from snow and ice; that there was found such metal as the Captain's *silver* whistle and the haft of a dagger belonging to one of the company which was gilt with *gold.* Being shown some copper, they pointed to the northward, and said it came from Saguenay. To this hill Cartier gave the name of *Montreal,* which it has ever since retained.

MILLY FRANCIS.

Duncan M'Krimmon, (a resident of Milledge ville, a Georgia militia man, stationed at Fort Gadsden,) being out one morning on a fishing excursion, in attempting to return, missed his way, and was several days lost in the surrounding wilderness. After wandering about in various directions he was espied and captured by a party of hostile Indians, headed by the well known prophet Francis. The Indians having obtained the satisfaction they wanted respecting the determination of government, the position of the American army, &c. they began to prepare for the intended sacrifice. M'Krimmon was bound to a stake, and the ruthless savages having shaved his head and reduced his body to a state of nudity, formed themselves into a circle and danced round him some hours, yelling most horribly. The youngest daughter of the prophet, about fifteen years of age, remained sad and silent the whole time. She participated not in the general joy, but was evidently, even to the affrighted prisoner, much pained at the savage scene she was compelled to witness. When the burning torches were about to be applied to the fagots which encompassed the prisoner, and the fatal tomahawk was raised to terminate forever his mortal existence, Milly Francis, (for that was her name,) like an angel of mercy, placed herself between it and death, resolutely bidding the astonished executioner, if he thirsted for human blood, to shed hers; being determined, she said, not to survive the prisoner's death.   A momentary pause was produced by this unexpected occurrence, and she took advantage of the circumstance to implore upon her knees the pity of the ferocious father, who finally yielded to her wishes; with the intention, however, it is suspected, of murdering them both, if he could not sell M'Krimmon to the Spaniards; which was luckily effected a few days after at St. Marks, for seven gallons and a half of rum. As long as M'Krimmon remained a prisoner his benefactress continued to show him acts of kindness.   The fortune of war since placed her in the power of the white people, being compelled, with a number of others of her tribe who were in a starving condition, to surrender themselves prisoners.   As soon as this fact was known to M'Krimmon, in manifestation of a due sense of the obligation which he owed to the woman who saved his life, at the hazard of her own, he sought her to alleviate her misfortune, and to offer her marriage; but Milly would not consent to become his wife as a consideration of having saved his life, declaring that she did no more than her duty, and that her intercessions were the same as they would ever have been on similar occasions

ADVENTURES OF SIMON BUTLER AMONG THE INDIANS.

Simon Kenton, *alias* Butler, from humble beginnings, made himself conspicuous by distinguished services and achievements, in the first settlement of this country, and ought to be recorded as one of the patriarchs of Kentucky. He was born in Virginia, in 1753. He grew to maturity without being able to read or write; but from his early exploits, he seems to have been endowed with feelings, which the educated, and those born in the upper walks of life appear to suppose a monopoly reserved for themselves. It is recorded of him, that at the age of nineteen he had a violent contest with another competitor for the favour of the lady of his love. She refused to make an election between them; and the subject of this notice indignantly exiled himself from his native place. After various peregrinations on the long rivers of the west, he fixed himself in Kentucky, and soon became a distinguished partizan against the savages. In 1774, he joined himself to Lord Dunmore, and was appointed one of his spies. He made various excursions, and performed important services in this employ. He finally selected a place for improvement on the site where Washington now is. Returning one day from hunting, he found one of his companions slain by the Indians, and his body thrown into the fire. He left Washington

in consequence, and joined himself to Colone.
Clark in his fortunate and gallant expedition
against Vincennes and Kaskaskia. He was
sent by that commander with despatches for
Kentucky. He passed through the streets of
Vincennes, then in possession of the British
and Indians, without discovery. Arriving at
White river, he and his party made a raft, on
which to cross with their guns and baggage,
driving their horses into the river, and com-
pelling them to swim it. A party of Indians
was concealed on the opposite bank, who took
possession of the horses as they mounted the
bank, after crossing the river. Butler and his
company seeing this, continued to float down
the river on their raft, without coming to land.
They concealed themselves in the bushes until
night, when they crossed the river, pursued
their journey, and delivered their despatches.

After this, Butler made a journey of discovery to the northern regions of the Ohio
country, and was made prisoner by the Indians. They painted him black, as is their custom, when a victim is devoted to torture; and
informed him that he was destined to be burned
at Chillicothe. Meanwhile, for their own amusement, and as a prelude to his torture, they manacled him hand and foot, placed him on an
unbridled and unbroken horse, and turned the
animal loose, driving it off at its utmost speed
with shouts, delighted with witnessing its mode
of managing under its living burden. The
horse, unable to shake off this new and strange

incumbrance, made for the thickest covert of woods and brambles, with the speed of the winds. It is easy to conjecture the position and sufferings of the victim. The terrified animal exhausted itself in fruitless efforts to shake off its load, and worn down and subdued, brought Butler back to the camp amidst the exulting yells of the savages.

Having arrived within a mile of Chillicothe, they halted, took Butler from his horse, and tied him to a stake, where he remained twenty-four hours in one position. He was taken from the stake to 'run the gauntlet.' The Indian mode of managing this kind of torture was as follows: The inhabitants of the tribe, old and young, were placed in parallel lines, armed with clubs and switches. The victim was to make his way to the council house, through these files, every member of which struggled to beat him, as he passed, as severely as possible. If he reached the council house alive, he was to be spared. In the lines were nearly six hundred Indians, and Butler had to make his way almost a mile in the endurance of this infernal sport. He was started by a blow; but soon broke through the files, and had almost reached the council house, when a stout warrior knocked him down with a club. He was severely beaten in this position, and taken back again into custody.

It seems incredible, that they sometimes rescued their prisoners from these tortures, adopted them, and treated them with the utmost lenity and even kindness. At other times, ingenuity was exhausted to invent tortures, and every renewed endurance of the victim seemed to stimulate their vengeance to new discoveries of cruelty. Butler was one of these ill-fated subjects. No way satisfied with what they had done, they marched him from village to village, to give all a spectacle of his sufferings. He ran the gauntlet thirteen times. He made various attempts to escape; and in one instance would have effected it, had he not been arrested by some savages who were accidentally returning to the village from which he was escaping. It was finally determined to burn him at the lower Sandusky, but an apparent accident changed his destiny.

In passing to the stake, the procession went by the cabin of Simon Girty, who had just returned from an unsuccessful expedition to the frontiers of Pennsylvania. The wretch burned with disappointment and revenge; and hearing that there was a white man going to the torture, determined to wreak his vengeance on him. He found the unfortunate Butler, threw him to the ground, and began to beat him. Butler, who instantly recognized in Girty a former companion of his youth, made himself known to him. His savage heart relented. He raised him up, and promised to use his influence to save him. Girty had a council called, and he moved the savages to give Butler up to him. He took the unfortunate man home, fed, and clothed him, and Butler began to recruit from his wounds and torture. But the relenting of the savages in his favour was only momentary. After five days, they repented of their relaxation in his favour, reclaimed him, and marched him to Lower Sandusky to be burned, according to their original purpose. By a surprising coincidence, he there met the Indian agent from Detroit, who from motives of humanity, exerted his influence with the savages for his release, and took him with him to Detroit Here he was paroled by the governor. He escaped, and by a march of thirty days through the wilderness, reached Kentucky.

14

INGENUITY IN TORTURE.

An instance of the keenness of Indian ingenuity, in the invention of original modes of
torture, is given in Flint's Indian Wars.   The
Indians captured a young man of the name of
Moses Hewitt, who lived on the Little Hock
hocking, and was a member of the Marietta
settlement.   He was remarkable for the sup-
pleness of his limbs, and the swiftness of his
running.   The Indians tested him with their
champion racers, and, although he could not
have run with much spirit, under his depressing
circumstances, he easily vanquished them all in
swiftness.   They affected to be pleased, but
their envy was piqued.   They were destitute
of provisions, and wished to secure their swift-
footed prisoner, while they were occupied in
their hunt.   With this view, and probably to
torture him at the same time, they fastened his
wrists by crossing them, and binding them
firmly with a cord.   They then tied his arms to
a stake, so as partly to raise the upper part of
his body.   They fastened his legs in the same
way, and partly cut off a young sapling, bending it down, so that the weight of the lower
part of his body would be a counterpoise to the
elastic force of the curved tree.   Thus was he
partially raised by his hands and feet, in a way
most horribly painful; and yet in a position
where death would be slow in arriving to his
release.   It was like the torture of killing by

dropping water on the head.   Fortunately the
young man had remarkably slender wrist bones.
When left alone to meditate upon his terrible
situation, he contrived, not without disengaging
the skin and flesh from his wrists, to disentangle
his arms from their manacles, and finally his
legs.   He picked up a little of the scraps of
jerked meat, which the Indians had left.   To
baffle their pursuit and that of their dogs, he
ran on the bodies of fallen trees, and meandered
his course in every direction.   Such was the
adroitness of his management, that he put them
completely at fault, escaped them, and came in
to the settlement of Marietta, wounded, his
flesh torn and mangled, and emaciated to a
skeleton — a living proof how much man can
survive before he suffers the mortal pang.   He
had been absent fourteen days.

OSCEOLA.

On one occasion, Osceola acted as guide to a party of horsemen, and finding that, at starting, they proceeded slowly, he enquired the cause. On being told that it was on his account, with one of those smiles he alone can give, he bade them proceed more rapidly.   They put spurs to their steeds, and he, a-foot, kept up with them during the entire route, nor did he exhibit the slightest symptoms of fatigue, at the close of day, but arrived at the point proposed, as early as the mounted body.   To Col. Gadsden, sole Commissioner at the Treaty of Payne's Landing, Osceola rendered good service, at the head of thirty or forty warriors, posting himself nearer to the Colonel's position than the other Indians, and saying, he was more like the white man than they.   He did not sign the treaty then and there made, nor did he refuse so to do.   The fact is, he was never asked to subscribe his name thereto, being at that time, but a Tuste-nugge and of little note.   This treaty must not be confounded with the subsequent agreement that Osceola finally signed, and into which he is said to have plunged his knife, when called on for his signature.   The negotiations at Payne's landing were in the time of Tuckasee Emathla, or the Ground Mole Warrior, Chief of the Micasuky tribe.   At that date it was not known of Powell, as Cotton Mather says of Roger Williams, that "the whole country was soon like to be set on fire by the rapid motion of a wind mill in the head of this one man

GRATITUDE OF OSCEOLA.

Osceola's agency, and that of his Lieutenant Tom, in Omathla's death, and his killing Gen. Thompson, with the rifle presented him by the General, militate against the favourable estimate of his character. But that all his goodly feelings were not utterly eradicated, is proven by an incident, in the interview with Gen. Gaines' command. On that occasion, Osceola anxiously inquired after Lieut. John Grahame, and on being informed that he was wounded, stoutly denied it. On being asked why he was so positive that Lieut. G. was unhurt, he replied that he had imperatively ordered his people never to molest that young man, and he knew no one who would dare disobey him; none should, and live! It was then admitted, that though the brothers, Grahame, had been wounded, yet Lt. G. had escaped injury; at which admission Osceola greatly joyed. It seems that Powell has a little daughter, to whom Lt. G. was kind, and had presented with frocks, in which the young girl, who grew very fond of him, always insisted on being dressed, whenever she perceived Lieut. G. (for whom she often looked out) coming to visit her. Osceola's motive in sparing Lieut. G. was gratitude for attention to his child, which he also endeavored to repay by teaching the Lieut. the Indian language, for he spoke a little English, and was very intelligent.

14*

THE CROWNING OF POWHATAN.

The Virginia company in London, deceived by false reports, and misled by their own sanguine imaginations, had conceived an expectation not only of finding precious metals in the country, but of discovering the South Sea, from the mountains at the head of James-river; and it was thought, that the journey thither, might be performed in eight or ten days. For the purpose of making this capital discovery, they put on board Newport's ship, a barge capable of being taken to pieces, and put together again at pleasure. This barge was to make a voyage to the head of the river, then to be carried in pieces across the mountains. and to descend the rivers which were supposed to run westward to the South Sea. To facilitate this plan, it was necessary to gain the favour of Powhatan, through whose country the passage must be made; and as means of winning him, a royal present was brought over, consisting of a bason and ewer, a bed and furniture, a chair of state, a suit of scarlet clothes, with a cloak and a crown, all which were to be presented to him in due form; and the crown placed on his head, with as much solemnity as possible. To a person who knew the country and its inhabitants so well as Smith, this project appeared chimerical, and the means whereby it was to be carried on, dangerous. With a small quantity of copper and a few beads, he could have kept

Powhatan in good humour, and made an advantage of it for the colony, whereas a profusion of presents he knew would but increase his pride and insolence. The project of travelling over unknown mountains with men already weakened by sickness, and worn out with fatigue, in a hot climate, and in the midst of enemies, who might easily cut off their retreat, was too romantic even for his sanguine and adventurous spirit. His opinion upon the matter cannot be expressed in more pointed language, than he used in a letter to the company. "If the quartered boat was burned to ashes, *one* might carry her in a bag, but as she is, five hundred cannot, to a navigable place above the falls." His dissent however was ineffectual, and when he found that the voice of the council was for executing it, he lent his assistance to effect as much of it as was practicable.

Previously to their setting out, he undertook, with four men only, to carry notice to Powhatan of the intended present, and invite him to come to James-Town, that he might receive it there. Having travelled by land twelve miles to Werocomoco, on Pamunky (York) river, where he expected to meet Powhatan, and not finding him there, whilst a messenger was dispatched thirty miles for him; his daughter Pocahontas, entertained Smith and his company with a dance, which for its singularity, merits a particular description.

In an open plain, a fire being made, the gentlemen were seated by it. Suddenly a noise was heard in the adjacent wood, which made them fly to their arms, and seize on two or three old men, as hostages for their own security, imagining that they were betrayed. Upon this the young princess came running to Smith, and passionately embracing him, offered herself to be killed, if any harm should happen to him or his company. Her assurances, seconded by all the Indians present, removed their fears. The noise which had alarmed them, was made by thirty girls, who were preparing for the intended ceremony. Immediately they made their appearance, with no other covering than a girdle of green leaves and their skins painted, each one of a different colour. Their leader had a pair of buck's horns on her head, an otter's skin as her girdle, and another on one arm; a bow and arrow in the other hand, and a quiver at her back. The rest of them had horns on their heads, and a wooden sword or staff in their hands. With shouting and singing, they formed a ring round the fire, and performed a circular dance for about an hour, after which they retired in the same order as they had advanced. The dance was followed by a feast, at which the savage nymphs were as eager with their caresses as with their attendance; and this being ended, they conducted the gentlemen to their lodging by the light of fire brands.

The next day Powhatan arrived, and Smith delivered the message from his father, Newport (as he always called him) to this effect. "That he had brought him from the King of England, a royal present, and wished to see him at James-Town, that he might deliver it to him; promising to assist him in prosecuting his revenge against the Monacans, whose country they would penetrate even to the sea beyond the mountains." To which the savage prince with equal subtility and haughtiness, answered, " If your King has sent me a present, I also am a King, and am on my own land. I will stay here eight days. Your father must come to me, I will not go to him, nor to your fort. As for the Monacans, I am able to revenge myself. If you have heard of salt water beyond the mountains, from any of my people, they have deceived you." Then with a stick he drew a plan of that region on the ground; and after many compliments the conference ended.

The present being put on board the boats, was carried down James-river and up the Pamunky, whilst Newport, with fifty men, went across by land and met the boats, in which he passed the river, and held the proposed interview. All things being prepared for the ceremony of coronation, the present was brought from the boats; the bason and ewer were deposited, the bed and chair were set up, the scarlet suit and cloak were put on, though not till Namontac (an Indian youth whom Newport had carried to England and brought back again) had assured him that these habiliments would do him no harm; but they had great difficulty in persuading him to receive the crown, nor would he bend his knee, or incline his head in the least degree. After many attempts, and with actual pressing on his shoulders, they at last made him stoop a little and put it on. Instantly, a signal being given, the men in the boats fired a volley, at which the monarch started with horror, imagining that a design was forming to destroy him in the summit of his glory; but being assured that it was meant as a compliment, his fear subsided, and in return for the baubles of royalty received from King James, he desired Newport to present him his old fur mantle and deer skin shoes, which in his estimation were doubtless a full equivalent; since all this finery could not prevail on the wary chief to allow them guides for the discovery of the inland country, or to approve their design of visiting it. Thus disappointed they returned to James-Town, determined to proceed without his assistance.

THE FLORIDA INDIANS.

The Palarches, Eamuses and Kaloosas, were the ancient possessors of Florida, and are all extinct. The present Florida Indians are the remains of that ancient and warlike tribe on the Mississippi, which being almost extirpated by the French, retreated along the Northern coast of the Gulf of Mexico, and united with broken bands of Biloxies, Red Sticks, and runaway Creeks, called Seminoles. The largest portion of these Indians are Lower Creeks, and are of the most dissolute, daring, and abandoned of that tribe.

The word Seminole signifies a wanderer or runaway, or it means a wild people or outsettlers, the ancestors of the tribe having detached themselves from the main body of the Creeks, and dwelt remotely, wherever the inducements of more game, or greater scope for freedom of action, might casually lead them. They settled in Florida about 115 years ago.

That this is the period of their becoming a separate community, is confirmed by the connection of their history with that of the Yemasees, of whom there occur frequent notices in the account of the early settlement of Georgia and South Carolina.

In a talk, which the Seminoles about the year 1820, transmitted to the American government, they say, alluding to their ancient independence: "An hundred summers have seen

the Seminole warrior reposing undisturbed under the shade of his live oak, and the suns of
an hundred winters have risen on his ardent
pursuit of the buck and the bear, with none to
question his bounds, or dispute his range."

The greater part of East Florida appears to
have been originally in possession of the Yemasees — a powerful people, who not only occupied this province, but spread themselves
over Georgia, and into the limits of South
Carolina, which on its first demarcation was
bounded on the South by the Altamaha. Some
of the tribes resided within the present limits
of that State, in and about Beaufort and Savannah River, and also the Sea Islands. Bartram relates that these people, after a hardy
contest, and many bloody defeats, were nearly
exterminated by their ancient enemies the
Creeks, who had a tradition, that a beautiful
race of Indians, whose women they called
Daughters of the Sun, resided amidst the re-
cesses of the great Oakefanokee wilderness,
where they enjoyed perpetual felicity, in ever
blooming islands, inaccessible to human approach.

Bartram with probability supposes, that this
fable took its rise from a fugitive remnant of
the Yemasees, who found a refuge in this
swamp, and were perhaps, after a lapse of
years, accidentally seen by some of the hunters
of the Creek nation.

There is frequent mention, in the early colo-
nial history of South Carolina of wars between

the first settlers and the Yemasees, the latter having been excited to attack the Colony by the Spanish authorities in St. Augustine.

A formidable war was kindled by these people, which would have proved destructive to the infant settlement of Carolina, had not timely intimation of the danger been obtained by means of one of the outsettlers to whom Sanute, a chief of the hostile Indians, from a feeling of friendship, gave notice of the impending attack. On this occasion the Indians were defeated by Gov. Grant, and driven out of the province. Dr. Ramsay mentions that the Yemasees retired into Florida, to which country they seem to have been subsequently restricted by the increasing power of the whites, and by the Creeks. No further mention of them occurs, until the Seminoles came into notice, by whom they were conquered, and nearly exterminated, in 1721, in the manner mentioned by Bartram. When in the year 1715, the Yemasees were driven within the limits of Florida, they became slaves to the Seminoles. Another account states, that the Yemasees left St. Augustine in a body, in 1722; or rather were expelled by the Spaniards, who essayed in vain to compel them to labours which were regarded as degrading drudgeries by the warriors of Yemasee.

The Yemasees were remarkably black people, and the Ocklewahaw tribe, who are of a deeper shade than the Seminoles, are descendants of the conquered race. The chief of the

Ocklewahaws, Yaha Hadgo, who was killed by
General Shelton in the campaign of '36, was
very dark; but generally, the Seminole's complexion is like that of the Creeks.

Under King Payne, grandfather of Micco-
nope, (the present Chief) the Seminoles invaded
and achieved the conquest of the territories
they lately occupied. He lived to near 100
years of age, and married a Yemasee woman,
his slave, by whom he had the late chief Payne,
who bore, in the darkness of his complexion, a
proof of his Yemasee descent.

The Indians were formerly very numerous
in Florida, perhaps as much so as in Mexico
They are now reduced to comparatively small
cands, in few villages.

GENERAL JACKSON'S CONQUEST OF THE INDIANS.

An artful impostor, Tecumseh of the Shaw nees, a man of most extraordinary abilities and consummate address, conceived the bold design of an union of the red against the white population of America, under a hope that by a general and continued assault along the whole line of our frontiers, the future extension of settlements might be checked, if the present inhabitants could not be driven into the ocean. Assuming the attributes of a prophet, and, among other things, assisted by the fortuitous occurrence of an earthquake, of which he had hazarded a prediction, a confidence began to be reposed in the sacredness of his character and mission. A majority of the Creek nation were enlisted in his cause, and the storm of an exterminating savage war hung over the West. Its first explosion was on Fort Mims, a rude stockade defence, into which the Southern inhabitants of Alabama had lately retreated for security. More than 300 persons, including women and children, fell victims to savage barbarity. " The slaughter was indiscriminate ; mercy was extended to none, and the tomahawk often transfixed mother and child at the same stroke. But seventeen of the whole number in the fort, escaped to give intelligence of the dreadful catastrophe." In the midst of an alarm which such an inhuman outrage was calculated to excite, the eyes of Tennessee were turned on Jackson. Though confined at this period to his house by a fractured arm, his characteristic firmness did not desert him, and he cheerfully yielded to a second call for his services in the cause of his country. Two thousand militia were ordered to assemble at Fayetteville in Tennessee, in addition to five hundred cavalry previously raised under the command of Gen. Coffee.

The alarming accounts of the concentration of the forces of the enemy, with a view of deluging the frontier in blood, compelled General Jackson (though individually in a most disabled state of body) to take the field before the ranks of his army had been filled, or his troops organized.

With this undisciplined force, he prepared for active operations; but the wisest dispositions were counteracted, and all his movements embarrassed, by the failure of unfeeling and speculating contractors.

The enemy were gathering strength, and on the advance; they had already threatened a fort of Indian allies. In this situation, to retreat was to abandon our frontier citizens to the mercy of savages; to advance, was with the certainty of exposure to every privation.

Jackson hesitated not on the alternative, and with but six days' rations of meat, and less than two of meal, he moved with his army upon the Coosa; and, with Coffee's command, gave a most decisive blow to the enemy at Tallushatchee, in less than twenty-five days after he had marched from the rendezvous at Fayetteville. The loss of the Creeks in this engagement, was 186 killed, and 84 prisoners.

Though compelled by the want of supplies to return to his depots on the frontier, we find him in less than six weeks in the field, at the well fought battle of Talledega, and in the subsequent conflicts at Emuckfau, Enotichopco, and Tohopka, annihilating the hopes and expectations of the Creeks, and crushing the hydra of savage hostility in the South.

MASSACRE OF MR. COOLY'S FAMILY.

On the 6th of January, 1836, whilst Mr
Cooly was from home, a party of about thirty
Indians made an attack upon his family, settled
at New River, about 12 miles from Cape Florida. They murdered his wife, three children,
and a Mr. Flinton, who was employed as their
teacher. The children were sitting in the hall,
getting their lessons, when the Indians came up
by stealth, and shot them down. Flinton was
killed on the threshold of the door; the little
girl about eleven years old was found dead,
with her book in her hand. As soon as the
firing commenced, Mrs. Cooly snatched up her
infant child, and endeavoured to effect their escape by a back way. She was shot at a distance of about one hundred and fifty yards
from the house: the ball entered between her
shoulders, and after passing through her breast,
broke the arm of the child which was cradled
on her bosom. The little boy, about eight or
nine years of age, was found in the yard with
his skull and arm fractured, probably done with
a billet of wood. Having destroyed all of the
white inhabitants, they shot the cattle, plun-
dered the house of property worth from one
thousand to twelve hundred dollars, took away
two negroes and all the horses, and finally set
fire to the house.

The circumstances attending the murder of
Mr Cooly's family, are well calculated to illus

trate the treachery of the Indian character. He
nad resided among them for many years, spoke
their language well, and treated them with uniform kindness and hospitality. Indeed, such
was his friendship for them, that he named two
of his sons after their chiefs Alnomock and
Montezuma. His wife had once been a captive among them, and was esteemed a great
favourite. Standing in this relation, and con-
fiding in their professions of friendship, which
lulled him into a fatal security, he left his home
for a few days, and returned to find it desolate.
It is a remarkable fact, that the villains who
perpetrated the deed of death, had not the
hardihood to scalp the poor mother and her
three innocent children. Was it the recollection
of former friendship, that induced them thus to
spare ? Or were they conscious that their own
savage colleagues would have blushed for the
chivalry of those warriors, who could find no
work more befitting their tomahawks and scalping knives, than the cruel butchery of women
and children ? Did they fear that some chief,
more feeling than the rest, would ask,

> " Oh wherefore strike the beautiful, the young,
> So innocent, unharming ?   Lift the knife,
> If need be, 'gainst the warrior ; but forbear
> The trembling woman."

The unfortunate schoolmaster shared a dif
ferent fate. To him they owed no obligations
of friendship ; he was a man, and as such, capable of resistance ; his scalp was therefore
torn from him, and borne off as a testimony of
their savage triumph.

PHYSICAL CHARACTER OF THE INDIANS.

In their physical character, the American Indians are considered by Blumenbach as forming a particular variety of the human species, differing, though not very widely, from the Mongolian. Believing, as we do, that the New World was peopled from the Old, and considering that the Mongol race was situated nearest to the point where Asia and America come almost into contact, we incline to ascribe these variations merely to a change of outward circumstances. The face is broad and flat, with high cheek-bones; more rounded and arched, however, than in the allied type, without having the visage expanded to the same breadth. The forehead is generally low; the eyes deep, small, and black; the nose rather diminutive, but prominent, with wide nostrils; and the mouth large, with somewhat thick lips. The stature, which varies remarkably throughout the Continent, is, in the quarter of which we treat, generally above the middle size. This property, however, is confined to the men, the females being usually below that standard, a fact which may be confidently ascribed to the oppressive drudgery they are compelled to undergo. The limbs, in both sexes, are well proportioned; and few instances of deformity ever occur.

The colour of the skin in the Indian is generally described as red or copper-coloured; or, according to Mr. Lawrence's more precise definition, it is "an obscure orange or rusty iron colour, not unlike the bark of the cinnamon-tree." Although we believe that climate is the chief cause of the diversities in human colour, yet it is certain that all savages are dark-tinted. This peculiarity may be accounted for by their constant exposure to the inclemency of the seasons, to sun, air, and tempests; and the same cause in civilized countries produces a similar effect on sailors, as well as on those who work constantly in the fields. In the Old World, the intermediate tints between white and black are generally varieties of brown and yellow. The *red* tint is considered characteristic of the New World. We must, however, observe, that the traveller Adair, who lived upward of thirty years among the Indians, positively asserts that it is artificially produced; that in the oil, grease, and other unctous substances with which they keep their skin constantly smeared, there is dissolved the juice of a root which gradually tinges it of this colour. He states, that a white man, who spent some years with the natives, and adorned himself in their manner, completely acquired it. Charlevoix seems also to lean to the same opinion. Weld, tho' on rather inclined to dissent from it, admits that such a notion was adopted by missionaries and others who had re-sided long in the country. It is certain that the inhabitants glory in this colour, and regard Europeans who have it not as nondescript beings, not fully entitled to the name of men. It may be noticed also, that this tint is by no

means so universal as is commonly supposed
Humboldt declares that the idea of its general
prevalence could never have arisen in equinoc-
tial America, or been suggested by the view of
the natives in that region : yet these provinces
include by far the larger part of the aboriginal
population.   The people of Nootka sound and
other districts of the north-western coast are
nearly as white as Europeans ; which may be
ascribed, we think, to their ample clothing and
spacious habitations.   Thus the red nations
appear limited to the eastern tribes of North
America, among whom generally prevails the
custom of painting or smearing the skin with
that favourite colour.   We are not prepared to
express a decided opinion on this subject ; but
it obviously requires a closer investigation than
it has yet received.

The hair is another particular in which the
races of mankind remarkably differ.   The ruder
classes are generally defective, either in the
abundance or quality of that graceful appen-
dage ; and the hair of the American Indians,
like that of their allied type the Mongols, is
coarse, black, thin, but strong, and growing to a
great length.   Like the latter, also, by a curious
coincidence, most of them remove it from every
part of the head, with the exception of a tuft
on the crown, which they cherish with much
care.   The circumstance, however, which has
excited the greatest attention, is the absence of
beard, apparently entire, among all the people
of the New World.   The early travellers viewed

it as a natural deficiency; whence Robertson and other eminent writers have even inferred the existence of something peculiarly feeble in their whole frame. But the assertion, with all the inferences founded upon it, so far as relates to the North American tribes, has been completely refuted by recent observation. The original growth has been found nearly, if not wholly, as ample as that of Europeans; but the moment it appears, every trace is studiously obliterated. This is effected by the aged females, originally with a species of clam-shell, but now by means of spiral pieces of brass-wire supplied by the traders. With these an old squaw will in a few minutes reduce the chin to a state of complete smoothness; and slight applications during the year clear away such straggling hairs as may happen to sprout. It is only among old men, who become careless of their appearance, that the beard begins to be perceptible. A late English traveller strongly recommends to his countrymen a practice which, though scarcely accordant with our ideas of manly dignity, would, at the expense of a few minutes' pain, save them much daily trouble. The Indians have probably adopted this usage, as it removes an obstacle to the fantastic painting of the face, which they value so highly. A full beard, at all events, when it was first seen on their French visiters, is said to have been viewed with peculiar antipathy, and to have greatly enhanced the pleasure with which they killed these foreigners.

The comparative physical strength of savage and civilized nations has been a subject of controversy. A general impression has obtained that the former, inured to simple and active habits, acquire a decided superiority; but experience appears to have proved that this conclusion is ill founded. On the field of battle, when a struggle takes place between man and man, the Indian is usually worsted. In sportive exercises, such as wrestling, he is most frequently thrown, and in leaping comes short of his antagonist. Even in walking or running, if for a short distance, he is left behind; but in these last movements he possesses a power of perseverance and continued exertion to which there is scarcely any parallel. An individual has been known to travel nearly eighty miles in a day, and arrive at his destination without any symptoms of fatigue. These long journeys, also, are frequently performed without any refreshment, and even having the shoulders loaded with heavy burdens, their capacity of supporting which is truly wonderful. For about twelve miles, indeed, a strong European will keep ahead of the Indian; but then he begins to flag, while the other, proceeding with unaltered pace, outstrips him considerably. Even powerful animals cannot equal them in this respect. Many of their civilized adversaries, when overcome in war, and fleeing before them on swift horses, have, after a long chase, been overtaken and scalped.

DRESS OF THE INDIANS.

Having thus given a view of the persons of the Indians, we may proceed to consider the manner in which they are clothed and ornamented. This last object might have been expected to be a very secondary one, among tribes whose means of subsistence are so scanty and precarious; but, so far is this from being the case, that there is scarcely any pursuit which occupies so much of their time and regard. They have availed themselves of European intercourse to procure each a small mirror, in which, from time to time, they view their personal decorations, taking care that everything shall be in the most perfect order. Embellishment, however, is not much expended on actual clothing, which is simple, and chiefly arranged with a view to convenience. Instead of shoes, they wear what are termed moccasins, consisting of one strip of soft leather wrapped round the foot, and fastened in front and behind. Europeans, walking over hard roads, soon knock these to pieces; but the Indian, tripping over snow or grass, finds them a light and agreeable *chaussure*. Upward to the middle of the thigh, a piece of leather or cloth, tightly fitted to the limb, serves instead of pantaloons, stockings, and boots; it is sometimes sewed on so close as never to be taken off. To a string or girdle round the waist are fastened two aprons, one before and the other at the

back, each somewhat more than a foot square,
and these are connected by a piece of cloth like
a truss, often used also as a capacious pocket.
The use of breeches they have always repelled
with contempt, as cumbrous and effeminate.
As an article of female dress, they would consider them less objectionable; but that the limbs
of a warrior should be thus manacled, appears
to them utterly preposterous. They were particularly scandalized at seeing an officer have
them fastened over the shoulder by braces, and
never after gave him any name but Tied-
Breech.

The garments now enumerated form the
whole of their permanent dress. On occasions
of ceremony, indeed, or when exposed to cold.
they put over it a short shirt fastened at the
neck and wrists, and above it a long loose robe,
closed or held together in front. For this purpose they now generally prefer an English
blanket. All these articles were originally fa-
bricated from the skins of wild animals; but at
present, unless for the moccasins, and sometimes the leggins, European stuffs are preferred.
The dress of the female scarcely differs from
that of the male, except that the apron reaches
down to the knees; and even this is said to
have been adopted since their acquaintance
with civilized nations. The early French writers relate an amusing anecdote to prove how
little dress was considered as making a dis
tinction between the sexes. The Ursuline nuns,
having educated a Huron girl, presented her,

on her marriage to one of her countrymen,
with a complete and handsome suit of clothes
in the Parisian style. They were much surprised, some days after, to see the husband,
who had ungenerously seized the whole of his
bride's attire and arrayed himself in it, parad-
ing back and forward in front of the convent,
and betraying every symptom of the most ex-
travagant exultation. This was farther height-
ened when he observed the ladies crowding to
the window to see him, and a universal smile
spread over their countenances.

These vestments, as already observed, are
simple, and adapted only for use. To gratify
his passionate love of ornament, the Indian
seeks chiefly to load his person with certain
glittering appendages. Before the arrival of
Europeans, shells and feathers took the lead;
but, since that period, these commodities have
been nearly supplanted by beads, rings, brace-
lets, and similar toys, which are inserted profusely into various parts of his apparel, particularly the little apron in front. The chiefs
usually wear a breastplate ornamented with
them; and among all classes it is an object of
the greatest ambition to have the largest possible number suspended from the ear. That
organ, therefore, is not bored, but slit to such
an extent that a stick of wax may be passed
through the aperture, which is then loaded with
all the baubles that can be mustered; and if
the weight of these gradually draw down the
yielding flap till it rest on the shoulder, and the

ornaments themselves cover the breast, the Indian has reached his utmost height of finery.
This, however, is a precarious splendour; the
ear becomes more and more unfit to support
the burden, when at length some accident, the
branch of a tree, or even a twitch by a wag-
gish comrade, lays at his feet all his decora
tions, with the portion of flesh to which they
were attached. Weld saw very few who had
preserved this organ entire through life. The
adjustment of the hair, again, is an object of
especial study. As already observed, the greater
part is generally eradicated, leaving only a tuft,
varying in shape and place, according to taste
and national custom, but usually encircling the
crown. This lock is stuck full of feathers,
wings of birds, shells, and every kind of fantastic ornament. The women wear theirs long
and flowing, and contrive to collect a considerable number of ornaments for it, as well as for
their ears and dress.

But it is upon his skin that the American
warrior chiefly lavishes his powers of embellishment. His taste in doing so is very different
from ours. "While the European," says Creuxius, "studies to keep his skin clean, and free
from every extraneous substance, the Indian's
aim is, that his, by the accumulation of oil,
grease, and paint, may shine like that of a
roasted pig." Soot scraped from the bottoms
of kettles, the juices of herbs, having a green,
yellow, and, above all, a vermilion tint, rendered adhesive by combination with oil and

grease, are lavishly employed to adorn his person, or, according to our idea, to render it hideous. Black and red, alternating with each other in varied stripes, are the favourite tints. Some blacken the face, leaving in the middle a red circle, including the upper lip and tip of the nose; others have a red spot on each ear, or one eye black and the other of a red colour. In war the black tint is profusely laid on, the others being only employed to heighten its effect, and give to the countenance a terrific expression. M. de Tracy, when governor of Canada, was told by his Indian allies, that, with his good-humoured face, he would never inspire the enemy with any degree of awe. They besought him to place himself under their brush, when they would soon make him such that his very aspect would strike terror. The breast, arms, and legs are the seat of more permanent impressions, analogous to the tattooing of the South Sea Islanders. The colours are either elaborately rubbed in, or fixed by slight incisions with needles and sharp-pointed bones. His guardian spirit, and the animal that forms the symbol of his tribe, are the first objects delineated. After this, every memorable exploit, and particularly the enemies whom he has slain and scalped, are diligently graven on some part of his figure; so that the body of an aged warrior contains the history of his life.

INDIAN HUNTING.

It is a mistake to suppose that hunting is pursued by the Indian merely as a means of suosistence. It is also his favourite sport; and no English gentleman who spends his thousands of pounds per annum on his horses and hounds, follows the sports of the field with a keener zest, than the wild Indian who has never beheld the face of a white man. The accounts of Catlin, who spent much time among the wildest tribes, show, that amusement, in its most liberal sense, is pursued by the Indians in this way. Hunting is not drudgery to them.

The means of procuring subsistence must always form an important branch of national economy. Writers take a superficial view of savage life, and, seeing how scanty the articles of food are, while the demand is necessarily urgent, have assumed that the efforts to attain them must absorb his whole mind, and scarcely leave room for any other thought. But, on the contrary, these are to him very subordinate objects. To perform a round of daily labour, even though ensuring the most ample provision for his wants, would be equally contrary to his inclination and supposed dignity. He will not deign to follow any pursuit which does not, at the same time, include enterprise, adventure, and excitement. Hunting, which the higher classes in the civilized parts of the world pursue for mere recreation, is almost the only occupation considered of sufficient importance to engage his attention. It is peculiarly endeared by its resemblance to war, being carried on with the same weapons, and nearly in the same manner. In his native state, the arrow was the favourite and almost exclusive instrument for assailing distant objects; but now the gun has nearly superseded it. The great hunts are rendered more animating, as well as more effectual, from being carried on in large parties, and even by whole tribes. The men are prepared for these by fasting, dreaming, and other superstitious observances, similar to those which we shall find employed in anticipation of war. In such expeditions, too, contrivance and skill, as well as boldness and enterprise, are largely employed. Sometimes a circle is formed, when all the animals surrounded by it are pressed closer and closer, till they are collected in the centre, and fall under the accumulated weight of weapons. On other occasions they are driven to the margin of a lake or river, in which, if they attempt to seek refuge, canoes are ready to intercept them. Elsewhere a space is enclosed by stakes, only a narrow opening being left, which, by clamour and shouts, the game are compelled to enter, and thereby secured. In autumn and spring, when the ice is newly formed and slight, they are pushed upon it, and their legs breaking through, they are easily

caught. In winter, when the snow begins to
fall, traps are set, in which planks are so arranged, that the animal, in snatching at the
bait, is crushed to death. Originally the deer,
both for food and clothing, was the most valuable object of chase; but, since the trade with
Europeans has given such a prominent importance to furs, the beaver has in some degree
supplanted it. In attacking this animal, great
care is taken to prevent his escape into the water, on which his habitation always borders;
and with this view various kinds of nets and
springes are employed. On some occasions the
Indians place themselves upon the dike which
encloses his amphibious village. They then
make an opening in it, when the inmates,
alarmed by seeing the water flowing out, hasten
to this barrier, where they encounter their ene
mies, armed with all the instruments of de
struction. At other times, when ice covers the
surface of the pond, a hole is made, at which
the animal comes to respire; he is then drawn
out and secured. The bear is a formidable
enemy, which must be assailed by the combined force of the hunters, who are ranged in
two rows, armed with bows or muskets. One
of them advances and wounds him, and, on
being furiously pursued, he retreats between
the files, followed in the same line by the animal, which is then overwhelmed by their united
onset. In killing these quadrupeds, the natives
seem to feel a sort of kindness and sympathy
for their victim. On vanquishing a beaver or

a bear, they celebrate its praises in a song, recounting those good qualities which it will never more be able to display, yet consoling themselves with the useful purposes to which its flesh and its skin will be applied.

Of the animals usually tamed and rendered subservient to useful purposes, the Indians have only the dog, that faithful friend of man. Though his services in hunting. are valuable he is treated with but little tenderness, and is left to roam about the dwelling, very sparingly supplied with food and shelter. A missionary. who resided in a Huron village, represents his life as having been rendered miserable by these animals. At night they laid themselves on his person for the benefit of the warmth; and, whenever his scanty meal was set down, their snouts were always first in the dish. Dog's flesh is eaten, and has even a peculiar sanctity attached to it. On all solemn festivals it is the principal meat, the use of which, on such occasions, seems to import some high and mysterious meaning.

But, besides the cheering avocations of the chase, other means must be used to ensure the comfort and subsistence of the Indian's family; all of which, however, are most ungenerously devolved upon the weaker sex. Women, according to Creuxius, serve them as domestics, as tailors, as peasants, and as oxen; and Long does not conceive that any other purposes of their existence are recognized, except those of bearing children and performing hard work

They till the ground, carry wood and water, build huts, make canoes, and fish; in which latter processes, however, and in reaping the harvest, their lords deign to give occasional aid. So habituated are they to such occupations, that when one of them saw a party of English soldiers collecting wood, she exclaimed that it was a shame to see men doing women's work, and began herself to carry a load.

Through the services of this enslaved portion of the tribe, those savages are enabled to combine in a certain degree the agricultural with the hunting state, without any mixture of the pastoral, usually considered as intermediate. Cultivation, however, is limited to small spots in the immediate vicinity of the villages, and these being usually at the distance of sixteen or seventeen miles from each other, it scarcely makes any impression on the immense expanse of forest. The women, in the beginning of summer, after having burned the stubble of the preceding crop, rudely stir the ground with a long, crooked piece of wood; they then throw in the grain, which is chiefly the coarse but productive species of maize peculiar to the Continent. The nations in the south have a considerable variety of fruits; whereas those of Canada appear to have raised only turnsols, watermelons, and pompions. Tobacco used to be grown largely; but that produced by the European settlers is now universally preferred, and has become a regular object of trade. The grain, after harvest (which is celebrated by a festival), is lodged in large subterraneous stores lined with bark, where it keeps extremely well. Previous to being placed in these, it is sometimes thrashed; on other occasions merely the ears are cut off, and thrown in. When first discovered by settlers from Europe, the degrees of culture were found to vary in different tribes. The Algonquins, who were the ruling people previous to the arrival of the French, wholly despised it, and branded as plebeian their neighbours, by whom it was practised. In general, the northern clans, and those near the mouth of the St. Lawrence, depended almost solely on hunting and fishing; and when these failed they were reduced to dreadful extremities, being often obliged to depend on the miserable resource of that species of lichen called *tripe de roche.*

The maize, when thrashed, is occasionally toasted on the coals, and sometimes made into a coarse kind of unleavened cake. But the most favourite preparation is that called *sagamity*, a species of pap formed after it has been roasted, bruised, and separated from the husk. It is insipid by itself; yet when thrown into the pot, along with the produce of the chase, it enriches the soup or stew, one of the principal dishes at their feasts. They never eat victuals raw, but rather overboiled; nor have they yet been brought to endure French ragouts, salt, pepper, or, indeed, any species of condiment. A chief, admitted to the governor's table, seeing the general use of mustard, was led by cu-

riosity to take a spoonful and put it into his
mouth. On feeling its violent effects, he made
incredible efforts to conceal them, and escape
the ridicule of the company; but severe sneez-
ings, and the tears starting from his eyes, soon
betrayed him, and raised a general laugh. He
was then shown the manner in which it should
be used; but nothing could ever induce him to
allow the "boiling yellow," as he termed it, to
enter his lips.

The Indians are capable of extraordinary
abstinence from food, in which they can persevere for successive days without complaint or
apparent suffering. They even take a pride in
long fasts, by which they usually prepare themselves for any great undertaking. Yet, when
once set down to a feast, their gluttony is described as enormous, and the capacity of their
stomachs almost incredible. They will go from
feast to feast, doing honour to each in succession.
The chief giving the entertainment does not
partake, but with his own hands distributes
portions among the guests. On solemn occasions, it is a rule that everything shall be eaten;
nor does this obligation seem to be felt as either
burdensome or unpleasant. In their native
state, they were not acquainted with any species
of intoxicating liquors; their love of ardent
spirits, attended with so many ruinous effects,
having been entirely consequent on their intercourse with Europeans.

HABITATIONS OF THE INDIANS.

There is great diversity among the various tribes of North American Indians in respect to manners and customs, dress, and modes of living. The inhabitants of the sultry regions of Florida and Texas, of course pay less atten tion to the texture of their garments, and the comfort of their dwellings, than those who re- side in the more northern regions; and other diversities of habit are produced by differences of climate and situation. Still there is a cer tain degree of simplicity inherent in savage life which pervades all the tribes:—it is the sim plicity which is the necessary consequence of poverty and ignorance.

The habitations of the Indians receive much less of their attention than the attire, or, at least, embellishment of their persons. Our countrymen, by common consent, give to them no better appellation than cabins. The bark of trees is their chief material both for houses and boats: they peel it off with considerable skill, sometimes stripping a whole tree in one piece. This coating, spread not unskilfully over a framework of poles, and fastened to them by strips of tough rind, forms their dwel- lings. The shape, according to the owner's fancy, resembles a tub, a cone, or a cart-shed, the mixture of which gives to the village a confused and chaotic appearance. Light and

heat are admitted on y by an aperture at the
top, through which also the smoke escapes,
after filling all the upper part of the mansion.
Little inconvenience is felt from this by the
natives, who, within doors, never think of any
position except sitting or lying; but to Europeans, who must occasionally stand or walk, the
abode is thereby rendered almost intolerable;
and matters become much worse when rain or
snow makes it necessary to close the roof.
These structures are sometimes upward of a
hundred feet long; but they are then the residence of two or three separate families. Four
of them occasionally compose a quadrangle,
each open on the inside, and having a common
fire in the centre. Formerly the Iroquois had
houses somewhat superior, adorned even with
some rude carving; but these were burned
down by the French in successive expeditions,
and were never after rebuilt in the same style.
The Canadians in this respect seem to be
surpassed by the Choctaws, Chickasaws, and
other tribes in the south, and even by the
Saukies in the west, whose mansions Carver
describes as constructed of well-hewn planks,
neatly jointed, and each capable of containing
several families.

In their expeditions, whether for war or
hunting, which often lead them through desolate
forests, several hundred miles from home, the
Indians have the art of rearing, with great expedition, temporary abodes. On arriving at
their evening station, a few poles, meeting at

the top in the form of a cone, are in half an hour covered with bark; and having spread a few pine-branches within by way of mattress, they sleep as soundly as on beds of down. Like the Esquimaux, they also understand how to convert snow into a material for building; and find it in the depth of winter the warmest and most comfortable. A few twigs platted together secure the roof. Our own countrymen, in their several campaigns, have, in cases of necessity, used with advantage this species of bivouac.

The furniture in these native huts is exceedingly simple. The chief articles are two or three pots or kettles for boiling their food, with a few wooden plates and spoons. The former, in the absence of metal, with which the inhabitants were unacquainted, were made of coarse earthenware that resisted the fire; and sometimes of a species of soft stone, which could be excavated with their rude hatchets. Nay, in some cases, their kitchen utensils were of wood, and the water made to boil by throwing in heated stones. Since their acquaintance with Europeans, the superiority of iron vessels has been found so decided, that they are now universally preferred. The great kettle or caldron, employed only on high festivals associated with religion, hunting, or war, attracts even a kind of veneration; and potent chiefs have assumed its name as their title of honour.

INTELLECTUAL CHARACTER OF THE INDIANS

The intellectual character of the American savage presents some very striking peculiarities. Considering his unfavourable condition, he of all other human beings might seem doomed to make the nearest approach to the brute; while, in point of fact, without any aid from letters or study, many of the higher faculties of his mind are developed in a very remarkable degree. He displays a decided superiority over the uninstructed labourer in a civilized community, whose mental energies are benumbed amid the daily round of mechanical occupation. The former spends a great part of his life in arduous enterprises, where much contrivance is requisite, and whence he must often extricate himself by presence of mind and ingenuity. His senses, particularly those of seeing and smelling, have acquired by practice an almost preternatural acuteness. He can trace an animal or a foe by indications which to a European eye would be wholly imperceptible; and in his wanderings he gathers a minute acquaintance with the geography of the countries which he traverses. He can even draw a rude outline of them by applying a mixture of charcoal and grease to prepared skins, and on seeing a regular map he soon understands its construction, and readily finds out places. His facility in discovering the most direct way to spots situated at the distance of hundreds of miles, and known perhaps only by the report of his countrymen, is truly astonishing. It has been ascribed by some to a mysterious and supernatural instinct, but it appears to be achieved by merely observing the different aspect of the trees or shrubs when exposed to the north or the south, as also the position of the sun, which he can point out, although hidden by clouds. Even where there is a beaten track, if at all circuitous, he strikes directly through the woods, and reaches his destination by the straightest possible line.

Other faculties of a higher order are developed by the scenes amid which the life of savages is spent. They are divided into a number of little communities, between which are actively carried on all the relations of war, negotiation, treaty, and alliance. As mighty revolutions, observes an eloquent writer, take place in these kingdoms of wood and cities of bark, as in the most powerful civilized states. To increase the influence and extend the possessions of their own tribe, to humble and, if possible, to destroy those hostile to them, are the constant aims of every member of those little commonwealths. For these ends, not only deeds of daring valour are achieved, but schemes are deeply laid, and pursued with the most accurate calculation. There is scarcely a refinement in European diplomacy to which they are strangers. The French once made an attempt to crush the confederacy of the Five Nations by attacking each in succession, but as they were on their march against the first tribe, they were met by the deputies of

17*

the others, who offered their mediation, intima-
ting that, f it were rejected, they would make
common cause with the one threatened.   That
association also showed that they completely
understood how to employ the hostility which
prevailed between their enemy and the English
for promoting their own aggrandizement.   Em-
bassies, announced by the calumet of peace, are
constantly passing from one tribe to another.

The same political circumstances develop in
an extraordinary degree the powers of oratory;
for nothing of any importance is transacted
without a speech.   On every emergency a
council of the tribe is called, when the aged and
wise hold long deliberations for the public weal
The best speakers are despatched to conduc
their negotiations, the object of which is unfolded in studied harangues.   The functions of
orator, among the Five Nations, had even become a separate profession, held in equal or
higher honour than that of the warrior; and
each clan appointed the most eloquent of their
number to speak for them in the public council.
Nay, there was a general orator for the whole
confederacy, who could say to the French
governor, "Ononthio, lend thine ear; I am the
mouth of all the country; you hear all the
Iroquois in hearing my word."   Decanesora,
their speaker at a later period, was greatly admired by the English, and his bust was though'.
to resemble that of Cicero.   In their diplomatic
discourses, each proposition is prefaced by the
delivery of a belt of wampum, of which what

follows is understood to be the explanation, and which is to be preserved as a record of the conference. The orator does not express his proposals in words only, but gives to every sentence its appropriate action. If he threatens war, he wildly brandishes the tomahawk; if he solicits alliance, he twines his arms closely with those of the chief whom he addresses; and if he invites friendly intercourse, he assumes all the attitudes of one who is forming a road in the Indian manner, by cutting down the trees, clearing them away, and carefully removing the leaves and branches. To a French writer, who witnessed the delivery of a solemn embassy, it suggested the idea of a company of actors performing on a stage. So expressive are their gestures, that negotiations have been conducted. and alliances concluded between petty states and communities who understood nothing of one another's language.

The composition of the Indian orators is studied and elaborate. The language of the Iroquois is even held to be susceptible of an Attic elegance, which few can attain so fully as to escape all criticism. It is figurative in the highest degree, every notion being expressed by images addressed to the senses. Thus, to throw up the hatchet or to put on the great caldron is to begin a war; to throw the hatchet to the sky is to wage open and terrible war; to take off the caldron or to bury the hatchet is to make peace; to plant the tree of peace on the highest mountain of the earth is to make a general pacification. To throw a prisoner into the caldron is to devote him to torture and death; to take him out, is to pardon and receive him as a member of the community. Ambassadors coming to propose a full and general treaty say, " We rend the clouds asunder, and drive away all darkness from the heavens, that the sun of peace may shine with brightness over us all." On another occasion, referring to their own violent conduct, they said, " We are glad that Assarigoa will bury in the pit what is past; let the earth be trodden hard over it, or, rather, let a strong stream run under the pit to wash away the evil." They afterward added, " We now plant a tree, whose top will reach the sun, and its branches spread far abroad, and we shall shelter ourselves under it, and live in peace." To send the collar under ground is to carry on a secret negotiation; but when expressing a desire that there might be no duplicity or concealment between them and the French, they said that " They wished to fix the sun in the top of the heaven, immediately above that pole, that it might beat directly down and leave nothing in obscurity." In pledging themselves to a firm and steady peace, they declared that they would not only throw down the great war-caldron, and cause all the water to flow out, but would break it in pieces This disposition to represent every thing by a sensible object extends to matters the most important. One powerful people assumed the appellation of Foxes, while another gloried in that of Cats. Even when the entire nation bore a different appellation, separate fraternities distinguished themselves as the tribe of the Bear, the Tortoise, and the Wolf. They did not disdain a reference even to inanimate things. The Black Caldron was at one time the chief warrior of the Five Nations; and Red Shoes was a person of distinction well known to Long the traveller. When the chiefs concluded treaties with Europeans, their signature consisted in a picture, often tolerably well executed, of the beast or object after which they chose to be named.

The absence among these tribes of any written or even pictorial mode of recording events, was supplied by the memories of their old men, which were so retentive, that a certain writer calls them living books. Their only remembrancer consisted in the wampum belts; of which one was appropriated to each division of a speech or treaty, and had seemingly a powerful effect in calling it to recollection. On the close of the transaction, these were deposited as public documents, to be drawn forth on great occasions, when the orators, and even the old women, could repeat verbatim the passage to which each referred. Europeans were thus enabled to collect information concerning the revolutions of different tribes, for several ages p eceding their own arrival.

SINGULAR EXECUTION OF AN INDIAN.

In March, 1823, a Choctaw savage, calling himself Doctor Sibley, belonging to a wander ing tribe of his nation, in the Arkansas Terri tory,—while in a state of intoxication, stabbed to the heart another Indian; who instantly ex- pired. This act called for revenge, founded on the *lex taliones*—that invariable custom of the aborigines. A brother of the deceased called upon Sibley, and told him, that he was come to take his life, in atonement for the death of his brother. With the composure of a philosopher, and the courage of a Roman, Sibley—readily, and without a murmur—yielded assent; only desiring the execution might be postponed until the following morning. This was granted;— the execution was postponed—and Sibley *left at large, under no restraint whatever!*

When the morning came, Sibley went out with the rest of the party, and, with perfect apathy, aided in digging a grave for the mur- dered Indian. The work being finished, he calmly observed to the by-standers, that he thought it large enough to contain two bodies;— signifying, at the same time, a wish to be buried in the same grave. This, too, was granted: and the murderer deliberately took a standing position over the grave, with out- stretched arms; and, giving a signal to fire, the brother drove a rifle ball through his heart— and he dropt into the hole he had assisted to make!

INDIAN VERACITY.

" He once told a lie"—was the emphatical expression of an Indian to me, in 1794, when I was attending to the surveying of a large body of lands in, what was then called, 'The French-Creek Country,' and West of the Alleghany River: and, as some of my people were killed by the Western Indians, I found it necessary, while the surveying was going on, to visit the Indian Towns on the Alleghany River frequently: — they were inhabited by the Senecas. General Wayne was then on his way, with his army, to the Indian settlements on the Miami River.

One day, when I was at the Cornplanter's town, the *'News-Spout,'* as it is called, was heard. All the Indians in the village immediately retired to their houses (and even their dogs went with them;) when an old man went out to meet the person who brought the news, and to take him to the Long, or Council-House, where a fire was made and refreshments were carried to him, and time given for him to dress and paint himself, so as to appear decent.

When sufficient time had elapsed for the preparatives to be performed, the chiefs went first to the house; and, as the young men were following, I asked an Indian — who spoke English, and to whom (as he professed to be a priest, physician, and conjurer) I gave the name of Doctor—whether there was any impropriety

in my going to hear the news. He said, " No"—
and that, as I was received as a friend and
visiter, all their houses were open to me : and
if I did not go without any ceremony, it would
appear as if *I doubted their words and hospitality ;* which was considered as the greatest
affront that could be put on an Indian. For
that, if there was any secret business going on
they would inform me of it, in a friendly way
and then I might retire.

I accordingly went into the house with him,
when the Chiefs immediately rose, and gave me
a seat among them.

All the Indians in the house were smoking
their pipes when I came in; and the stranger
was sitting opposite the Chiefs, in a seat, or
rather a platform, by himself. The time appeared to me very long, as I was anxious to
hear the news; being much interested in the
event, as the Indians had been deliberating,
whether or not they would permit me to continue surveying, or send me out of the country :
and, what surprised me, was, that no one—contrary to their usual custom—asked him for the
news; and I was at a loss to account for their
conduct. Eventually, the Indian himself—after
prefacing the business, with telling them, he
had no doubt,—as they knew he had been to
the West—they would be gratified in hearing
his news. But no one appeared to signify his
assent or negative. The Indian then gave an
account of an affair between a convoy of
Americans—who were carrying reinforcements

and provisions to one of our frontier posts—
and the Indians; and they had killed the commanding officer and a number of our men:
and, after he had related all he had to say, no
one asked for any particulars of the action, or
for any corroborating circumstance; as I had
formerly observed, they were particularly polite
to strangers and visiters, and were very cautious
to say or do any thing to hurt their feelings.
and, soon after, the chiefs and other Indians
began to leave the house.

I left the house with the Doctor; and, as
soon as we had passed the door, I expressed my
surprise to him, at the manner they treated the
man who brought the news, as it was so
different from any treatment I had before seen,
when visited by strangers; and that I would
thank him to inform me of the cause of it:—
when he, without any hesitation, and with
considerable emphasis, answered, "He once
told a lie"—and continued: "What that man
said, may be so true; may be so not. We
always listen to what a newsman has to say,—
even when we know him to be a liar. But,
whether we believe him or not, it is not our
custom to let him know; or to say any thing
on the subject: for, if we had asked him any
questions about the fight, it would have been
a great gratification to him; as he would have
concluded some of the company did believe
him: which is a thing we do not indulge any
person in, who has been guilty of telling a lie."
He concluded, by saying, "*He all one as dead.*"

18

Peter Otsaquette was the son of a man of consideration among the Oneida Indians of New York.   At the close of the Revolutionary war, he was noticed by the Marquis de La Fayette, who, to a noble zeal for liberty, united the most philanthropic feelings.   Viewing, therefore, this young savage with peculiar interest, and anticipating the happy results to be derived from his moral regeneration, he took him, though scarcely twelve years old, to France.   Peter arrived at that period when Louis XVI. and Maria Antoinette were in the zenith of their glory. There he was taught the accomplishments of a gentleman ;—music, drawing, and fencing, were made familiar to him, and he danced with a grace that a Vestris could not but admire.   At about eighteen, his separation from a country in which he had spent his time so agreeably and so profitably, became necessary.   Laden with favours from the Marquis, and the miniatures of those friends he had left behind. Peter departed for America—inflated, perhaps, with the idea, that the deep ignorance of his nation, with that of the Indians of the whole continent, might be dispelled by his efforts, and he become the proud instrument of the civili zation of thousands.

Prosecuting his route to the land of his parents, he came to the city of Albany ; not the uncivilized savage, not with any of those marks which bespoke a birth in the forest, or years spent in toiling the wilds of a desert, but possessing a fine commanding figure, an expressive countenance, an intelligent eye, with a face scarcely indicative of the race from which he was descended. He presented, at this period, an interesting spectacle : a child of the wilderness was beheld about to proceed to the home of his forefathers, having received the brilliant advantages of a cultivated mind, and on his way to impart to the nation that owned him, the benefits which civilization had given him. It was an opportunity for the philosopher to contemplate, and to reflect on the future good this young Indian might be the means of producing.

Shortly after his arrival in Albany—where he visited the first families—he took advantage of Governor Clinton's journey to Fort Stanwix (where a treaty was to be held with the Indians,) to return to his tribe. On the route, Otsaquette amused the company (among whom were the French Minister, Count De Moustiers, and several gentlemen of respectability) by his powers on various instruments of music. At Fort Stanwix, he found himself again with the companions of his early days, who saw and recognised him. His friends and relations had not forgotten him, and he was welcomed to his home and to his blanket.

But that which occurred soon after his reception, led him to a too fearful anticipation of an unsuccessful project; for the Oneidas, as if they could not acknowledge Otsaquette, attired in the dress with which he appeared before them, — a mark which did not disclose his nation, — and, thinking that he had assumed it. as if ashamed of his own native costume, the garb of his ancestors, they tore it from him with a savage avidity, and a fiend-like ferociousness, daubed on the paint to which he had been so long unused, and clothed him with the uncouth habiliments held sacred by his tribe. Their fiery ferocity, in the performance of the act, showed but too well the bold stand they were about to take against the innovations they supposed Otsaquette was to be the agent for affecting against their immemorial manners and customs, and which, from the venerable antiquity of their structure, it would be nothing short of sacrilege to destroy.

Thus the reformed savage was taken back again to his native barbarity, and—as if to cap the climax of degradation to a mind just susceptible of its own powers—was *married to a squaw!*

From that day, Otsaquette was no longer the accomplished Indian, from whom every wish of philanthropy was expected to be realized. He was no longer the instrument by whose power the emancipation of his countrymen from the thraldom of ignorance and superstition, was to be effected. From that day, he was again an inmate with the forest; was once more buried in his original obscurity, and his nation only viewed him as *an equal.* Even a liberal grant from the State, failed of securing to him that superior consideration among them which his civilization had procured for him with the rest of mankind. The commanding pre-eminence acquired from instruction, from which it was expected ambition would have sprung up, and acted as a double stimulant, from either the natural inferiority of the savage mind, or the predetermination of his countrymen—became of no effect, and, in a little time, was wholly annihilated. Otsaquette was lost! His moral perdition began from the hour he left Fort Stanwix. Three short months had hardly transpired, when Intemperance had marked him as her own, and soon hurried him to the grave. And, as if the very transition had deadened all the finer feelings of his nature, the picture given him by the Marquis—the very portrait of his affectionate friend and benefactor himself—he parted with!

Extraordinary and unnatural as the conduct of this educated savage may appear, the anecdote is not of a kind altogether unique; which proves, that little or nothing is to be expected from conferring a literary education upon those children of the forest: — An Indian, named George White-Eyes, was taken, while a boy, to the college at Princeton, where he received a classical education. On returning to his nation, he made some little stay in Philadelphia. He was amiable in his manners, and of modest demeanour, without exhibiting any trait of the savage whatever; but, no sooner had he re joined his friends and former companions, in

18*

the land of his nativity, than he dropped the garb and manners of civilization, and resumed those of the savage, and, drinking deep of their intoxicating cup, soon put a period to his existence.

Many other instances might be adduced, to show how ineffectual have been the attempts to plant civilization on savage habits, by means of *literary* education—" Can the leopard change his spots?"

THE CATASTROPHE.

The son of a Kickapoo Chief, being engaged to a Ouiattanon girl, came in quest of her to fort Knox, at Vincennes—though an Indian war was then waging against the United States; and, in this, the Kickapoos were among the most formidable. We happened to be there at this time. It was summer, and the weather very warm. The young Kickapoo was admitted into the fort, and, among other presents, threw down several joints of venison; observing to the commanding officer, that, if he could not eat them himself, (for they were tainted,) they might answer for his *hogs* and *dogs*—muttering at the same time, and making the sign of a halter round his neck, that perhaps they might hang him for appearing among them; alluding, no doubt, to the then Indian war.

On the evening of the same day the young Kickapoo got into a drunken frolic, with other savages, among whom was the before mentioned Indian. The latter said to the Kickapoo, "May be I shall kill you:" and, without further preface, he plunged a knife into him—which instantly proved fatal. At this moment the Ouiattanons in company took the alarm—fearful of the consequences that might befal their tribe, from the death of the son of a powerful chieftain. It was therefore determined to propitiate the Kickapoo's father, by sending a deputation to him with the present of a ten gallon keg of whisky as a peace offering. This was furnished for the purpose, on request, by the commanding officer of the fort. They had not gone far when the precious liquor proved too great a temptation : the keg was broached, and soon emptied. What then was to be done?

Next morning, however, they appeared again at the fort—deplored the '*accident*,' (as they called it,) and begged for another keg of liquor. This too was granted—and off they went again. But this keg met with the fate of the former : its contents proved an irresistible temptation. As no more whisky could now be obtained, the mission fell through.

Upon this, the Indians appeared before the fort, with the murderer in custody, under the window of the writer, and demanded justice to be done on the prisoner. He told them it was an affair for themselves to settle, as it was confined to themselves alone. They now marched in Indian file, carrying off the murderer, who, every now and then, looked fearfully behind him—for the brother of the deceased's sweetheart had taken post next in his rear. They had not proceeded far, when this brother plunged a knife into the prisoner's back, which broke, and a part was left buried in the wound. The whole party now returned before the fort—the wounded man singing his death-song. He was borne off by his friends into a thicket, in the prairie, where all their efforts to extract the broken blade proved ineffectual ; and the next day or two he died.

The Spider, a brother of the murderer, and then at Kaskaskia, hearing of the predicament which had befallen the latter, hastened to Vincennes—but death had closed the scene. He came in time, however, to attend the funeral. When the body was about to be consigned to the earth, he opened the blanket which enveloped the corpse, and taking off a silver ornament which encompassed his head, he bound it around that of the defunct, saying, "There, brother! this will bring you respect in the land of Spirits."

The buffalo, more properly called the bison, is the great object of Indian hunting in the west. These animals abound in the prairies; and they are often seen coursing over the plains in immense herds. Thousands of them appear under the direction of one of their number, who acts as leader. This propensity to follow a leader affords a ready means to the Indians of destroying them. The manner in which this is accomplished is graphically described in the following extract from the account of a late writer. It affords a wild picture of the scenes which present themselves to the notice of the traveller as he passes through the great prairies of the west.

We passed a precipice of about one hundred and twenty feet high, under which lay scattered the fragments of at least one hundred carcases of buffaloes, although the water, which had washed away the lower part of the hill, must have carried off many of the dead. These buffaloes had been chased down the precipice, in a way very common on the Missouri, and by which vast herds are destroyed in a moment. The mode of hunting is, to select one of the most active and fleet young men, who is disguised, by a buffalo skin around his body, the skin of the head, with the ears and the horns, fastened on his own head, in such a way as to deceive the buffalo. Thus dressed, he fixes nimself at a convenient distance, between a herd of buffaloes and any of the river precipices, which sometimes extend for some miles. His companions, in the meantime, get into the rear, and on the side of the herd, and, at a given signal, show themselves, and advance towards the buffalo: they instantly take the alarm; and, finding the hunters beside them, they run towards the disguised Indian or decoy, who leads them on at full speed toward the river, when, suddenly securing himself in some crevice of the cliff which he had previously fixed on, the herd is left on the brink of the precipice. It is then in vain for the foremost to retreat, or even to stop—they are pressed on by the hindmost rank, who, seeing no danger, but from the hunters, goad on those before them, till the whole are precipitated, and the shore is strewed with their dead bodies. Sometimes, in this perilous seduction, the Indian is himself either trodden under foot, by the rapid movements of the buffaloes or missing his footing in the cliff, is urged down the precipice along with the falling herd.

The Indians now select as much meat as they choose, and the rest is abandoned to the wolves, and creates a most dreadful stench. The wolves who had been feasting on these carcases were very fat, and so gentle, that one of them was killed with an espontoon.

RELIGION OF THE INDIANS

The earliest visiters of the New World, on seeing among the Indians neither priests, temples, idols, nor sacrifices, represented them as a people wholly destitute of religious opinions. Closer inquiry, however, showed that a belief in the spiritual world, however imperfect, had a commanding influence over almost all their actions. Their creed includes even some lofty and pure conceptions. Under the title of the Great Spirit, the Master of Life, the Maker of heaven and earth, they distinctly recognise a supreme ruler of the universe and an arbiter of their destiny. A party of them, when informed by the missionaries of the existence of a being of infinite power, who had created the heavens and the earth, with one consent exclaimed, "*Atahocan! Atahocan!*" that being the name of their principal deity. According to Long, the Indians among whom he resided ascribe every event, propitious or unfortunate, to the favour or anger of the Master of Life. They address him for their daily subsistence; they believe him to convey to them presence of mind in battle, and amid tortures they thank him for inspiring them with courage. Yet though this one elevated and just conception is deeply graven on their minds, it is combined with others which show all the imperfection of unassisted reason in attempting to think rightly on this great subject. It may even be observed, that the term, rendered into our language "great spirit," does not really convey the idea of an immaterial nature. It imports with them merely some being possesed of lofty and mysterious powers, and in this sense is applied to men, and even to animals. The brute creation, which occupies a prominent place in all their ideas, is often viewed by them as invested, to a great extent, with supernatural powers; an extreme absurdity, which, however, they share with the civilized creeds of Egypt and India.

When the missionaries, on their first arrival, attempted to form an idea of the Indian mythology, it appeared to them extremely complicated, more especially because those who attempted to explain it had no fixed opinions. Each man differed from his neighbour, and at another time from himself; and when the discrepances were pointed out, no attempt was made to reconcile them. The southern tribes, who had a more settled faith, are described by Adair as intoxicated with spiritual pride, and denouncing even their European allies as "the accursed people." The native Canadian, on the contrary, is said to have been so little tenacious, that he would at any time renounce all his theological errors for a pipe of tobacco, though, as soon as it was smoked, he immediately relapsed. An idea was found prevalent respecting a certain mystical animal, called Mesou or Messessagen, who, when the earth was buried in water, had drawn it up and restored it. Others spoke of a contest between the hare, the fox, the beaver, and

19

the seal, for the empire of the world.   Among
the principal nations of Canada, the hare is
thought to have attained a decided preeminence ;
and hence the Great Spirit and the Great Hare
are sometimes used as synonymous terms.
What should have raised this creature to such
distinction seems rather unaccountable ; unless
it were that its extreme swiftness might appear
something supernatural.   Among the Ottowas
alone the heavenly bodies become an object of
veneration ; the sun appears to rank as their
supreme deity.

To dive into the abyss of futurity has always
been a favourite object of superstition.   It has
been attempted by various means ; but the
Indian seeks it chiefly through his dreams, which
always bear with him a sacred character.   Be
fore engaging in any high undertaking, especi
ally in hunting or war, the dreams of the prin
cipal chiefs are carefully watched and studiously
examined ; and according to the interpretation
their conduct is guided.   A whole nation has
been set in motion by the sleeping fancies of a
single man.   Sometimes a person imagines in
his sleep that he has been presented with an
article of value by another, who then cannot,
without impropriety, leave the omen unfulfilled.
When Sir William Johnson, during the Ameri
can war, was negotiating an alliance with a
friendly tribe, the chief confidentially disclosed
that, during his slumbers, he had been favoured
with a vision of Sir William bestowing upon
him the rich laced coat which formed his ful'

dress. The fulfilment of this revelation was very inconvenient; yet, on being assured that it positively occurred, the English commander found it advisable to resign his uniform. Soon after, however, he unfolded to the Indian a dream with which he had himself been favored, and in which the former was seen presenting him with a large tract of fertile land most commodiously situated. The native ruler admitted that, since the vision had been vouchsafed, it must be realized, yet earnestly proposed to cease this mutual dreaming, which he found had turned much to his own disadvantage.

The manitou is an object of peculiar veneration; and the fixing upon this guardian power is not only the most important event in the history of a youth, but even constitutes his initiation into active life. As a preliminary, his face is painted black, and he undergoes a severe fast, which is, if possible, prolonged for eight days. This is preparatory to the dream in which he is to behold the idol destined ever after to afford him aid and protection. In this state of excited expectation, and while every nocturnal vision is carefully watched, there seldom fails to occur to his mind something which, as it makes a deep impression, is pronounced his manitou. Most commonly it is a trifling and even fantastic article; the head, beak, or claw of a bird, the hoof of a cow, or even a piece of wood. However, having undergone a thorough perspiration in one of their vapour-baths, he is laid on his back, and a picture of it is drawn upon his breast by needles of fish-bone dipped in vermilion. A good specimen of the original being procured, it is carefully treasured up; and to it he applies in every emergency, hoping that it will inspire his dreams, and secure to him every kind of good fortune. When, however, notwithstanding every means of propitiating its favour, misfortunes befall him, the manitou is considered as having exposed itself to just and serious reproach. He begins with remonstrances, representing all that has been done for it, the disgrace it incurs by not protecting its votary, and, finally, the danger that, in case of repeated neglect, it may be discarded for another. Nor is this considered merely as an empty threat; for if the manitou is judged incorrigible, it is thrown away; and by means of a fresh course of fasting, dreaming, sweating, and painting, another is installed, from whom better success may be hoped.

The absence of temples, worship, sacrifices, and all the observances to which superstition prompts the untutored mind, is a remarkable circumstance, and, as we have already remarked, led the early visiters to believe that the Indians were strangers to all religious ideas. Yet the missionaries found room to suspect that some of their great feasts, in which every thing presented must be eaten, bore an idolatrous character, and were held in honour of the Great Hare. The Ottawas, whose mythological system seems to have been the most complicated, were wont to keep a regular festival to celebrate the beneficence of the sun; on which occasion the luminary was told that this service was in return for the good hunting he had procured for his people, and as an encouragement to persevere in his friendly cares. They were also observed to erect an idol in the middle of their town, and sacrifice to it; but such ceremonies were by no means general. On first witnessing Christian worship, the only idea suggested by it was that of their asking some temporal good, which was either granted or refused. The missionaries mention two Hurons, who arrived from the woods soon after the congregation had assembled. Standing without, they began to speculate what it was the white men were asking, and then whether they were getting it. As the service continued beyond expectation, it was concluded they were *not* getting it; and as the devotional duties still proceeded, they admired the perseverance with which this rejected suit was urged. At length, when the vesper hymn began, one of the savages observed to the other: " Listen to them now in despair, crying with all their might."

The grand doctrine of a life beyond the grave was, among all the tribes of America, most deeply cherished and most sincerely believed. They had even formed a distinct idea of the region whither they hoped to be transported, and of the new and happier mode of existence, free from those wars, tortures, and cruelties which throw so dark a shade over their lot upon earth Yet their conceptions on this subject

19 *

were by no means either exalted or spiritualized
They expected simply a prolongation of their
present life and enjoyments, under more fa
vourable circumstances, and with the same
objects furnished in greater choice and abundance In that brighter land the sun ever shines
unclouded, the forests abound with deer, the
lakes and rivers with fish; benefits which are
farther enhanced in their imagination by a faithful wife and dutiful children. They do not reach
it, however, till after a journey of several months,
and encountering various obstacles; a broad
river, a chain of lofty mountains, and the attack
of a furious dog. This favoured country lies
far in the west, at the remotest boundary of
the earth, which is supposed to terminate in a
steep precipice, with the ocean rolling beneath.
Sometimes, in the too eager pursuit of game,
the spirits fall over, and are converted into
fishes. The local position of their paradise appears connected with certain obscure intimations
received from their wandering neighbours of
the Mississippi, the Rocky Mountains, and the
distant shores of the Pacific. This system of
belief labours under a great defect, inasmuch as
it scarcely connects felicity in the future world
with virtuous conduct in the present. The one
is held to be simply a continuation of the other;
and under this impression, the arms, ornaments,
and everything that had contributed to the welfare of the deceased, are interred along with
him. This supposed assurance of a future life
so conformable to their gross habits and con-

ceptions, was found by the missionaries a serious obstacle when they attempted to allure them by the hope of a destiny, purer and higher indeed, but less accordant with their untutored conceptions. Upon being told that in the promised world they would neither hunt, eat, drink, nor marry, many of them declared that, far from endeavouring to reach such an abode, they would consider their arrival there as the greatest calamity. Mention is made of a Huron girl whom one of the Christian ministers was endeavouring to instruct, and whose first question was what she would find to eat. The answer being "Nothing," she then asked what she would see; and being informed that she would see the Maker of heaven and earth, she expressed herself much at a loss how she should address him.

INDIAN FUNERALS.

Another sentiment, congenial with that now described, is most deeply rooted in the mind of the Indians. This is reverence for the dead, with which Chateaubriand, though somewhat hastily, considers them more deeply imbued than any other people. During life they are by no means lavish in their expressions of tenderness, but on the hour of final separation it is displayed with extraordinary force. When any member of a family becomes seriously ill, all the resources of magic and medicine are exhausted in order to procure his recovery. When the fatal moment arrives, all the kindred burst into loud lamentations, which continue till some person possessing the requisite authority desires them to cease. These expressions of grief, however, are renewed for a considerable time at sunrise and sunset. After three days the funeral takes place, when all the provisions which the family can procure are expended in a feast, to which the neighbours are generally invited; and, although on all solemn occasions it is required that every thing should be eaten, the relations do not partake. These last cut off their hair, cover their heads, paint their faces of a black colour, and continue long to deny themselves every species of amusement. The deceased is then interred with his arms and ornaments, his face painted, and his person attired in the richest robes which they can furnish. It was the opinion of one of the early missionaries, that the chief object of the Hurons in their traffic with the French was to procure materials for honouring their dead; and, as a proof of this, many of them have been seen shivering half naked in the cold, while their hut contained rich robes to be wrapped round them after their decease. The body is placed in the tomb in an upright posture, and skins are carefully spread round it, so that no part may touch the earth This, however, is by no means the final cere mony, being followed by another still more solemn and singular. Every eighth, tenth, or twelfth year, according to the custom of the different nations, is celebrated the festival of the dead; and, till then, the souls are supposed to hover round their former tenement, and not to depart for their final abode in the west. On this occasion the people march in procession to the places of interment, open the tombs, and, on beholding the mortal remains of their friends, continue some time fixed in mournful silence. The women then break out into loud cries, and the party begin to collect the bones, removing every remnant of flesh. The remains are then wrapped in fresh and valuable robes, and con- veyed amid continual lamentation to the family cabin. A feast is then given, followed during several days by dances, games, and prize-com- bats, to which strangers often repair from a great distance. This mode of celebration cer- tainly accords very ill with the sad occasion · yet the Greek and Roman obsequies were

solemnized in a similar manner; nay, in many
parts of Scotland, till very recently, they were
accompanied by festival, and often by revelry.
The relics are then carried to the council-house
of the nation, where they are hung for exhibi-
tion along the walls, with fresh presents destined
to be interred along with them.   Sometimes
they are even displayed from village to village.
At length, being deposited in a pit previously
dug in the earth, and lined with the richest furs,
they are finally entombed.   Tears and lamentations are again lavished; and during a few
days food is brought to the place.   The bones
of their fathers are considered by the Indians
the strongest ties to their native soil; and when
calamity forces them to quit it, these mouldering
fragments are, if possible, conveyed along with
them.

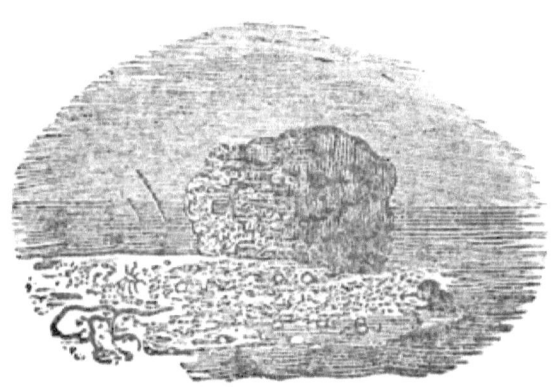

INDIAN CANNIBALISM.

It has been made a question whether the Indians can be justly charged with cannibalism. It is certain that all the terms by which they designate their inhuman mode of putting a prisoner to death bear reference to this horrid practice. The expressions are to throw him into the caldron, to devour him, to eat soup made of his flesh. It has hence been plausibly inferred that this enormity really prevailed in early times, but was changed, we can scarcely say mitigated, into the present system of torture. Yet, as every action is described by them in terms highly figurative, those now quoted may have been used as expressing most fully the complete gratification of their revenge. Of this charge they cannot now be either condemned or wholly acquitted. In the excited fury of their passions, portions of the flesh are often seized, roasted, and eaten, and draughts taken of the blood. To eat an enemy's heart is considered a peculiar enjoyment. Long mentions a gentleman who came upon a party who were busy broiling a human heart, when he with difficulty prevailed on them to desist. There is little hesitation among them, in periods of scarcity, to relieve hunger with the flesh of their captives; and during one war, this fate is said to have befallen many French soldiers who fell into the hands of the Five Nations. Colone! Schuyler told Colden, that, having entered the cabin of a chief who had some rich soup before him, he was invited to partake. Being hungry and tired, he readily agreed, till the ladle, being put into the great caldron, brought up a human hand, the sight of which put an immediate end to his appetite and meal.

INDIAN DANCES.

The dances of the Indians, even those at common festivals, are on an extensive scale, requiring to a complete performance forty or fifty persons, who execute their evolutions by following each other round a great fire kindled in the centre. Their movements, monotonous but violent, consist in stamping furiously on the ground, and often brandishing their arms in a manner compared by an able writer to a baker converting flour into dough. They keep good time; but the music is so exceedingly simple that this implies little merit. They conclude with a loud shout or howl, which echoes frightfully through the woods. The dances in celebration of particular events are of a more varied character, and often form a very expressive pantomime. The war-dance is the most favourite and frequent. In this extraordinary performance, a complete image is given of the terrible reality; the war-whoop is sounded with the most frightful yells; the tomahawk is wildly brandished; and the enemy are surprised, seized, and scalped, or carried off for torture. The calumet-dance, which celebrates peace between nations, and the marriage-dance, which repre· rents domestic life, are much more pleasing. Some mention is made of a mystic dance, carried on by the jugglers or doctors, with strange superstitious ceremonies, and in which a supernatural personage, termed by some the devil, rises and performs; but it does not seem to have been witnessed by any European, an' is said to be now in a great measure disused.

INDIAN GAMES.

There are games to which the Indians are fondly attached, which, though they be only ranked under the head of amusement, are yet constructed in the same serious manner as their other transactions. Their great parties are said to be collected by supernatural authority, communicated by the jugglers; and they are preceded, like their wars and hunts, by a course of fasting, dreaming, and other means of propitiating fortune. The favourite game is that of the bone, in which small pieces of that substance, resembling dice, and painted of different colours, are thrown in the air, and according to the manner in which they fall, the game is decided. Only two persons can play; but a numerous party, and sometimes whole villages, embrace one side or the other, and look on with intense interest. At each throw, especially if it be de- ·isive, tremendous shouts are raised; the players

and spectators equally resemble persons pos
sessed; the air rings with invocations to the
bones and to the manitous. Their eagerness
sometimes leads to quarreling and even fighting,
which on no other occasion ever disturb the
interior of these societies. To such a pitch are
they occasionally worked up, that they stake
successively all they possess, and even their
personal liberty; but this description must apply
only to the more southern nations, as slavery
was unknown among the Canadian Indians.

A temporary interval of wild license, of
emancipation from all the restraints of dignity
and decorum, seems to afford an enjoyment
highly prized in all rude societies. Corresponding
with the saturnalia and bacchanals of antiquity,
the Indians have their festivals of dreams, which,
during fifteen days, enlivens the inaction of the
coldest season. Laying aside all their usual
order and gravity, they run about, frightfully
disguised, and committing every imaginable
extravagance. He who meets another demands
an explanation of his visions, and if not satisfied,
imposes some fantastic penalty. He throws
upon him cold water, hot ashes, or filth; sometimes, rushing into his cabin, he breaks and
destroys the furniture. Although everything
appears wild and unpremeditated, it is alleged
that opportunities are often taken to give vent
to old and secret resentments. The period
having elapsed, a feast is given, order is restored,
and the damages done are carefully repaired.

BEAUTIFUL TRAIT OF CHARACTER.

One M'Dougal, a native of Argyleshire, hav
ing emigrated to Upper Canada, from anxiety
to make the most of his scanty capital, or some
other motive, he purchased a location, where
the price of land is merely nominal, in a country
thinly peopled, and on the extreme verge of
civilization. His first care was to construct a
house, and plant in the wild. This task finished,
he spent his whole time, early and late, in the
garden and the fields. By vigorous exertions,
and occasional assistance, he brought a few
acres of ground under crop; acquired a stock
of cattle, sheep and hogs; made additional inroads on the glade and the forest, and, though
his toils were hard, gradually and imperceptibly
became, in a rough way, " well enough to live,"
as compared with the poverty he had abandoned
at home.

His greatest discomforts were, distance from
his neighbours, the church, markets, and even
the mill; and, along with these, the suspension
(or rather, the enjoyment) after long intervals
of time, of those endearing charities and friendly
offices, which lend such a charm to social life.

On one occasion, M'Dougal had a melder of
corn to grind, and as the distance was considerable, and the roads none of the smoothest, this
important part of his duty could only be performed by starting with the sun, and returning
with the going down of the same. In his ab-

sence, the care of the cattle devolved on his
spouse, and as they did not return at the usual
hour, the careful matron went out in quest of
them. Beyond its mere outskirts, the forest was,
to her, *terra incognita,* in the most emphatic
sense of the term; and with no compass, or
notched trees to guide, it is not to be wondered
at that she wandered long and wearily to very
little purpose. Like alps on alps, tall trees arose
on every side—a boundless continuity of shade
—and, fatigued with the search, she deemed it
prudent to retrace her steps, while it was yet
time.   But this resolution was much easier
formed than executed; returning was as dangerous as "going o'er," and, after wandering
for hours, she sunk on the ground, her eyes
swollen and filled with tears, and her mind
agitated almost to distraction. But here she had
not rested many minutes, before she was startled
by the sound of approaching footsteps, and,
anon, an Indian hunter stood before her, "a
stoic of the woods, a man without fear." Mrs.
M'Dougal knew that Indians lived at no great
distance, but as she had never seen a member
of the tribe, her emotions were those of terror
—quickening, it may be said, every pulse, and
yet paralyzing every limb. The Indian's views
were more comprehensive; constantly on the
look out, in search of the quarry, and accustomed
to make circuits, comprising the superficies of
many a highland mountain and glen, he had
observed her, without being observed himself,
knew her home, recognized her person, com-

prehended her mishap, divined her errand, and
immediately beckoned her to follow him. The
unfortunate woman understood his signal, and
obeyed it, as far as terror left her power; and,
after a lengthened sweep, which added not a
little to her previous fatigue, they arrived at the
door of an Indian wigwam.

Her conductor invited her to enter, by signs:
but this she sternly refused to do, dreading the
consequence, and preferring death in the open
air to the tender mercies of cannibals within.
Perceiving her reluctance, and scanning her
feelings the hospitable Indian darted into the
wigwam, and communed with his wife, who,
in a few minutes, also appeared: and, by certain
signs and sympathies, known only to females,
calmed the stranger's fears, and induced her to
enter their lowly abode. Venison was instantly
prepared for supper, and Mrs. M'Dougal—
though still alarmed at the novelty of her situation, found the viands delicious, and had rarely,
if ever, partaken of so savoury a meal. Aware
that she was wearied, the Indians removed from
their place near the roof, two beautiful deer
skins, and, by stretching and fixing them across,
divided the wigwam into two apartments. Mats
were also spread in both, and next, the stranger
was given to understand, that the further dor-
mitory was expressly designed for her acom-
modation. But here again her courage failed
her, and to the most pressing intreaties, she
replied by signs, as well as she could, that she
would prefer to sit and sleep by the fire. This

20*

determination seemed to puzzle the Indian and
his squaw sadly.   Often they looked at each
other, and conversed softly in their own language: and, at last, the Red took the White
woman by the hand, led her to her couch, and
became her bedfellow.   In the morning she
awoke, greatly refreshed, and anxious to depart,
without further delay—but the Indian would
on no account permit it.   Breakfast was prepared—another savoury and well-cooked meal
—and then the Indian accompanied his guest,
and conducted her to the very spot where the
cattle were grazing.   These he kindly drove
from the wood, on the verge of which Mrs.
M'Dougal descried her husband, running about
every where, hallooing and seeking for her, in
a state of absolute distraction.   Great was his
joy, and great his gratitude to her Indian benefactor, who was invited to the house, and treated
to the best the larder afforded, and presented,
on his departure, with a suit of clothes.

In about three days he returned, and endeavoured, by every wile, to induce Mr. M'Dougal
to follow him into the forest.   But this invita-
tion the other positively declined—and the poor
Indian went on his way, obviously grieved and
disappointed.   But again he returned; and,
though words were wanting, renewed his intreaties—but still vainly, and without effect:
and then, as a last desperate effort, he hit upon
an expedient, which none, save an Indian
hunter, would have thought of.   Mrs. M'Dougal
had a nursling only a few months old—a fact

the Indian failed not to notice. After his pan-
tomimic eloquence had been thrown away, he
approached the cradle, seized the child, and
darted out of the house with the speed of an
antelope. The alarmed parents instantly followed, supplicating and imploring, at the top
of their voices. But the Indian's resolves were
as fixed as fate—and away he went, slow
enough to encourage his pursuers, but still in
the van by a good many paces, and far enough
ahead to achieve the secret purpose he had
formed—like the parent-bird, skimming the
ground, when she wishes to wile the enemy
from her nest. Again and again Mr. M'Dougal
wished to continue the chase alone—but mater-
nal anxiety baffled every remonstrance ; and
this anxiety was, if possible, increased, when
she saw the painted savage enter the wood, and
steer, as she thought, his course towards his
own cabin. The Indian, however, was in no
hurry;—occasionally, he cast a glance behind,
poised the child almost like a feather, treading
his way with admirable dexterity, and kept the
swaddling clothes so closely drawn around it,
that not even the winds of heaven were permitted to visit it roughly. It is, of course, need-
less to go into all the details of this singular
journey, further than to say, that the Indian, at
length, called a halt on the margin of a most
beautiful prairie, teeming with the richest vegetation, and comprising many thousands of acres.
In a moment the child was restored to its parents
—who, wondering what so strange a procedure

could mean, stood, for some minutes, panting
for breath and eying one another in silent and
speechless astonishment.

The Indian, on the other hand, appeared
overjoyed at the success of his manœuvre—
and never did a human being frisk about and
gesticulate with greater animation. We have
heard, or read, of a professor of signs: and
supposing such a character were wanted, the
selection could not—or, at least should not—be
a matter of difficulty, so long as even a remnant
remains of the aborigines of North America.
All travellers agree in describing their gestures
as highly dignified, eloquent, and intellgent:
and we have the authority of Mr. M'Dougal
for saying, that the hero of the present strictly
authentic tale, proved himself to be a perfect
master of the art. The restoration of the child
—the beauty and wide extent of the prairies,
and various other circumstances combined—
flashed across our countryman's mind—opera-
ting convicting where jealousy and distrust had
lurked before. Mr. M'Dougal, in a trice, examined the soil and immediately saw the pro-
priety of the advice given by the *untutored one*.
By a sort of tacit agreement, a day was fixed
for the removal of the materials of our countryman's cabin, goods and chattels;—and the
Indian, true to his word, brought a detachment
of his tribe to assist in one of the most romantic
" flittings " that ever was undertaken either in
the old or new world. In a few days a roomy
log-house was fashioned, and a garden formed

in a convenient section of the beautiful prairie, from which the smoke was seen curling, and the woodpecker tapping at no great distance. M'Dougal was greatly pleased at the change— and no wonder, seeing that he could almost boast of a body-guard as bold as the bowmen of Robin Hood. His Indian friend speedily became a sort of foster brother, and his tribe as faithful as the most attached Tail of Gillies that ever surrounded a Highland chieftain. Even the stupid kine lowed, on finding themselves suddenly transferred to a boundless range of richest pasture:—and, up to the date of the latest advices, were improving rapidly in condition, and increasing in numbers.

The little garden was smiling like a rose in the desert—grass, overabundant, was gradually giving way to thriving crops, and the kine so well satisfied with their *gang*, that the herds and enclosures were alike unheeded to keep them from the corn. The Indians continued friendly and faithful—occasionally bringing presents of venison and other game, and were uniformly rewarded from the stores of a dairy, overflowing with milk, butter, and cheese.

Attached as the Red man was to his own mode of life, he was induced at length to form a part of the establishment, in the capacity of grieve, or head shepherd—a duty he undertook most cheerfully, as it still left him opportunities of meeting and communing with his friends, and reconnoitering the altering denizens of the forest. Let us hope, therefore, that no untoward accident will occur to mar this beautiful picture of sylvan life; that the M'Dougal colony will wax stronger, till every section of the prairie is forced to yield tribute to the spade and the plough.

THE REFORMED INDIAN.

Some of the Indians believe, that the "Evil Spirit" is the maker of spirituous liquors, from which, notwithstanding, hardly one of them can refrain. An Indian near the Delaware Water Gap, told Mr. Heckewelder, a missionary, that he had once, when under the influence of strong liquor, killed the best Indian friend he had, fancying him to be his worst avowed enemy. He said that the deception was complete; and that while intoxicated, the face of his friend presented to *his* eyes all the features of the man with whom he was in a state of hostility. It is impossible to express the horror which struck him, when he awoke from that delusion. He was so shocked that from that moment, he resolved never more to taste of the maddening potion, of which he was convinced the devil was the inventor; for that it could only be the "Evil Spirit" who made him see his enemy when his friend was before him, and produced so strong a delusion on his bewildered senses, that he actually killed him. From that time until his death, which happened thirty years afterwards, he never drank a drop of ardent spirits, which he always called "the devil's blood;" and was firmly persuaded that the devil, or some of his infernal spirits, had a hand in preparing it.

FIDELITY.

Among the North American Indians, one of the first lessons they inculcate on their children, is duty to their parents, and respect for old age; and there is not among the most civilized nations, any people who more strictly observe the duty of filial obedience. A father need only to say, in the presence of his children, "I want such a thing done "—"I want one of my children to go upon such an errand "—"Let me see who is the good child that will do it." The word *good* operates as it were by magic, and the children immediately vie with each other to comply with the parent's wishes. If a father sees an old decrepid man or woman pass by, led along by a child, he will draw the attention of his own children to the object, by saying, "What a *good* child that must be, which pays such attention to the aged! That child, indeed, looks forward to the time when it will likewise be old, and need its children's help." Or he will say, "May the Great Spirit, who looks upon him, grant this *good* child a long life!"

STRATAGEM DEFEATED.

Early in the war of the American revolution, a Sergeant, who traveled through the woods of New Hampshire, on his way to the American army, met with a singular adventure, which ended much to his credit.

He had twelve men with him. Their route was far from any settlement, and they were obliged every night to encamp in the woods. The Sergeant had seen a good deal of the Indians, and understood them well;—early in the afternoon, one day, as they were marching on, over bogs, swamps, and brooks, under the towering maple trees, a body of Indians, exceeding their own number, rushed out upon a hill in front of them.

They appeared to be pleased at meeting with the Sergeant and his party. They considered them, they said, as their best friends; for themselves they had taken up the hatchet for the Americans, and would scalp and strip those rascally English for them, like so many wild cats. "How do you do, pro?" (meaning brother) said one. "How do you do, pro?" said another, and so they went about, shaking hands with the Sergeant and his twelve men.

They went off, at last, and the Sergeant, having marched onward a mile or two, halted his men, and addressed them,—"My brave fellows," said he, "we must use all possible caution, or before morning we shall all of us be dead men. You are amazed, but depend upon me, these Indians have tried to put our suspicion to sleep; you will see more of them bye-and-bye."

It was concluded, finally, to adopt the following scheme for defence: they encamped for the night, near a stream of water, which protected them from behind. A large oak was felled, and a brilliant fire kindled; each man cut a log of wood, about the size of his body, rolled it nicely up in his blanket, placed his hat on the end of it, and laid it before the fire, that the enemy might take it for a man.

Thirteen logs were fitted out in this way, representing the Sergeant and his twelve men. They then placed themselves, with loaded guns, behind the fallen tree; by this time it was dark, but the fire was kept burning till midnight. The Sergeant knew, that if the savages ever came, they would come now.

A tall Indian was seen, at length, through the glimmering of the fire, which was getting low.   He moved cautiously towards them, skulking, as an Indian always does. He seemed to suspect, at first, that a guard might be watching, but seeing none, he came forward more boldly, rested on his toes, and was seen to move his finger, as he counted the thirteen men, sleeping, as he supposed, by the fire. He counted them again, and retired; another came up, and did the same. Then the whole party, sixteen in number, came up and glared silently at the logs, till they seemed to be satisfied they

21

were fast asleep. Presently they took aim,
fired their whole number of guns upon the logs,
yelled the horrid war-whoop, and pushed forward to murder and scalp their supposed victims.
The Sergeant and his men were ready for them;
they fired upon them, and not one of the Indians
was left to tell the story of that night. The
Sergeant reached the army in safety.

SCENES IN KING WILLIAM'S WAR, 1689.

SURPRISE OF DOVER.

Thirteen years had almost elapsed since the
seizure of the 400 Indians, at Cocheco, by
Major Waldron; during all which time an
inextinguishable thirst of revenge had been
cherished among them, which never till now
found opportunity for gratification. Wonolanset,
one of the sachems of Penacook, who was
dismissed with his people at the time of the
seizure, always observed his father's dying
charge, not to quarrel with the English; but
Hagkins, another sachem, who had been treated
with neglect by Cranfield, was more ready to
listen to the seducing invitations of Castine's
emissaries. Some of those Indians, who were
then seized and sold into slavery abroad, had
found their way home, and could not rest till
they had their revenge. Accordingly a confederacy being formed between the tribes of
Penacook and Pigwacket, and the strange

Indians (as they were called) who were incor-
porated with them, it was determined to surprise the major and his neighbors, among
whom they had all this time been peaceably
conversant.

In that part of the town of Dover which lies
about the first falls in the river Cochceo, were
five garrisoned houses, three on the north side,
called respectively, Waldron, Otis, and Heard;
and two on the south side, Peter Coffin and his
son's. These houses were surrounded with
timber walls, the gates of which, as well as the
house doors, were secured with bolts and bars.
The neighboring families retired to these houses
by night; but by an unaccountable negligence,
no watch was kept. The Indians who were
daily passing through the town, visiting and
trading with the inhabitants, as usual in time of
peace, viewed their situation with an attentive
eye. Some hints of a mischievous design had
been given out by their squaws; but in such
dark and ambiguous terms that no one could
comprehend their meaning. Some of the people
were uneasy; but Waldron, who, from a long
course of experience, was intimately acquainted
with the Indians, and on other occasions had
been ready enough to suspect them, was now so
thoroughly secure, that when some of the people
hinted their fears to him, he merrily bade them
to go and plant their pumpkins, saying that he
would tell them when the Indians would break
out. The very evening before the mischief
was done, being told by a young man that the

town was full of Indians, and the people were much concerned; he answered that he knew the Indians very well, and there was no danger.

· The plan which the Indians had preconcerted was, that two squaws should go to each of the garrisoned houses in the evening, and ask leave to lodge by the fire; that in the night when the people were asleep they should open the doors and gates, and give the signal by a whistle, upon which the strange Indians, who were to be within hearing, should rush in, and take their long meditated revenge.   This plan being ripe for execution, on the evening of Thursday the 27th of June, two squaws applied to each of the garrisons for lodging, as they frequently did in time of peace.   They were admitted into all but the younger Coffin's, and the people, at their request, shewed them how to open the doors, in case they should have occasion to go out in the night.   Mesandowit, one of their chiefs, went to Waldron's garrison, and was kindly entertained, as he had often been before. The squaws told the major, that a number of Indians were coming to trade with him the next day, and Mesandowit, while at supper, with his usual familiarity, said, "Brother Waldron, what would you do if the strange Indians should come?"   The major carelessly answered, that he could assemble 100 men, by lifting up his finger.   In this unsuspecting confidence the family retired to rest.

When all was quiet, the gates were opened and the signal given.   The Indians entered, set a guard at the door, and rushed into the major's apartment which was an inner room. Awakened by the noise, he jumped out of bed, and though now advanced in life to the age of eighty years, he retained so much vigor as to drive them with his sword through two or three doors, but as he was returning for his other arms, they came behind him, stunned him with a hatchet, drew him into his hall, and seating him in an' elbow chair on a long table insultingly asked him, " Who shall judge Indians now?" They then obliged the people in the house to get them some victuals; and when they had done eating, they cut the major across the breast and belly with knives, each one with a stroke saying, " I cross out my account." They then cut off his nose and ears, forcing them into his mouth— and when, spent with the loss of blood, he was falling down from the table, one of them held his own sword under him, which put an end to his misery. They also killed his son-in-law Abraham Lee; but took his daughter Lee with several others, and having pillaged the house, left it on fire. Otis's garrison, which was next to the major's, met with the same fate; he was killed with several others, and his wife and child were captured. Heard's was saved by the barking of a dog just as the Indians were entering: Elder Wentworth, who was awakened by the noise, pushed them out, and falling on his back, set his feet against the gate and held it till he had alarmed the people; two balls were fired through it but both missed him. Cof=

fin's house was surprised, but as the Indians
had no particular enmity to him, they spared
his life, and the lives of his family, and con-
tented themselves with pillaging the house.
Finding a bag of money, they made him throw
it by handfulls on the floor, while they amused
themselves in scrambling for it. They then
went to the house of his son who would not
admit the squaws in the evening, and summoned
him to surrender, promising him quarter: he
declined their offer, and determined to defend his
house, till they brought out his father and
threatened to kill him before his eyes; filial affection then overcame his resolution, and he
surrendered. They put both families together
into a deserted house, intending to reserve them
for prisoners; but while the Indians were busy
in plundering, they all escaped.

Twenty-three people were killed in this sur-
prisal, and twenty-nine were captured; five or
six houses with the mills were burned; and so
expeditious were the Indians in the execution
of their plot, that before the people could be
collected from the other parts of the town to
oppose them, they fled with their prisoners and
booty. As they passed by Heard's garrison in
their retreat, they fired upon it, but the people
bring prepared and resolved to defend it, and
the enemy being in haste, it was preserved. The
preservation of its owner was more remarkable.

Elizabeth Heard, with her three sons and a
daughter, and some others, were returning in
the night from Portsmouth; they passed up the

river in their boat unperceived by the Indians, who were then in possession of the houses; but suspecting danger by the noise which they heard, after they had landed they betook themselves to Waldron'a garrison, where they saw lights, which they imagined were set up for direction to those who might be seeking a refuge. They knocked and begged earnestly for admission, but no answer being given, a young man of the company climbed up the wall, and saw, to his inexpressible surprise, an Indian standing in the door of the house with his gun. The woman was so overcome with the fright that she was unable to fly, but begged her children to shift for themselves, and they with heavy hearts left her. When she had a little recovered she crawled into some bushes, and lay there till day-light: she then perceived an Indian coming toward her with a pistol in his hand, he looked at her and went away; returning, he looked at her again, and she asked him what he would have. He made no answer, but ran yelling to the house, and she saw him no more. She kept her place till the house was burned and the Indians were gone, and then returning home found her own house safe. Her preservation in these dangerous circumstances was more remarkable, if (as it is supposed) it was an instance of justice and gratitude in the Indians: for at the time when the 400 were seized in 1676, a young Indian escaped and took refuge in her house, where she concealed him; in return for which kindness he promised her that he never would kill her, nor any of her family in any future war, and that he would use his influence with the other Indians to the same purpose. This Indian was one of the party who surprised the place, and she was well known to the most of them.   •

The same day after the mischief was done, a letter from Secretary Addington, written by order of the government, directed to Major Waldron, giving him notice of the intention of the Indians to surprise him under pretense of trade, fell into the hands of his son.   This design was communicated to Governor Bradstreet by Major Henchman of Chelmsford, who had learned it of the Indians.   The letter was dispatched from Boston, the day before, by Mr. Weare; but some delay which he met with at Newbury ferry prevented his arrival in season.

The prisoners taken at this time were mostly carried to Canada, and sold to the French; and these, so far as can be learned, were the first that ever were carried hither.   One of these prisoners was Sarah Gerrish, a remarkably fine child, of seven years old, and grand-daughter of Major Waldron, in whose house she lodged that fatal night.   Some circumstances attending her captivity are truly affecting.   When she was awakened by the noise of the Indians in the house, she crept into another bed, and hid herself under the clothes to escape their search.   She remained in their hands till the next winter, and was sold from one to another several times.   An Indian girl once pushed her into a river; but, catching by the bushes, she escaped drowning, yet durst not tell how she came to be wet. Once she was so weary with travelling, that she did not awake in the morning till the Indians were gone, and then found herself alone in the woods, covered with snow, and without any food; having found their tracks, she went crying after them till they heard her and took her with them. At another time they kindled a great fire, and the young Indians told her she was to be roasted. She burst into tears, threw her arms round her master's neck, and begged him to save her, which he promised to do if she would behave well. Being arrived in Canada, she was bought by the Intendant's lady, who treated her courteously, and sent her to a nunnery for education. But when Sir William Phips was at Quebec she was exchanged, and returned to her friends, with whom she lived till she was sixteen years old.

The wife of Richard Otis was taken at the same time, with an infant daughter of three months old. The French priests took this child under their care, baptised her by the name of Christina, and educated her in the Romish religion. She passed some time in a nunnery, but declined taking the veil, and was married to a Frenchman, by whom she had two children. But her desire to see New England was so strong, that upon an exchange of prisoners in 1714, being then a widow, she left both her children, who were not permitted to come with her, and returned home, where she abjured the Romish faith. M. Siguenot, her former confessor, wrote her a flattering letter, warning her of her danger, inviting her to return to the bosom of the catholic church, and repeating many gross calumnies which had formerly been vented against Luther and the other reformers. This letter being shown to Governor Burnet, he wrote her a sensible and masterly answer, refuting the arguments, and detecting the falsehoods it contained : both these letters were printed. She was married afterwards to Captain Thomas Baker, who had been taken at Deerfield, in 1704, and lived in Dover, where she was born, till the year 1773. The Indians had been seduced to the French interest by popish emissaries, who had begun to fascinate them with their religious and national prejudices. They had now learned to call the English heretics, and that to extirpate them as such was meritorious in the sight of heaven. When their minds were filled with religious frenzy, they became more bitter and implacable enemies than before; and finding the sale of scalps and prisoners turn to good account in Canada, they had still farther incitement to continue their depredations and prosecute their vengeance.

TREATMENT OF THE PRISONERS AT SALMON FALLS IN 1690.

The following instances of cruelty, exercised towards the prisoners taken at Salmon falls, are mentioned by Dr. Mather. Robert Rogers, a corpulent man, being unable to carry the burden which the Indians imposed upon him, threw it in the path and went aside in the woods to conceal himself. They found him by his track, stripped, beat, and pricked him with their swords: then tied him to a tree and danced round him till they had kindled a fire. They gave him time to pray, and take leave of his fellow prisoners, who were placed round the fire to see his death. They pushed the fire toward him, and when he was almost stifled, took it away to give him time to breathe, and thus prolong his misery; they drowned his dying groans with their hideous singing and yelling, all the while dancing round the fire, cutting off pieces of his flesh and throwing them in his face. When he was dead they left his body broiling on the coals, in which state it was found by his friends and buried. Mehetabel Goodwin was taken with a child of five months old; when it cried they threatened to kill it, which made the mother go aside and sit for hours together in the snow to lull it to sleep, her master seeing that this hindered her from travelling, took the child, struck its head against a tree, and hung it on one of the branches; she

would have buried it but he would not let her
telling her that if she came again that way she
might have the pleasure of seeing it.   She was
carried to Canada, and after five years returned
home.   Mary Plaisted was taken out of her
bed, having lain in but three weeks : they made
her travel with them through the snow and " to
ease her of her burden," as they said, struck
the child's head against a tree, and threw it into
a river.   An anecdote of another kind may
relieve the reader after these tragical accounts.
Thomas Toogood was pursued by three Indians
and overtaken by one of them, who having
enquired his name, was preparing strings to
bind him, holding his gun under his arm, which
Toogood seized and went backward, keeping
the gun presented at him, and protesting that he
would shoot him if he alarmed the others who
had stopped on the opposite side of the hill.
By this dexterity he escaped and got safe into
Cocheco ; while his adversary had no recompense in his power but to call after him by the
name of Nogood.